MOUNTAINEERS ARE ALWAYS FREE

MOUNTAINEERS ARE ALWAYS FREE

Heritage, Dissent, and a West Virginia Icon

ROSEMARY V. HATHAWAY

West Virginia University Press
Morgantown

ISBN
Cloth 978-1-949199-30-7
Paper 978-1-949199-31-4
Ebook 978-1-949199-32-1

Library of Congress Cataloging-in-Publication Data
Names: Hathaway, Rosemary V., author. | West Virginia University Press.
Title: Mountaineers are always free : heritage, dissent, and a West Virginia icon /
    Rosemary V. Hathaway.
Other titles: Heritage, dissent, and a West Virginia icon
Description: First Edition. | Morgantown : West Virginia University Press, 2020. |
    Includes bibliographical references and index.
Identifiers: LCCN 2019044561 | ISBN 9781949199307 (Cloth) | ISBN
    9781949199314 (Paperback) | ISBN 9781949199321 (eBook)
Subjects: LCSH: West Virginia University—History. | School mascots. | West
    Virginia—History—20th century. | West Virginia University Mountaineer.
Classification: LCC GV958.W4 H37 2020 | DDC 796.332/630975452—dc23
LC record available at https://lccn.loc.gov/2019044561

Book and cover design by Than Saffel / WVU Press

To the memory of my Mountaineers,
David Barr Hathaway and Joyce Toothman Hathaway.
This is your book as much as it is mine.

Contents

Acknowledgments

THIS BOOK would not have been possible without the collaboration of many, many people. First and foremost, I want to thank my parents, David and Joyce (Toothman) Hathaway, both proud West Virginia natives. Their love of the state and of family stories are at the heart of this project. In my wildest dreams I never imagined that those stories would become a significant part of my own life's work, but I am so grateful that they did. Very few academics get to combine their personal lives and professional interests so neatly. This book is, in every way, dedicated to them. I only wish they had been around to see the project to its completion.

I am also indebted to the former residents of Trinity Hall for their stories about Morgantown and college life; truly, these stories, which I'd heard throughout my childhood, shaped everything I knew about West Virginia University (WVU) and are part of what brought me to teach here in 2007.

When I started thinking about how to turn what began as an article for *West Virginia History* into a book-length project, I realized that to really understand the Mountaineer, I needed to talk to the people who knew best what it means to be one: the men and women who have served as the official WVU Mountaineer. Connecting with them would not have been possible without the generous help of the superwoman I refer to as the "Mountaineer wrangler," Sonja Wilson, who worked as the Mountaineer adviser—and as the organizer of Mountaineer Week—for many years before her retirement in March 2019 (and even in retirement, she is continuing her advisory work). Sonja helped me reach out to former Mountaineers and was always available to answer my (many) questions. Thank you, Sonja.

I was moved and humbled by the magnanimity of all the former Mountaineers I interviewed. They willingly agreed to talk to me and did so with enthusiasm, humor, and candor. Their passion fueled my progress and taught me what it takes to be a real Mountaineer: boundless energy, compassion, a fine sense of where the limits are, and an unwavering love of this state. Thank you so much, Dave Ellis, Lou Garvin, Doug Townshend, Bob Lowe, Ken Fonville, Mark Boggs, Matt Zervos, Natalie Tennant, Brady Campbell, Michael Squires, Rebecca Durst, and Brock Burwell. I hope, in time, to interview all of the former Mountaineers who are still with us, and to archive those interviews at the West Virginia and Regional History Center in the WVU Libraries for future researchers.

There are so many others who helped me along the way: many thanks to Ronald Lewis, WVU professor emeritus of history, who led me to exactly the right materials in the West Virginia and Regional History Center. And speaking of the West Virginia and Regional History Center, I am deeply grateful to everyone on the staff there; they always made me feel welcome, regularly brought new things to my attention, and, through their love of archival research, helped me refine my own. Ken Fones-Wolf in the WVU history department was invaluable in getting this project focused and off the ground when he asked me to submit an article based on my initial research to *West Virginia History*. And he was always ready with great recommendations when I (frequently) found myself out of my depth in the waters of history. Kelly Diamond helped get all my sources straight for the bibliography, proving again that librarians truly are information superheroes. I am also indebted to the West Virginia Humanities Council, which supported this project in multiple ways: first through a summer fellowship that helped me get started on the fieldwork and then by giving me the chance to get feedback from an audience via its Little Lectures series.

I'm also grateful to Randy McNutt, author of *King Records of Cincinnati* and *The Cincinnati Sound* (both on Arcadia Publishing) for the King Records ad that appears in chapter 2, and to Affrilachian poet and activist Crystal Good and Pastor Matthew Watts of the Grace Bible Church in Charleston for providing the image of the *Black Triangle* mural that appears in chapter 5. Conversations with Pastor Watts reminded me that there's much more to be written about the history of African American students at WVU, particularly during the 1960s. Thanks to him, I think I may have discovered my next project.

I am indebted to several people I met while doing archival research at the West Virginia and Regional History Center. First among these is Scott L. Bills, a history major and student activist at WVU during the late 1960s and early 1970s, who went on to earn his PhD and become Regents Professor of History at Stephen F. Austin State University in Texas. His book on the Kent State shootings, *Kent State/May 4: Echoes through a Decade*, remains, twenty-plus years after its publication, one of the best histories of that terrible day. I was astounded at Bills's prescience in keeping every flyer, pamphlet, and piece of correspondence about his time at WVU, but I am so grateful to him for doing so. When I came across his collections, I hoped to talk with him—but sadly, I learned that he died at the age of fifty-three in 2001. That was a real blow. Nevertheless, his work, both as a student activist and as a historian, is the backbone of chapter 3.

And I'm also grateful to Patrick Ward Gainer, the WVU English department's legendary folklorist, who taught thousands of students at the university (and also at Glenville State College) for decades, from the 1940s until the 1970s. He left some mighty big shoes for us later WVU folklorists to fill. In researching his papers in the West Virginia and Regional History Center, I came across a nearly complete manuscript titled "The Hillbilly" (see chapter 2) that either Gainer or one of his students wrote in the early 1970s. That manuscript's preface makes it clear that the author was doing exactly the same work I embarked on forty years later: trying to tease out the intertwining images of the hillbilly and the frontiersman. Clearly this is a perennial puzzle for WVU folklorists. I hope I've done my esteemed predecessor justice.

A number of my contemporary folklore colleagues provided invaluable feedback and support at every stage of this project. Their unflagging belief in what I was doing got me through some rough moments when this all seemed trivial and arcane. Sheila Bock Alarid, Emily Hilliard, Debra Lattanzi Shutika, and Martha Sims: you're my folk heroes, and your fingerprints are all over this text.

And finally, to Tom Bredehoft, who makes writing books look easy. Thank you for your unflagging faith in my ability to write one, too.

Introduction

I START THIS BOOK about the West Virginia Mountaineer by confessing that I am a Buckeye. Not only was I born and raised in Ohio, but I am also an alumna of The Ohio State University. But as the daughter of parents who both graduated from West Virginia University and who grew up in West Virginia—my father, David Barr Hathaway, in Grantsville (Calhoun County), and my mother, Joyce Toothman Hathaway, in Athens (Mercer County)—I was no stranger to the Mountaineer, either specifically as the WVU mascot, or more broadly, as a moniker for West Virginians. Growing up in the 1930s and 1940s, my parents heard the folk saying that the three Rs in West Virginia were "readin', writin', and Route 33" (elsewhere identified as Route 23, or "the road to Columbus," if that was the closer path out of the state). Like many others, they were part of the out-migration of West Virginians who left the state for better job opportunities in the 1950s. But like so many West Virginia expats, my parents never lost their love for their home state and wore their Mountaineer identity proudly: my father, in particular, took a deep and subversive pleasure in flying the West Virginia state flag alongside the US and Ohio flags on major holidays, including on June 20, West Virginia Day. And trust me, the West Virginia flag drew some curious looks and questions in that Columbus suburb, much to my father's delight.

So it was ironic when I—the only one of their four children not to be born in Morgantown—was hired by WVU's English department in 2007 and moved from my then-home of Colorado back to a gentler and greener set of mountains. Though my family had made frequent trips back to Grantsville and Athens to visit family while I was growing up, we never visited Morgantown. And yet, for the first few months I lived here, I had an unshakeable sense of déjà vu as I kept coming across places familiar to me through family stories: the site of Trinity Episcopal Church on the corner of Spruce and Willey Streets was where my dad's rooming house, Trinity Hall, formerly stood; Stansbury Hall, where the English department was then located, was the former fieldhouse where he watched Hot Rod Hundley astonish the crowds with his basketball showmanship. Woman's Hall, where my mother lived before the two were married, loomed over the campus, and my dad passed along to me an object I'd never seen before: the phone he "liberated" from the foyer of Woman's Hall on an occasion when Mom kept him waiting there too long before a date. Every day on my walk to campus I stepped on or over the star for Don Knotts in front of the Metropolitan Theater. Knotts had been a student during the same time as my dad and sometimes worked as the intermission act between sets when my dad performed with dance bands in town. It was uncanny, like coming home to a place I'd never been. I was haunted, in all the best ways.

When I started teaching at WVU in the fall semester of 2007, I began to understand and to be curious about the significance of the Mountaineer. I thought I knew college mascots from my experiences at Ohio State; as a graduate teaching assistant, I'd even taught a student who was the Brutus Buckeye mascot. But none of that prepared me for the depth and the complexity of the connection that West Virginians feel to the Mountaineer. During that first semester, it became clear to me that the Mountaineer was far more than just a mascot: West Virginians identified with the Mountaineer in ways that went well beyond sports fandom. Indeed, as a number of people who served as the WVU Mountaineer stressed when I interviewed them, they don't consider the Mountaineer to be a mascot at all: a mascot is some anonymous person in a costume and a cartoonish, oversized foam head. The Mountaineer, they told me, is a symbol of, and a representative for, the entire state. Many of them brought this distinction up without prompting, and they talked about their service as that representative with tremendous pride.

Of course, West Virginia University teams aren't the only college athletics programs to call themselves Mountaineers: that moniker is shared by athletes, students, and alumni at Appalachian State University (North Carolina), Berea College (Kentucky), Mount St. Mary's University (Maryland), Schreiner University (Texas), Western Colorado University, Eastern Oregon University, Eastern Oklahoma State College, and Southern Vermont College. Of all of those teams, Appalachian State's mascot, Yosef, is most akin to WVU's Mountaineer in terms of its symbolism. According to Appalachian State's website, the name "'Yosef' is mountain talk for 'yourself,' with the idea being that if you are an Appalachian alumnus, fan or friend and have a heart filled with black and gold, you are Yosef." The histories of the WVU Mountaineer and Yosef are remarkably similar: Yosef came into being in the late 1940s, conceived of as a hillbilly caricature for Appalachian State's 1948 yearbook. And the following year, 1949, saw John Geffrich, "a 48-year-old World War II veteran," become the unofficial Appalachian State Mountaineer mascot. Like WVU Mountaineers of the time, the Appalachian State Mountaineer was depicted by "male undergraduates [as] a bearded man with coveralls, a pipe and a straw hat," and carrying a musket.[1] As we shall see in chapter 2, this portrayal is very similar to the iconography of the WVU Mountaineer of the time and reflects a surprisingly urbane sense of Appalachian identity.

But the Appalachian State's Mountaineer and the WVU Mountaineer part ways in the 1980s, when Appalachian State "modernized Yosef's look through a cartoon-type head and body."[2] WVU maintained its tradition of having a single, identifiable student portray the Mountaineer, which proved to be a crucial decision (or lack of decision). Having a real person serve as the Mountaineer is a physical reminder that the figure symbolizes the independence and individuality of West Virginians, both historically and in the present. However, in the late 1980s, WVU would discover that this tradition was also problematic when Natalie Tennant competed to become, and then was named, the first woman to serve as the Mountaineer. Chapter 4 demonstrates that while the WVU Mountaineer might be all about freedom, some students and fans felt that only men were qualified to fill the role. In fact, it was a similar resistance to Rebecca Durst's selection as the second female Mountaineer in 2009 that became the spark that ignited this book project. When some students—including a large number of female students—complained that a woman couldn't be the Mountaineer, I began to see the complexity of Mountaineer identity, and how it is in a constant balancing act between tradition and change.

In many ways, then, this book is the result of a fascination with what it means to be a Mountaineer, something that has consumed me since my arrival in Morgantown in 2007. What I've discovered is that even though the *image* of the Mountaineer has changed over time, *ideas* about who and what the Mountaineer represents have been remarkably consistent and persistent since the term first emerged as a synonym for residents of western Virginia in the early nineteenth century. The Mountaineer is a mirror for a deep range of intangible values and ideals: It represents pride in one's history and heritage. It personifies the rebellious, independent spirit reflected in the state motto, *Montani semper liberi* (Mountaineers are always free). It has stood, at various points in time, as both the personification of and an antidote to the stereotype of the poor "white trash" hillbilly. It has been a lightning rod that attracts and absorbs larger cultural concerns about race, class, and gender. It has been a tool students use to release their inhibitions, and a tool the university's admin-istration has used to rein in student misbehavior. Individuals use the Mountaineer figure to enact what they believe it means to be a student at West Virginia University, a citizen of the state, and a resident of the Appalachian region. Those enactments vary radi-cally, sometimes coming into direct conflict with each other, and have adapted to reflect changing historical and cultural contexts. And yet despite its flexibility, the Mountaineer identity retains a remarkably stable core that has allowed it to continue to reflect a crucial part of West Virginians' identity for over two hundred years. What is it about the Mountaineer identity that is unique and perennially appealing?

Hillbillies, Frontiersmen, and Tricksters

In order to understand the present-day Mountaineer, we need to understand where the figure comes from. As will be discussed in more detail in chapter 1, the Mountaineer has its roots in two long-standing American icons: the hillbilly and the frontiersman. Both of these figures have an extensive cultural history that long predates the founding of the state of West Virginia—and in some cases predates the founding of the United States. I argue that the personas of the frontiersman and the hillbilly, which developed separately, merge in the figure of the Mountaineer. While these two figures share some qualities—fierce independence, plainspo-kenness—they also differ in significant ways. The frontiersman represents the natural gentleman of the backwoods, who—while not worldly or formally educated—is nevertheless intelligent, articulate, and forthright. With the frontiersman, what you see is what you get; he is the proverbial salt-of-the-earth guy, with a hefty dose of rugged individualism and bravery. The hillbilly, on the other hand, is a barely civilized rabble-rouser, one who acts first and thinks later. His pleasures are of the flesh: carousing, drinking, fighting. If he is even aware of the status quo, the hillbilly fails to understand why it matters and may actively defy it. What he is keenly aware of, however, is that outsiders often see him as a fool, and in fact he sometimes plays the fool deliberately in order to trick outsiders and put them in their place.

It may seem impossible that these two distinct figures could coexist in the single figure of the Mountaineer, but they do. In combining the seemingly opposed figures of the frontiersman and the hillbilly, the Mountaineer becomes a wholly different kind of icon than either the hillbilly or the frontiersman alone: he becomes a trickster. Lewis Hyde defines the trickster as a "boundary-crosser" who exists at the boundaries between "right and wrong, sacred and profane, clean and dirty, male and female, young and old, living and dead."[3] The trickster is amoral in the sense of being oblivious to convention: he does and says what he pleases, and if deceit and trickery are needed to accomplish his goals, he willingly engages in deceit and trickery without shame. It's this aspect of shamelessness that makes tricksters so appealing; but as Hyde (and others) have argued, the trickster isn't a sociopath or a chaos agent. Rather, through its "relationship to other powers, to people and institutions and traditions," the trickster functions "to uncover and disrupt the very things that cultures are based on."[4] In short, every cultural group needs a trickster figure to stand guard at the boundaries of the group's values, both to police and to challenge the limits of group behavior.

Trickster figures exist in virtually every culture,[5] and tales about them are part of nearly every cultural group's narrative folklore: familiar examples are Brer Rabbit, Coyote, Anansi, and—in Appalachian tradition—Jack of the Jack tales. In these stories, tricksters outwit others—especially those seeking to harm them—by deceit, cleverness, and wit. We will see how the Mountaineer plays this same role in nineteenth-century stories about backwoodsmen outsmarting dandies. But the trickster can also be a culture hero, a figure who embodies the ideals of a particular group—and certainly the Mountaineer is a culture hero. The Mountaineer represents everything central to West Virginia's mythology: he is the pioneer who first ventured into the region and settled it; he is the principled, if poor, citizen whose resistance to slavery led to the formation of the state of West Virginia; he is the stoic, self-sufficient, and naturally hospitable gentleman who judges people and situations by his own standards and acts accordingly, even if his actions are unconventional. In all of those qualities, we can also see how the Mountaineer's virtues straddle the boundary between civility and order: he is not afraid to leave civilization behind and confront the ambiguities and dangers of the natural world, and he is willing to fight for what he believes in, even if it means rejecting the status quo. There's a fine balance between the Mountaineer's laudable qualities—independence and forthrightness—and his potentially disruptive ones—his willingness to reject and resist social norms.

The idea of a single figure who is both culture hero and trickster may seem an unlikely and paradoxical combination. And in fact, folklorists and anthropologists in the late nineteenth and early twentieth centuries carried on a long debate about this tendency for a single character to embody both roles, when one would expect these roles to be carried out by separate and opposing characters in a tale.[6] The trickster is generally a comic figure, like the fool or clown, while the culture hero is more often a tragic one. Nevertheless, as anthropologist Franz Boas noted, there is "a uniform tendency to attribute coarse buffoonery or moral delinquencies of the worst sort to an ideal culture-hero."[7] And such is the case with the Mountaineer: he can be both stalwart frontiersman and coarse hillbilly, depending on the context. Notably, both roles are built into the duties of the WVU Mountaineer, who is required both to be a well-behaved, articulate public-relations agent for the university and an effective rabble-rouser, one who can excite fans with his or her game-day antics.

Folklorist Barbara Babcock-Abrahams resolves the problem of combining the culture hero and the trickster in a single figure by recalling that the trickster "embodies the fundamental contradiction of our existence: the contradiction between the individual and society, between freedom and constraint."[8] Hyde, too, observes that the trickster lives at the boundary between civilized, sanctioned behavior and misbehavior, sometimes obscuring, challenging, and moving that boundary by engaging in activities that test the boundary's limits. The trickster's testing function is essential, and not just because that's what tricksters do: this boundary testing is also essential to the very groups and institutions whose conventions the trickster challenges. These groups and institutions understand that "their liveliness depends on having those boundaries regularly disrupted."[9] The trickster's challenges make visible the unstated, invisible values of a group or institution. This visibility, in turn, gives the group or institution a chance to revisit its core values and to restate and modify those values, if need be. Just as small tears and injuries to a muscle allow it to become stronger, so the trickster's challenges to a group's values allow those values to be transformed and strengthened.

The need of cultural groups and institutions to have their boundaries disrupted occasionally is crucial to understanding the role of the Mountaineer in general and of the WVU Mountaineer more specifically. As noted above, the official WVU Mountaineer already embodies the paradoxical double role of being both the upstanding representative for the institution and a rabble-rousing cheerleader for students, fans, and alumni. Where does the balance between those two aspects of the WVU Mountaineer's identity and function lie? And how far can the individual portraying the WVU Mountaineer push that boundary in either direction before upsetting the balance between the two?

The boundaries that regularly get tested at WVU are the very ones Babcock-Abrahams articulates: the ones that lie "between the individual and society, between freedom and constraint." As we shall see, the Mountaineer comes by these contradictions honestly, through its twin roots in the earlier figures of the squatter and the hillbilly on one side, and the backwoodsman and frontiersman on the other side. While both the hillbilly and the frontiersman are symbols of freedom, the hillbilly represents a more disruptive, unrestrained kind of freedom than the frontiersman. As both Babcock-Abrahams and Hyde suggest, these hillbilly and frontiersman aspects of the Mountaineer don't cancel each other out; rather, they complement each other. They give the Mountaineer a wider range of characteristics than either figure alone would, and they also give individuals more latitude for performing Mountaineer identity. Depending on the context, people who identify as Mountaineers can choose either to reinforce or to push the boundary between the two: when discussing West Virginia with people outside the state, they might enact the frontiersman side of the identity, stressing the grit, hardiness, and humility of West Virginians. After a big WVU football win (or loss), however, they might get drunk and set a couch on fire. Whether the university likes it or not, these are both performances consistent with the dual nature of Mountaineer identity.

Here and throughout the text, when I use the term *performance*, I'm not referring solely to the formal performance of WVU's official Mountaineer mascot but also to the informal performances that people who identify themselves as Mountaineers engage in, such as the two described above: the serious conversation with outsiders and the couch burning. How do Mountaineers understand what it means to be a Mountaineer, and how do they demonstrate to themselves and to outsiders what it means? In other words, how do they perform Mountaineer identity? And how has that performance changed over time?

That, in a nutshell, is the work of this book.

What fascinated me as I did my research was discovering that over time there has been a regular, almost predictable oscillation between the frontiersman and hillbilly ends of the Mountaineer spectrum. For much of the Mountaineer's existence—first, as a moniker for the people of western Virginia generally, then as a name for the citizens of the new state of West Virginia, and then as a specific term for WVU students, fans, and alumni—the frontiersman and hillbilly have coexisted peacefully. But with great regularity, the two identities come into conflict over those cultural boundaries described above. And specifically, West Virginia University has tried, at various times, to kill the boundary-pushing trickster—the hillbilly—and to elevate the more constrained and civilized frontiersman.

Chapter 1 explores the roots of the Mountaineer by looking at its earlier incarnations from colonial times until the turn of the twentieth century. To truly understand the debate about the Mountaineer's identity—in particular, the conflict between the untamed, wild man side and the stalwart frontiersman side—we have to understand how far back the roots of both halves of that identity extend: they go back not only to pre-Revolutionary days but to England itself. As the United States expanded westward, the figures of the squatter and the backwoodsman entered American popular imagination and became powerful political tools that could be used both to the advantage and the disadvantage of people living in the Appalachians. After the Civil War, emancipation, Reconstruction, and the flood of European immigrants to the United States, rural whites were held up—at varying turns—as objects of scorn, charity, and romantic racism by outsiders.

Chapter 2 looks at how the idea of the Mountaineer was impacted in the early twentieth century by the invention of the popular culture hillbilly, a figure that—by the 1930s and 1940s—was ubiquitous in films, music, comics, and other media. The hillbilly gained popularity at exactly the moment that WVU decided to make the Mountaineer its official mascot, forever cementing the link between the two figures, despite later attempts by university administrators to sever that link. This connection will be traced through research and fieldwork with men who attended

WVU immediately after World War II, a time when the university's student body grew enormously, not just in terms of numbers but in terms of cultural diversity, as former servicemen from ethnic, working-class backgrounds became first-generation college students on the GI Bill. This was also the era when the portrayal of the Mountaineer as a hillbilly reached its peak, when Mountaineer Day (later Mountaineer Week) came into existence, and also—in the 1950s—when the hillbilly image was formally banished by the university administration.

Chapter 3 focuses on the Mountaineer during the 1960s into the early 1970s, a time of social and political upheaval that affected West Virginia and WVU as surely as it affected other places and college campuses. And yet, this was also the decade when Lyndon Johnson declared the War on Poverty, which focused heavily on Appalachia and which all too often was justified by selling the same old combination of romance and repulsion that has shaped how people perceive Appalachia not just for decades but for centuries. In an era when young men were being drafted to carry rifles for their country in an unpopular war, and students at home were pushing back against institutional authority, the Mountaineer again became a locus for playing with ideas about rebellion, dissent, patriotism, and Appalachian identity.

In chapter 4 I turn to the experiences of the only two women ever to serve as WVU Mountaineers, Natalie Tennant and Rebecca Durst. Despite serving nearly twenty years apart, both women faced intense criticism and sexism during their time as Mountaineers. While early chapters focus on the ways that Mountaineer identity has always been linked to ideas about race and social class, chapter 4 examines the ways in which Tennant and Durst exposed the link between the Mountaineer and masculinity.

The final chapter looks at more recent controversies surrounding Mountaineer identity, following on the controversy created by Rebecca Durst's service as the second female Mountaineer. From MTV's short-lived series *Buckwild* to J. D. Vance's surprise best-seller *Hillbilly Elegy* to the West Virginia teachers' strike of 2018, Appalachian culture has been very much in the national spotlight in recent years. And the WVU Mountaineer itself has undergone an enormous shift with the rollout of the university's Go First publicity campaign, which seems designed to decouple Mountaineer values from a specific Mountaineer body. And yet conflicts endure about what it means to be a Mountaineer, as students continue to embrace the Mountaineer's wild side and administrators continue to quash it. More than two hundred years after the term was first used to describe western Virginians, what is it about the Mountaineer that keeps it so relevant and controversial? And in an increasingly globalized world—and in particular, on an increasingly diverse campus—what is the future of the Mountaineer?

The Battle of the Mountaineers, Official and Unofficial

———

Not all readers will agree with the aspects of Mountaineer identity that I focus on in the following chapters, and I suspect some will be disappointed that this is not a book that chronicles the service of every person who has served as the WVU Mountaineer. That is certainly a book that deserves to be written. This book, though, is a cultural history of the figure of the Mountaineer in a broad sense, not just a history of the official WVU Mountaineer. To be sure, the two figures and their histories are related: the official WVU Mountaineer is, of course, based on the larger idea that the Mountaineer stands for all West Virginians, representing their history, heritage, and values. But these two incarnations of the Mountaineer do not always intersect neatly. In fact, the book focuses frequently on moments when the university's official idea of who and what the Mountaineer should be came into conflict with broader ideas about the Mountaineer's identity.

After all, the term *Mountaineer* existed for over a century before the university adopted it, and thus has a much longer, more complex, and broader-ranging history than just that of the WVU Mountaineer. (This is why I will, insofar as possible, use the term *WVU Mountaineer* to indicate that I'm referring specifically to the university's mascot, and *Mountaineer* to indicate that I'm referring to the larger, older idea of the Mountaineer.) Some might even argue that the university has exercised too much control in shaping and defining the idea of the Mountaineer: after all, the name belongs to all West Virginians, not just those affiliated with the university. Little did WVU know when it adopted the nickname in the early twentieth century that it was also agreeing to accept the baggage that the Mountaineer brought with it from its hundred-plus years of circulation. In some ways, the history of the WVU Mountaineer chronicles the university's slow realization of just how complicated and contentious its choice of mascot was, not to mention its ongoing attempts to regulate and control the concept of the Mountaineer.

As a folklorist, I'm fascinated by this interaction between traditional folk ideas about the Mountaineer and the university's "official" ones. Spoiler alert: in this sort of battle, the folk version almost always wins. And I do approach this project as a folklorist, not as a trained historian. As such, while I want to get the historical facts right and provide as deep and detailed a sense of cultural context as possible, ultimately it's stories that matter to me: the stories of the students and alumni who so generously talked to me about their experiences at WVU but also the larger narratives that those stories helped me understand.

My prior experience in folklore fieldwork may have prepared me for the work of doing oral history and archival research, but it did not prepare me for the challenges (and deep pleasures) of doing historiography. Even just dipping my toe into those waters has given me tremendous respect for historians. How do you know when to stop? There is always another archival source to check out, another book to read. To that end, I am incredibly grateful to those historians whose work helped me to situate my research in the larger context of West Virginia and Appalachian history: John Alexander Williams's *West Virginia: A History* provided vital facts and details, and I am especially appreciative of Williams's insistence on actively resisting the usual way of telling the state's history. Apart from personal interviews and archival research, a number of books were particularly useful in helping shape my thinking about this project. Nancy Isenberg's paradigm-shifting *White Trash: The 400-Year Untold History of Class in America* and Steven Stoll's *Ramp Hollow: The Ordeal of Appalachia* were hugely influential, particularly in terms of understanding the ways that Mountaineer identity was shaped by much larger and much older economic and social systems. Anthony Harkins's *Hillbilly: A Cultural History*—a study of the popular culture incarnations and meanings of the hillbilly that is both sweeping and incredibly precise—helped me frame the long history of the hillbilly icon, which is so closely linked to that of the Mountaineer. These are but a few of the book-length sources that undergird my work, and I mention them specifically for readers who are interested in exploring the broader history of West Virginia and Appalachia in more depth and detail.

Mascot or Not?

As a college sports mascot, the Mountaineer is one of the very few that is portrayed by a single, identifiable individual. Most mascots are of the type I refer to as "foam heads"; the identity of the individual portraying the mascot is obscured by an outsized costume, especially by elaborate headgear that goes beyond a basic mask. These typical mascot costumes exaggerate the mascot's size, making an already unhuman figure seem even less human by virtue of its enormous physical proportions. But mascots' individuality is disguised in other ways, too. In the course of my research, I had the great pleasure of interviewing master puppeteer and puppet maker Ingrid Crepeau, who designed and built the mascot costumes for the Washington Nationals Presidents, among many other college and professional sports teams. It was Crepeau who told me about the "mascot code," a set of informal rules among sports mascots that create and protect a mascot's magical otherness. One of the most important of these rules is that the identity of the performers who occupy the mascot costumes be kept secret. Teams rarely reveal the names of the person (or people) who inhabit the mascot costume. Another piece of the code is that if the mascot is, in fact, portrayed by multiple people, two people cannot portray the mascot simultaneously, even if their appearances are at different venues. Most crucially, however, mascots are not allowed to talk. They learn to communicate with fans through gestures and movements, but they cannot speak.[10]

Clearly, WVU Mountaineers break all the usual rules of mascotry: there is only one WVU Mountaineer (and an alternate) at any given time; the identity of the person is not only known but essential both to their selection and to their service; and the mascot absolutely talks. In fact, over the years, the WVU Mountaineer's service has become as much, if not more, about being a public-relations spokesperson for the university as it is about cheering at sports events. Whereas early Mountaineers were only expected to show up and cheer at sporting events, recent Mountaineers have put in an average of 250 non-sports-related public appearances a year, showing up for alumni events and fund-raisers, giving speeches at schools, and visiting children in hospitals. When I explained all of this to Crepeau, she, too, opined that she wouldn't call the WVU Mountaineer a mascot—which a number of former Mountaineers had already told me. Crepeau just helped me understand why. So, to paraphrase the movie *Stand By Me*, if not a mascot, then what the hell *is* the Mountaineer?

While a Mountaineer's face is visible, he or she does wear a costume—although at least one former Mountaineer said he didn't think of it as a costume since that evokes ideas about disguise and playacting and phoniness in general. Throughout this book, then, I'll refer to the WVU Mountaineer's typical outfit as the Mountaineer's *kit*, borrowing the British slang term for kit in the sense of "a set of things, such as tools or clothes, used for a particular purpose or activity."[11] Notably, *kit* is also used by Civil War reenactors to describe their clothing and accessories—an especially apt connection, given West Virginia's birth as a product of the Civil War. *Kit* also acknowledges that the Mountaineer doesn't just put on the buckskins and head out the door. The coonskin cap, the moccasins, the musket, and all its accoutrements are a necessary part of the kit as well. One might say that in recent years, a beard has also become part of the unofficial kit. The beard is contentious in many ways: as we'll see in chapter 4, both of the women who served as the Mountaineer were subjected to endless criticism and ridicule for not having or being able to grow one (indeed, many cited that as the primary reason why women should not be allowed to serve as Mountaineer). Because of these incidents, the university has consistently emphasized that the beard is not a required part of the Mountaineer's kit (though a WVU web page does say that "male Mountaineers customarily grow a beard during their tenure"[12]). However, very few Mountaineers wore beards at all for the first thirty years of the official mascot's existence; it was not until male facial hair became more widely accepted that the beard became part of the customary kit of the WVU Mountaineer.

Taken as a whole, the Mountaineer's kit is remarkably similar to the garb described by West Virginia clergyman and writer Joseph Doddridge, whose backwoodsman appears in a "hunting shirt, a shotpouch, with his powderhorn on his right side, with his feet and legs, dressed, of course, in leggins and mockasons."[13] That description, though written in 1823, is a pretty accurate summary of the general appearance of today's WVU

Mountaineer. Several former Mountaineers told me that putting on the kit was a transformative experience: that it changed
them from an individual into the icon of the Mountaineer. This is
remarkable to me, since, as noted above, what separates the WVU
Mountaineer from other mascots is that the person in the kit is a
recognizable individual. And yet, they also are *not* individuals: in
donning the kit, they transcend individual identity and assume
a communal identity that links them not only to previous WVU
Mountaineers but to state history and to a whole set of intangible values and beliefs. It seems like a paradox: how can the WVU
Mountaineer be both a recognizable individual *and* the symbolic
embodiment of state identity? Looked at more closely, though,
there's no paradox at all: given that Mountaineer identity is all
about individualism, it makes perfect sense to have a mascot who
is both a unique individual and—by virtue of that very individualism—the embodiment of larger ideals about autonomy and
freedom.

As we'll see in chapter 2, however, it hasn't always been the
case that only one person can portray the WVU Mountaineer. In
fact, the designation of an official Mountaineer seems to have
been a response to the fact that before the 1930s many university
men informally played Mountaineer at sporting events, showing
up for games in "overalls, a flannel shirt, coonskin cap, a sheep
or bear skin type vest" and carrying a rifle.[14] That outfit—with its
overalls and flannel shirt—is clearly more evocative of the hillbilly
figure than the frontiersman.

Even after the university formalized the selection of a single
Mountaineer in 1937, however, other men continued to play
Mountaineer at games and in other contexts, donning outfits
all along the range of the hillbilly-to-frontiersman spectrum,
depending on what any individual man had available. The look
of either frontiersman or hillbilly is easy to replicate, and in
those early years of the Mountaineer's existence, when there
was no authorized logo gear available, students dressing up in
their own interpretation of the Mountaineer's garb was a way to

display their fandom. I think many of the students who played Mountaineer in the early days of the mascot's existence did so because it created, for them, the same sense of transformation that several former WVU Mountaineers described to me: putting on the outfit connected them to a deeper, more collective sense of identity, one that incorporated not only fellow students and fans, but all West Virginians, past and present. It's a remarkable bit of magic, in some ways, and is part of what has always captivated and intrigued me about the Mountaineer.

The Origins of the Mountaineer

MONTANI SEMPER LIBERI: Mountaineers are always free. West Virginia's state motto neatly encapsulates the anti-elite, anti-establishment attitude that lies at the heart of Mountaineer identity. Over 150 years later, a phrase that began as a declaration of the state's independence from Virginia continues to reflect an iconoclastic spirit with which contemporary residents still identify; surely not many other state mottoes remain as relevant to their residents' contemporary identities. In a June 2016 newsletter, Senator Joe Manchin neatly encapsulated this idea when he wrote that "West Virginians have always abandoned the status quo to fight for what is right."[1]

The Mountaineer identity long predates the formation of the state. Well before the Civil War, residents of the western part of Virginia felt themselves to be culturally and economically different from their eastern counterparts. Most mountain residents were independent, geographically dispersed small farmers who did not own the land that they farmed, whereas the eastern part of the state was dominated by wealthy, slaveholding landowners. When the state of Virginia drew up its constitution in 1776, it granted voting rights only to "white males owning at least 25 acres of improved or 50 acres of unimproved land."[2] This requirement clearly favored residents in the already culti-

Figure 1.1. The Great Seal of the State of West Virginia, designed by Joseph H. Diss Debar.

vated eastern part of the state. Western Virginians were also disenfranchised by Virginia's law allowing only "two delegates per county, regardless of population."[3] Western residents bristled under these restrictions, and in 1803 John G. Jackson, the state representative from Harrison County in western Virginia, wrote a letter to the *Richmond Examiner* condemning these practices. Notably, he signed it not with his name but instead as "A Mountaineer."[4]

West Virginia historian John Alexander Williams downplays this eastern/western Virginia split, arguing that the belief that "western Virginia [was] by 1861 a society so radically different from eastern Virginia that a division of the state was inevitable" is more of "a long-established West Virginia tradition" than a historical fact. The split, he says, was neither inevitable nor unique:

> The conflict in Virginia was no worse than the conflict between eastern and western Tennessee or upstate and downstate Illinois or northern and southern California. What distinguishes Virginia from these states is that the Civil War threw a military line across the state. The line remained relatively stationary for more than two years, cordoning off the most dissatisfied section of the state, the northwestern corner, from the rest of the Old Dominion. If this had happened elsewhere, other states might have divided, but it happened only in Virginia and only Virginia split.[5]

To be sure, the "line across the state" was chosen not along cultural lines, but for purposes of transportation, infrastructure, and military strategy. However, Williams's offhand comment about the way the line "cordon[ed] off the most dissatisfied section of the state" glosses over a crucial piece of cultural information. "The most dissatisfied section of the state" suggests that there was, in fact, a broad consensus of feeling and opinion in the western part of Virginia that was markedly different from the sentiments of its more eastern population. There were certainly many in western Virginia who did not want to break from Virginia and who supported the Confederate cause in the war. In *West Virginia: A History*, Williams goes to great lengths to suggest that as it developed its sense of statehood, West Virginia looked like and aspired to be more like Virginia—culturally and politically—than not.

While Williams is correct in pointing us away from tradition and back to historical fact, tradition, myth, and legend have power in the real world and are a big part of what this chapter will explore. Folklorists have on occasion used the terms *local legend* and *local history* interchangeably in an effort to show how community histories, whether oral or written, often home in on a very few, significant events—events that in some way are emblematic not only of the community's past but also of its present character. These stories usually have a factual basis, but certain aspects of the narrative get emphasized, exaggerated, and even embellished over time as the story becomes less about what actually happened and more about what tellers want audiences to understand about its larger significance. Almost always, these stories say more about what contemporary people want to believe about their past than about the past itself. And the values emphasized in these narratives are usually those that the community wants to reclaim and reinforce rather than ones that it sees as no longer relevant.

Very few historical myths and legends have the staying power of the Mountaineer. From its first appearance in print in 1803 as a synonym for a resident of western Virginia, the idea of the Mountaineer has been integral to West Virginians' identity, conjuring up notions of rebelliousness, independence, and dissent—although *how* those notions manifested themselves changed over time.

The Mountaineer is a peculiar hybrid of two distinct but inextricably linked figures: that of the frontiersman, or backwoodsman, as he was known in his earlier incarnations—and that of the hillbilly, or squatter, as he was previously known. In the nineteenth century, these two figures came together in a unique way in Appalachia and especially in western Virginia, where residents identified themselves as Mountaineers even before West Virginia became a state. How these figures merged is the subject of this chapter, which also examines the ways in which all of the above terms were markers of race and class in nineteenth-century America. Mountaineers are always free, and—as the term and the identity emerged over the course of the nineteenth century—they were also always assumed to be white and nearly always poor. In fact, during the Civil War and especially afterward, the term *Mountaineer* took on an additional level of meaning as it was used to distinguish "Anglo-Saxon" whites from "white trash," Southern whites who were perceived as having been irredeemably corrupted by the slave economy.

The Split Roots of the Mountaineer's Family Tree

The figure of the Mountaineer has its roots in the colonial American figure of the rural rube, itself based on the stock character of the Yorkshireman "Hodge" in British theater.[6] The earliest American example can be found in Virginia planter William Byrd's account of his 1728 expedition to survey the contested

Figure 1.2. *The Map of Lubberland or the Ile of Lasye*, British cartoon circa 1670.

boundary between Virginia and North Carolina, in which he describes lazy men who "lye and Snore . . . light their Pipes . . . [and] loiter away their lives" while their women do all the work—an image made concrete by Billy deBeck some two hundred years later in the comic strip character of Snuffy Smith.[7] Byrd cast the area as the New World's "Lubberland," a fictional realm from

English folklore, where "sloth was contagious" and even dogs were so lazy that they rested their heads against the wall when they barked.[8]

Byrd's New World "lubbers" would morph into the "squatters" and "crackers" of the eighteenth and early nineteenth centuries and then into "white trash" and "hillbillies" in the nineteenth and twentieth centuries. The Mountaineer's roots can be found in all of these figures, but the Mountaineer's family tree has a second and equally important branch in the figures of the backwoodsman and the frontiersman. Understanding the complicated and inextricable links between these two sources of the Mountaineer's identity is crucial to understanding not only how and why West Virginia, and WVU in particular, adopted the Mountaineer as its moniker but also why the figure of the Mountaineer has been contested and regulated over the years. As noted in the introduction, the Mountaineer is both trickster and culture hero, and while these two roles work in tandem much of the time, occasionally they come into conflict with each other.

The westward expansion of America's frontier in the eighteenth and early nineteenth centuries meant that the territory of the lubbers, which Byrd "discovered" at the boundary between Virginia and North Carolina, soon extended well beyond that area. Eventually, it came to include all of the mountainous region between western Virginia and Arkansas, including Georgia and Alabama—though Nancy Isenberg traces this backwoods figure "as far north as Maine, as far south as Florida, and across the Northwest and Southeast territories."[9] During this era, the two branches of the Mountaineer's identity were only beginning to emerge as separate identities; pejorative terms like *cracker* and *squatter* were used more or less interchangeably with the term *backwoodsman*, although writers clearly were trying to establish some kind of social distinction or hierarchy among poor rural whites. *Squatter* and *cracker* were terms used specifically to refer to settlers occupying land that they held no title to, land that generally they did not cultivate or farm but used instead for timber, hunting, and fishing.[10] Squatters were largely itinerant, moving from place to place rather than claiming and occupying a particular plot of land.

But another American personage was beginning to emerge at this time: the noble backwoodsman, or frontiersman, exemplified by Natty Bumppo of James Fenimore Cooper's *Leatherstocking Tales*. Although the backwoodsman, too, was an itinerant hunter and explorer, he was distinguished from the average squatter by his common sense, wit, and generosity. The backwoodsman had "a folksy appeal: though coarse and ragged in his dress and manners, the post-Revolutionary backwoodsman was at times described as hospitable and generous, someone who invited weary travelers into his humble cabin."[11]

The backwoodsman wasn't universally regarded this way, however: as Isenberg describes it, the "'Adam' of the American wilderness had a split personality: he was half hearty rustic and half dirk-carrying highwayman. In his most favorable cast as backwoodsman, he was a homespun philosopher, an independent spirit, and a strong and courageous man who shunned fame and wealth. But turn him over and he became the white savage, a ruthless brawler and eye-gouger."[12] This implied connection between the backwoodsman and the "savage" is another important piece of the puzzle of the Mountaineer's identity. As will be discussed at greater length in chapter 2, it's no coincidence that the WVU Mountaineer is attired in buckskins and moccasins. Though other factors seem to have impacted the university's decision to promote that version of the Mountaineer, aspects of the Mountaineer's dress connect him squarely to Native American cultures—albeit an inaccurate and highly romanticized idea of those cultures. With his buckskin moccasins and clothes, the Mountaineer aligns himself with Appalachia's white and native histories, suggesting that backwoodsmen and American Indians shared a common set of values about the land—what it can provide and how it should be revered—and a common set of skills to practice those values.

Of course, this doesn't reflect the actual history of the region, which largely involved white settlers taking native lands and displacing—often violently—the groups that had lived or hunted on those lands for thousands of years. And many backwoodsmen, such as Simon Kenton, made names for themselves specifically for being ferocious hunters of American Indians. But, as is the case in most parts of the eastern and midwestern United States, once the native peoples were gone, it became acceptable, even necessary, to ennoble and romanticize them. The Mountaineer's garb is, on this level, a sort of homage to the state's native past.

There's an additional irony here. Early observers often placed backwoodsmen and squatters below Native Americans on the social scale, arguing that "at least American Indians belonged in the woods."[13] Later, in the mid-nineteenth century, southern industrialist William Gregg would bump them up a notch, noting that poor rural whites lived "in a state but one step in advance of the Indian of the forest."[14] The business of ordering classes of people on a social hierarchy based on race was (and continues to be) a persistent practice, and isn't limited to Native Americans; more often, poor rural whites were measured against African Americans, both enslaved and free, as we shall later see. However, while whiteness was and is often measured against racial and cultural Others, it is notable that both in the past and present, whiteness can incorporate a certain degree of "Indianness." Claiming some degree of Native American identity does not dilute one's claim to a white identity but can in fact enhance it by giving it the luster of historical rootedness and authenticity. Witness the longevity of some white families' claims to have a Cherokee princess in their family tree, a fallacious but tenacious practice that dates back to the 1840s.[15] As long as American Indians are kept in the past, their (imagined) legacy can be displayed proudly.

But in the early days of the Republic, it was the squatter or cracker against whom wealthier whites measured their own social status. In 1817 Thomas Jefferson's granddaughter Cornelia wrote a letter to her sister, describing a visit she and her grandfather made to Jefferson's property at Natural Bridge, Virginia. There, Cornelia came face-to-face with a family of squatters, whom she described as a "half civiliz'd race who lived beyond the ridge." The children were barely dressed, one man was shirtless, and between all of them, she noted, they had only "two or three pairs of shoes." She was shocked by their coarse speech and even more shocked that the family seemed to have no sense of shame about how they lived. Given the horror she felt, it's surprising that Cornelia was able to write to her sister about such shocking things, but write she did. The only part she left out was the fact that the "half civiliz'd" family was probably just as perplexed by her.[16]

In Cornelia Jefferson's observations, we see traces of the stereotypical hillbilly that are still with us today: the inadequate clothing, the bare feet, the peculiar dialect, and the ignorance of social convention. But Cornelia didn't invent these traits; in fact, her descriptions about poor frontier whites were likely informed by preexisting ideas that she'd encountered many times before. Isenberg neatly sums up these ideas: "The ubiquity of squatters across the United States turned them into a powerful political trope. They came to be associated with five traits: (1) crude habitations; (2) boastful vocabulary; (3) distrust of civilization and city folk; (4) an instinctive love of liberty (read: licentiousness); and (5) degenerate patterns of breeding. Yet even with such unappealing traits, the squatter also acquired some favorable qualities: the simple backwoodsman welcomed strangers into his cabin, the outrageous storyteller entertained them through the night."[17]

In this list, we see the full range of stereotypes that persisted about squatters through their being redubbed *white trash* and *hillbillies*. The stereotypes include squalid homes, interbreeding, hostility toward outsiders, and unbridled indulgence in vice, as well as more positive attributes such as hospitality and a love of storytelling.

While this combination of traits may seem paradoxical, it was, in fact, central to a growing cultural trope in the United States in the early nineteenth century: that of the unlettered, unsophisticated rustic who nevertheless has the brains and the brawn to deal handily with more "cultured" men who try to take advantage of him. Cecil Eby nicely summarizes this figure as "that enduring and ubiquitous American hero, a robustly innocent creature fabricated of roughly equal parts of simple heart and common sense, who, while docile and modest under normal circumstances, possesses the power to outwit or over-throw smart alecks who encroach upon his cultural dominion."[18] Contemporarily, we recognize this as the country bumpkin versus city slicker trope that continues to be a mainstay of jokes, television shows, films, and other entertainment.

So prevalent was this theme in nineteenth-century American writing that its type is sometimes referred to generically as "the squatter versus the dandy," and stories incorporating this theme could plausibly be called a folktale type. Mark Twain's first pub-lished story, "The Dandy Frightening the Squatter" (1852), is a notable example. In it, the dandy alights from a steamboat and, spotting a rustic backwoodsman on the shore, decides to take the opportunity to impress the single ladies on board the steam-boat. "Ladies, if you wish to enjoy a good laugh, step out on the guards," he calls out, announcing that he "intend[s] to frighten that gentleman into fits who stands on the bank." He approaches the backwoodsman and shouts, "Found you at last, have I? You are the very man I've been looking for these three weeks! Say your prayers! . . . You'll make a capital barn door, and I shall drill the key-hole myself!" The backwoodsman says nothing, respond-ing instead with a massive punch that knocks the dandy into the Mississippi. When the dandy surfaces, the squatter cries, "I say, yeou, next time yeou come around drillin' key-holes, don't forget yer old acquaintances!"[19] The squatter takes the first punch and gets the last laugh.

Most dandy/squatter stories end with this one-two combination of punch and punch line, but a more complex and relevant version of the story can actually be found in the writings of West Virginia's own Joseph Doddridge, a clergyman, writer, and historian who lived and worked in the areas around Lewisburg and Clarksburg (and for whom Doddridge County is named). In 1823, nearly thirty years before Twain's story was published, Doddridge wrote a short play titled *Dialogue of the Backwoodsman and the Dandy*. Doddridge sets the scene as follows: "The curtain rises and presents the Back-woods-man in an hunting shirt, a shotpouch, with his powderhorn on his right side, with his feet and legs, dressed, of course, in leggins and mockasons. A Spruce little Dandy in the dress of his order approaches him. The dialogue then begins."[20] The Dandy proceeds, in the mode of an early ethnographer, to ask the Backwoodsman all sorts of questions about his way of life. And as was often the case with early ethnographers, the Dandy's questions are really designed to confirm what he already believes he knows about frontier life, not to actually learn anything new. The Backwoodsman humors him for a while, but then the Dandy goes a step too far:

> I perceive from all you have said Mr. Back-woodsman, that you must have been in a deplorable condition—your country a wilderness; your habitations wretched hovels, or cabins; your furniture gourds, your marriages scenes of riot and obscenity: No places of worship; no schools, courts, nor civil government of any sort; a continual warfare with the Indians. No comforts; no elegancies for the body, and no means of improvement for the mind-Heavens! What a condition of human society! Was this country a Tartary or a Siberia? Surely, Sir, you must have been neither more nor less than a set of semi barbarians![21]

The Backwoodsman does what he feels naturally inclined to do, which is to punch the Dandy in the face. He responds to the label of "barbarian" by calling the Dandy, well, a Dandy, wondering aloud why "I suffer such a little finikin, puny pinched up thing, to call me and the rest of the first settlers of this country, simple barbarians?"[22] Unlike Twain's story, Doddridge's doesn't end with a joke, but with a lecture, as the Backwoodsman follows his punch with a lesson about the true nature of frontier life and frontier people:

> A Backwoodsman is a queer sort of fellow . . . If he's not a man of larnin, he had plain good sense. If his dress is not fine, his inside works are good and his heart is sound. If he is not rich or great, he knows that he is the father of his country. . . . You little dandies, and other big folk may freely enjoy the fruits of our hardships; you may feast, where we had to starve; and frolic, where we had to fight; but at peril of all of you, give the Backwoodsman none of your slack-jaw.[23]

For additional comic effect—and to underscore the frivolousness of the Dandy's life—the Backwoodsman has to help the Dandy back to his feet to hear this lecture, since the Dandy's tight corsets render him unable to get up on his own.

There are a couple of notable things about Doddridge's play. The first is its link to larger forces of Romantic Nationalism in the early nineteenth century. In Europe, concerns about how industrialization and urbanization might alter traditional cultures drove the brothers Grimm to collect German fairy tales and Wordsworth to wax poetic about English leech gatherers. Romantic Nationalism was a potent force in the newly formed United States, as well—but the trouble was, who constituted the United States' peasant class? Who were the simple folk who had lived on the land for centuries and who represented the soul of the nation's identity? The closest analogue was the backwoodsman, even though (as Doddridge's play suggests) he'd only been on the frontier for fifty years. Nevertheless, Doddridge's Dandy approaches the Backwoodsman with the same odd blend of reverence and snobbery that upper-class scholars in Europe approached their subjects. The difference is that Doddridge's Backwoodsman

The Origins of the Mountaineer   **31**

refuses—quite forcefully—to be relegated to the past and to barbarism. It's a stunningly modern tale in some ways, since the Backwoodsman is quite conscious of how the Dandy is trying to represent him and lets him know that he is alive and well and a hell of a lot smarter than the Dandy imagines him to be.

Also notable is the Backwoodsman's two-pronged approach to countering stereotypes: with physical force first and reason second. Doddridge's Backwoodsman follows up his immediate and violent response with a reasoned lecture that both explains the Backwoodsman's true nature to the Dandy and shows the Backwoodsman to be a truer and harder-working citizen, one whose unrecognized toil allows "little dandies" to have easy lives. This is a very different take on the squatter/dandy story, and what is most remarkable about it is how much its themes still resonate in contemporary West Virginia. In Doddridge's "Backwoodsman," we see the emergence of the figure that would eventually become the Mountaineer: he exhibits good sense, wears practical clothing, has a sound heart, and—most tellingly—is more than a little resentful of those who place themselves above him. This latter quality—that of a defensive pride in the face of elitism—is a particularly important one that lingers to this day. We see it, for example, in the rhetoric about the "war on coal," whose proponents are quick to remind today's "little dandies" and "big folk" that "coal keeps America's lights on." Eby characterizes "the mood" of Doddridge's later book, *Notes on the Settlement and Indian Wars of the Western Parts of Virginia and Pennsylvania* (1824) as "nostalgic and defensive," traits that, in many ways, came to be part of the Mountaineer identity as a whole.[24]

It's important to note how early Doddridge's account seems for frontier nostalgia, since today we imagine the early nineteenth century to be the very apex of frontier life. We make this association for specific reasons that will be discussed in the section about Andrew Jackson and Davy Crockett. But Doddridge's play reveals that by the 1820s, there was already a sense that the "real" frontier days were already over. In the *Dialogue of the Backwoodsman and the Dandy*, both characters talk about the frontier as though it no longer exists, as though the Backwoodsman is already an anachronism:

> Dandy. Good morning sir. I am glad to see you; I have often heard and read of the Back-woods-man: and supposing, from your dress you are one of them, I should like to have a little conversation with you, concerning the first settlement of this country, and your wars with the Indians.
>
> Back-woods-man. With all my heart.
>
> Dan[dy]. I have no doubt your tales of former times are highly interesting and entertaining, and of course worthy of remembrance.
>
> Back[woodsman]. For the matter of that, I cannot say much in their favor. I have no larnin, an I never was much of a hand at tellin tales; howenever, I will do with you as I have often seed them do in the Court, in West Liberty, I will answer such questons [*sic*] as you will ax me.
>
> Dan[dy]. What time did you come to this country?
>
> Back[woodsman]. In the year 1773, the summer before Dunmore's war, my father came over the mountins, and settled in this part of the country. I was then a thumpin chunk of a boy, may be ten or a dozen years old.
>
> Dan[dy]. What was the external appearance of the country at your first recollection of it?
>
> Back[woodsman]. Why, Sir, the tarnal appearance of the country was, that it was all wild woods, and full of deers, and bears, and turkies, and rattlesnakes—and in the summer time, the weeds was so high, that you could track a man on horseback, at full galop.
>
> Dan[dy]. I suppose, Sir, you had then but few of the comforts of civilized life.
>
> Back[woodsman]. Why, we was not very fine to be sure, but we was civil enough; for the war which placed our night caps in danger

every day, made us very lovin to one another; one man then was worth as much as twenty is now.[25]

Already, by 1823, Doddridge's Backwoodsman feels that the good old days are past, and that the succeeding generations have lost frontier virtues. In his preface to the play, Doddridge frames the piece not as a comedy or even as an invention, but as history, insisting that "the state of society which it describes is precisely such as existed at the period of time alluded to. Even the facts stated by 'the Back-woods-man' are historical. Its language that which was in current use among our first settlers."[26]

So what had been lost by 1823, less than fifty years into nationhood? Doddridge's recasting of the Backwoodsman as "the father of his country" gives us an important hint. M. J. Heale argues that "frontier heroes were in great demand during the second quarter of the nineteenth century," explaining that "the West represented a rejection of the Old World. It was the West which seemed to be unique to the United States. Anxious to establish an identity that was not European, many Americans began to think of western characteristics as American, or national, characteristics."[27]

This anxiety to establish a uniquely American identity wasn't just political, but cultural and literary as well: Heale notes the popularity of Sir Walter Scott's novels in the United States at this time, aligning them with the aforementioned *Leatherstocking Tales*; both Scott's and Fenimore Cooper's works emphasized the Romantic virtue of men living in harmony with nature.[28] The eminent folklorist Benjamin Botkin opens his classic 1944 tome, *A Treasury of American Folklore*, with a discussion of the centrality of the figure of what he terms the "irrepressible backwoodsman," noting that "the backwoodsman was the first of our tall men, whose words were tall talk and whose deeds were tall tales." "Romantic fiction has made much of his fierce, wild independence," Botkin writes, adding the now familiar contrast, that this early American folk hero also possessed a "'rough diamond' chivalry" and "skill with the rifle." Notably, Botkin dates the heyday of the backwoodsman figure to precisely the same time period as Doddridge's play: somewhere between 1815 and 1822, when comedian Noah Ludlow first performed his song "The Hunters of Kentucky," which "marked the passing of the backwoodsman from history into legend" as the American frontier shifted further west.[29]

It is easy to see how the backwoodsman morphed into the Mountaineer, given the backwoodsman's particular combination of values and ideas: he is a person whose separation from the trappings of society—the rules that govern the dandy—makes him more civil, more honest, certainly more manly, and possibly more deeply "American" than city dwellers. Doddridge's play also shows us how deeply aware people living on the frontier in the early nineteenth century were of outsiders' perceptions of them. Like the fictional Backwoodsman, frontierspeople were eager to challenge stereotypes about them and also anxious to prove that they were just as civilized as those who lived in more settled, populated areas. This potent combination of pride in one's heritage and anxiety about outsiders' perceptions lives on to this day in West Virginia, where news stories and other widely disseminated representations of the state are either scrutinized and castigated for perpetuating stereotypes or are praised for making West Virginia look civilized and progressive. Often, as we shall see, these tensions have been played out directly through the figure of the WVU Mountaineer.

Doddridge's play was published only six years after Cornelia Jefferson wrote to her sister about the "half civiliz'd race" she encountered in Natural Bridge, Virginia. The close proximity of these two documents indicates that the squatter and the backwoodsman were well-established types already and that there was a lively debate brewing as to how to define these types and who had the authority to define them. In the decade following the publication of Doddridge's play, this conflict would play out on the national stage in the person of two Tennessee men with very different interpretations of the backwoodsman's identity, each of whom leveraged his particular brand of backwoods capital for political gain: David Crockett and Andrew Jackson.

Jackson versus Crockett

————

The fact that squatter/dandy stories gained widespread popularity in the early to mid-nineteenth century tells us that by that time, isolation was more a part of the frontier myth than of frontier reality: Doddridge's sense that the real frontier days were already over by the 1820s is borne out by the fact that by 1800 a full 20 percent of the US population lived on the frontier between the Appalachian Mountains and the Mississippi River.[30] Speculators and other outsiders were, by this point, very much a part of frontier life, and people back east were curious about these places and the people who lived there. While squatter/dandy stories provided amusement for outsider audiences, for people living on the frontier, such stories provided a kind of narrative reclamation of independence and identity. Eby explains the popularity of such stories among frontierspeople as follows: "Threatened as they were by the lengthening shadows of social change and the diminution of local autonomy, backcountry audiences seemed to find irresistible those skits and stories which focused upon the drubbing of a dandy. Here was their vicarious revenge upon the encroaching swarms of flush-time speculators, Philadelphia lawyers, and Yankefied visitors from bourns east of the Hudson."[31] Claiming the label of *squatter* or *backwoodsman* was a way to gain control over it, to turn it into a badge of honor—or at least into a shield against outside forces. But as with all such linguistic wrestling matches, there was no agreement even among "insiders"—those who identified themselves as squatters or backwoodsmen—about the definition and meaning of those terms or how best to deploy and perform those identities.

This dispute is clearly illustrated by the contrasting images of the backwoodsman offered up to the public by Andrew Jackson and David Crockett. Both men hailed from Tennessee, although their respective birthplaces were at the time of their births still part of western North Carolina. Both rose to political and cultural prominence in the 1820s, though many forget that in addition to being "king of the wild frontier," as the TV theme song would have it, Crockett was also a "militia scout and lieutenant, justice of the peace, town commissioner, state representative, and finally a U.S. congressman," first elected in 1827.[32]

Of the two, it was Jackson who most fit the contemporary stereotype of the cracker or squatter. As Isenberg diplomatically phrases it, Jackson "was not admired for statesmanlike qualities," but rather for his "rough edges, his land hunger, and his close identification with the Tennessee wilderness."[33] The presidential campaigns of 1824, 1828, and 1832 worked hard to sell the positive aspects of Jackson's "wild" nature while downplaying the violent and licentious parts of his biography—the facts that he shot lawyer Charles Dickinson to death in a duel in 1806; that he had an adulterous affair with Rachel Donelson Robards, the woman he would eventually marry; and that in 1818, during his service as an army general, he led an unauthorized military invasion of a Spanish fortification in Pensacola, Florida. These were but a few of his notable exploits. To Old Hickory's supporters, all of this was evidence of his independence and willingness to act rather than to overthink; to his detractors, it was evidence that he was unfit to be a statesman.

However, as Botkin notes, this was precisely the moment when the backwoodsman emerged as the prototypical American folk hero—so who better to represent the growing Republic in the nation's capital? Jackson's first (unsuccessful) run for the presidency took place in 1824, the year after Doddridge published *Dialogue of the Backwoodsman and the Dandy* and the same year in which Doddridge published his *Notes on the Settlement and Indian Wars of the Western Parts of Virginia and Pennsylvania*.

The American public had a seemingly insatiable appetite for frontier tales, whether factual or fictitious. Heale attributes the public fascination with the frontier at this time to the fact that although "once feared by conservatives as a nursery of barbarism, the West was now accepted by almost all easterners. It may be that the benign, if uncouth, images of western heroes like Crockett helped to allay conservative fears; the West, it might be said, was tamed by its myths."[34] Reading audiences and voters in the 1820s were clearly fascinated by the figure of the backwoodsman, even if they still were not sure whether he was, as Doddridge suggested, "the father of our country" or a barbarian. Jackson and Crockett offered up versions of both for public consumption and judgment.

Jackson's approach was to embrace, if not outright exploit, the perception of frontiersmen as rude, aggressive men of action, promoting the efficacy of that approach in contrast to the studied, measured approach of the effete, dandified statesmen of the early Republic. Such dandies, the implication went, couldn't understand, much less function, in the harsh reality of the American frontier. Ironically, Jackson—best remembered for being the author of the Indian Removal Bill that forced native groups out of the Southeast—was often likened by critics to Native Americans in his violent barbarism. Henry Clay described Jackson in 1825 as a "military chieftain," and Jackson himself acknowledged that "great pains had been taken to represent me as having a savage disposition; who allways [sic] carried a Scalping Knife in one hand & a tomahawk in the other."[35] Here again we see the ways in which the identity of the frontiersman was linked with that of the American Indian. In Jackson's case, the link draws on the perception of Indians as violent, fearsome savages; other connections had more to do with the perception of Indians as lazy, stereotypes that fed into ideas about squatters and crackers.

A very different image was offered up by David Crockett. Initially allies, Crockett famously broke from Jackson over

Jackson's Indian Removal Bill, which Crockett opposed. Pressured to toe the party line and stop criticizing Jackson, Crockett claimed that he "would not wear a collar 'round my neck, with 'my dog' written on it, and the name of ANDREW JACKSON on the collar."[36] In so doing, Crockett exemplified the freethinking defiance that characterized the backwoodsman, but in a less abrasive way than Jackson. Jackson's backers, however, responded by tagging Crockett with the stereotypical traits of the squatter, calling him "unsavory and uneducated."[37]

And in fact, Crockett's objections to Jackson's Indian Removal Bill had more to do with its potential impact on the squatters of the frontier than its impact on Native Americans. In the forced removal of Indians, Crockett saw a parallel to—and a legal precedent for—the expulsion of white squatters from the land they had claimed and cleared. Having been a squatter himself, Crockett understood the precarious nature of squatters' rights, and the key issue of his political career was to protect squatters from the unscrupulous land-grab schemes of speculators, backing a "bill that would have sold land directly from the federal government to squatters."[38]

Lest we paint Crockett in too positive a light, we should recall that both Crockett and Jackson were slaveholders, and Crockett is infamously credited for boasting that he could "run like a fox, swim like a eel, yell like an Indian, and swallow a nigger whole."[39] In the end, it was this crass, outlandish bragging and Crockett's larger-than-life persona that secured his legacy, even in his own lifetime, as volumes of the unauthorized *Davy Crockett's Almanack* began being published in 1835. For a man whose life was relatively short (he died at the Alamo at the age of fifty) and whose political career was even shorter, Crockett made the most of his few years of notoriety, playing the role of the backwoodsman so successfully that his name is now almost synonymous with the term. Heale suggests that "Crockett was one of the first Americans to make a living, at least some of the time, as a celebrity. As a farmer and as a politician his record was patchy, but as a celebrity he was a huge success."[40] And Crockett crafted his public image very carefully (fig. 1.3), understanding just what his political handlers and his audiences admired and wanted to hear from him; Crockett "exploited the fondness that the American public had for the self-made man," even directing the publishers of his books to leave in the misspellings and bad grammar, "as I make no literary pretensions."[41] The cultivated image of the uneducated, boastful rube was just that: highly cultivated.

The consciousness of Crockett's performance is deeply significant, both for what it tells us about what was going on in his own time, as well as the ways it foreshadows the performances of the Mountaineer identity that will be discussed in later chapters. Crockett so masterfully embodied the role of frontiersman that more than a hundred years after his death, films and television shows continue to put him forward as the archetypal frontiersman. And, as will be discussed in the next chapter, Crockett's fame—as well as his link to the WVU Mountaineer—was updated and sealed with the Walt Disney television series of the 1950s. Jackson was no less a consummate performer of the backwoodsman identity; in many ways, he was the far more successful, given his greater political influence. Both men played an enormous part in shaping popular notions of what mountain men were like. Where their performances differed is equally important: Jackson recognized the power inherent in the threat of being seen as uncivilized and violent, while Crockett moved toward the other end of the spectrum, embodying the fearless, adventurous, but innately chivalrous natural man. Again, as we shall see, these twin roots of the Mountaineer's origins continue to play a part in its identity to this day.

By the end of the Jacksonian era, the figure of the squatter had become a fixture of the American political scene; during the presidential campaign of 1840, "the squatter morphed into the colloquial common man of democratic lore. Both parties now embraced him . . . [with] depictions of log cabins, popular nicknames, hard-cider drinking, and coonskin caps."[42] Presidential

Figure 1.3. David Crockett, engraved by C. Stuart from the
original portrait by J. G. Chapman, 1839.

candidate Daniel Webster "lamented that he had not been born in a log cabin but claimed vicarious virtue through the fact that his elder brothers and sisters had been."[43] Far from being an outsider, the squatter/backwoodsman was now a stand-in for the American everyman—at least, the poor, landless everyman who lived outside the power centers of the eastern United States. What Doddridge had implied in 1821—that the backwoodsman was "the father of his country"—had now become a far more widespread belief.

However, while Jackson and other politicians of his era milked their rough origins for political gain, their policies actively displaced and impoverished the squatters living on the frontier, who—as Steven Stoll phrases it in *Ramp Hollow*—"lost their lands under the same assumptions, if not the same tactics, deployed against Indians."[44] Simply occupying a piece of land no longer constituted ownership of it. In the emerging capitalist economy of the Jacksonian era, land was a commodity to be held in large swathes by absentee landlords, and squatters who hunted and farmed on those lands were usurpers whose lack of participation in a monetary economy made them lazy drains on the economy, wasted laborers who needed to be put to work in "real" jobs. Thus it is no coincidence that just at the moment that the squatter succeeded in partially defining his identity on his own terms, a different term for the same class of people would emerge: *poor white trash*.

Fussin' and Feudin' White Trash

As the country geared up for Civil War, terms such as *cracker* and *squatter* gave way to a newer, more insidious and lasting label for poor whites living on the margins: *white trash*, a term that "appeared in print as early as 1821 [and] gained widespread popularity in the 1850s."[45] Although we tend to associate the term almost exclusively with the South these days, when it first emerged, it was a term that could be applied to any poor white person living on the frontier. Even Abraham Lincoln was not spared the label; in 1862 Union general David Hunter described Lincoln as having been born a "poor white in a slave state [Kentucky]."[46]

However, as James C. Klotter notes, "Mountain society remained historically apart from that of the southern 'poor whites,' and people who shaped opinion soon grasped this difference. This would in time prove a vitally important distinction, for Mountaineers came to be considered a separate people worthy of uplift."[47] Consequently, while *squatters* and *crackers* morphed into *white trash* and later *hillbillies*, the backwoodsman was being transformed into the noble frontiersman, personified in that notable Confederate general, Stonewall Jackson. Jackson is, of course, one of West Virginia's most illustrious native sons, having been born in what was then Clarksburg, Virginia, in 1824. But while West Virginia might claim Jackson, Jackson did not claim West Virginia. He staunchly opposed dividing his home state of Virginia and identified himself as a Virginian until his death.[48] As Williams notes,

> Most biographers . . . slide over the problem [of Jackson's identifying himself as a Virginian] by trying to fit Stonewall into some sort of "typical Mountaineer" mold, creating a personage who may be identified with West Virginia not by virtue of his conscious choices and acts, but as a social creature who represents in his character, if not his behavior, the salient features of the society that made him. Thus Frank Vandiver in *Mighty Stonewall* presents Jackson as "a mountain man [with] the blunt honesty, the firmness, and the self-reliance of a frontiersman from the remote western parts of Virginia."[49]

This appeal to enthrone Stonewall Jackson as the prototypical Mountaineer is especially notable since it was West Virginia's break from Virginia to stay in the Union and Kentucky's refusal to join the Confederacy that led Northerners to praise the "loyal mountaineers."[50] Jackson managed to maintain his Mountaineer identity despite being a Confederate loyalist; his politics, apparently, were overridden by the "blunt honesty, firmness, and self-reliance" that Vandiver attributes to him. It's this sense of stoicism and indomitable will that Stonewall Jackson shares with the contemporary Mountaineer: he is a man of honor, not a barely civilized fool or "harlequin," as Frederick Douglass characterized Crockett.[51] Nevertheless, as we shall see, these polarized qualities of both rowdy rebelliousness and daring forthrightness shaped the WVU Mountaineer's image, and they continue to battle each other for precedence to this day.

The rowdy, rebellious version of the Mountaineer can be traced back to the figure of the squatter and his subsequent incarnation as white trash, which then evolved into the figure of the hillbilly that will be discussed at the end of this chapter and in the next. What is notable about the terms *white trash* and *hillbilly* is their link—explicit in the first and implied in the second—to specific, evolving ideas about race and whiteness in the late nineteenth and early twentieth centuries. As noted above, squatters, crackers, and backwoodsman were often defined by their likeness to Native American "savages." With the forced expulsion of actual indigenous people from the frontier, that link no longer had the relevance or the sting it had previously.

In the absence of a clear Other against which to measure the racial identity of impoverished frontierspeople, the idea of racial difference got built directly into the label for poor whites. They were not "white," but "white *trash*": racially separate from more urban and urbane white people. Descriptions of the era point to the desire of northern whites to distance themselves from this "Cracker race," as one newspaper article put it, and also to place "white trash" in a hierarchy of whiteness and pseudo-whiteness that would prevent such people from advancement. In 1866 a Boston newspaperman contended that poor southern whites

Figure 1.4. Illustration from George Washington Harris's short story "Sut Lovingood's Daddy, Acting Horse," 1867.

lived in "such filthy poverty, such foul ignorance, such idiotic imbecility" that while "time and effort will lead the Negro up to intelligent manhood . . . I almost doubt if it will be possible to ever lift this 'white trash' into respectability."[52] A New York artillery officer, William Wheeler, expressed his disbelief that the white refugees he encountered in Alabama after the war were truly "Caucasians," doubting that they were of the same "flesh and blood as ourselves." Other observers were slightly more sympathetic, if no less racist; a Union chaplain, Hallock Armstrong, expressed his hope that "the war would knock off the shackles of millions of poor whites, whose bondage was really worse than the African."[53] Regardless of the viewer's take, however, people labeled white trash were white only in name.

American literature of this era also chronicles the tenuous claims to whiteness among the poor in the trans-Appalachian region. Most notable among the "white trash" characters of the time is George Washington Harris's Sut Lovingood, who has the dubious honor of being the first poor white Appalachian character in American fiction (fig. 1.4).[54] Sut is a crass, racist, and vicious prankster who sets the stage for later incarnations of the Mountaineer in the way he revels in putting one over on authority figures, but he just as often ends up being the victim of these tricks due to his own gullibility. In this sense, Sut sets the stage for the intertwined and seemingly paradoxical notion of the Mountaineer as having a razor-sharp native intelligence combined with inexhaustible naivete. A similar figure emerges with the Arkansas traveler, a folkloric and pop-culture phenomenon of the mid- to late nineteenth century, in which the outsider—the traveler—is taken in by the seemingly foolish native.[55] This trope is perhaps best reflected in Twain's *The Adventures of Huckleberry Finn*, in which the Duke, a seasoned conman, adds a line to his ad for *The Royal Nonesuch*, saying "Ladies and children not admitted" with the gleeful prediction that "if that line don't fetch them, I don't know Arkansaw!"[56] Of course, the fact that the natives catch on and show up for the third and final performance with sixty-four dead cats echoes the parallel trope of the fool being duped only for so long. In fact, the descriptions of Arkansas in Twain's novel point to the conflation of Appalachia and the Ozarks—which Anthony Harkins describes more fully in his cultural history *Hillbilly*—a conflation that would continue into the twentieth century, most notably in Al Capp's comic strip *L'il Abner*, whose community of Dogpatch was initially located in Kentucky but later shifted to the Ozarks.[57]

Twain's novel also points to another emerging aspect of Mountaineer identity in the late nineteenth century in the feud episode between the rival Sheperdson and Grangerford families, also located in Arkansas. As Harkins notes, "From the 1870s through the first decade of the next century, regional and national newspapers reported on dozens of family-oriented conflicts, forty-one between 1874 and 1893 alone," including that of West Virginia's Hatfields and McCoys.[58] Historians now attribute the violence to a whole slate of postbellum social and economic woes and see it as the only means many had for maintaining local autonomy. At the time, however, the violence was constructed as the inevitable response of people descended from "wild Scottish highland ancestors."[59] In fact, while these clashes were initially labeled *vendettas*, the terminology gradually shifted to label them as *feuds* between clans, thus underscoring the allegedly Scottish explanation of the violence. This fallacious connection between Scottish ancestry and feuding persists to this day, most notably in J. D. Vance's memoir *Hillbilly Elegy*, in which he repeatedly connects his own family's violence to their Scots-Irish heritage.

In perhaps the first instance of someone actively playing hillbilly, "Devil" Anse Hatfield apparently posed with his rifle—solo and with other members of his family, also armed—for illustrations and photos (fig. 1.5).[60] But Anse Hatfield's performance was very consciously that: a performance. He was a savvy, diversified businessman and a patient legatee who "had faith enough in [his] titles to wait out the lawsuits," who lived "to enjoy a comfortable old age on the money from coal leases," and whose descendants "tended to wear white collars in the industrial era" following the feud years.[61] Hatfield's nephew Henry D. Hatfield went to medical school in Louisville, returned to practice in Mingo County, and in

Figure 1.5. "Devil" Anse Hatfield and family, 1897.

1912 became governor of West Virginia, the first to be born in the state of West Virginia, rather than in old Virginia.[62] As many historians have noted, the Hatfield-McCoy feud was far more about politics and economics than any innate Scottish proclivity to fussin' and feudin'; the same was true for other reported feuds in the 1880s and 1890s, when "some Mountaineers took down their rifles and fired warning shots across the paths of the new breed of surveyors who appeared in the mountains"—shots that, predictably, "were often reported by metropolitan newspapers as new repercussions of feuding."[63]

As all of this indicates, the outside public's appetite for stories about white trash squatters continued to be strong into the late nineteenth century, and newspapers were willing to oblige. But so, too, were some of the subjects of those stories, like Anse Hatfield himself, with his willingness to let people take photos of him with his rifle. Just as Andrew Jackson and Davy Crockett had realized a couple of generations earlier, it was not only possible but lucrative to milk capital from outsiders' stereotypes. As Williams notes, West Virginians were (and in many ways still are) conflicted about this dynamic: on the one hand, they "resented the publicity at the time" but also "[made] the feud a permanent part of their folklore."[64] According to Williams, the feuds "helped to make the southern highlander a stock figure in American popular culture, reinforcing the picturesque image of the stalwart Mountaineer, but also helping to create the negative stereotype of the hillbilly, with his period costume of slouch hat and jeans, a full beard, a rifle, a whiskey jug, and a demeanor that one of the Hatfield chroniclers . . . neatly characterized as dull when sober, dangerous when drunk."[65] Williams's description perfectly summarizes the twin poles of the Mountaineer's emerging identity; while he is stalwart, or "sober," on the one hand, he is also a dangerous hillbilly. Just as the previous era struggled to distinguish the noble backwoodsman from the degenerate squatter, this emerging figure was also one of contradictions and complexities.

It might seem ironic that this figure would emerge in the late nineteenth century at the very moment when "the mountaineer's way of life was beginning to disappear."[66] But of course, there's nothing ironic about that at all: the two dynamics are inextricably related. Just as Native Americans did not become romantic figures in white, eastern US culture until after they had been forcibly removed from the land, so the Mountaineer could not become a romantic figure until he, too, was an endangered species. Portraying feuding families as "barbaric Mountaineers"—as did T. C. Crawford, author of *An American Vendetta: A Story of Barbarism* (1889)—satisfied outsiders' curiosity about these Other Americans while also allowing outsiders to wash their hands of them. Or more accurately, such a portrayal allowed outsiders to feel perfectly comfortable with the economic and environmental exploitation of the region, since it bolstered the perception that only highly educated outside philanthropists and industrialists could redeem such a backward place and people. During this era, Elizabeth Catte says, "Narratives that presented mountaineers as helpless and otherwise doomed without industrial purpose abounded. Coal barons credited their industry with bringing order and harmony to an uncivilized place."[67]

Of course, as we have seen in Doddridge's play, the sense that the frontier and its spirit had been lost was already present in the 1820s. But in the late nineteenth century, West Virginians saw enormous economic and legal changes that regulated or removed traditional ways of living off the land: the forests, which had "provided an indispensable harvest in the form of game meats for the table, of ramps (wild leeks), sassafras, berries, nuts . . . and in the form of skins and herbs, especially ginseng, which could be exchanged for cash or, more commonly, bartered" had been so heavily clear-cut by the timber industry that the state's ten million acres of virgin forest that existed in 1870 was completely gone by 1920.[68] Fishing and hunting regulations, designed to curb the depletion of game and fish stocks, further limited the ability to provide one's own food.[69] These radical changes at the end of the nineteenth century marked the endpoint of the backwoodsman's story arc. In many ways, West Virginians had a longer run with that story than other places, but as the Hatfield family's own history indicates, "Mountaineers had to abandon traditional ways of living and working and adopt new ways."[70]

The abandonment of that way of life created an enormous vacuum that could only be filled with nostalgia. As Williams notes, "The frontier had lived on in West Virginia's interior for more than a century, but it had irreversibly been set on the road to extinction by 1900. A great nostalgia for some of its habits and customs welled up in subsequent years, but there was no returning to the old ways, no matter how unpalatable the new industrial frontier might be."[71] It is vital to note the timing here: nostalgia for the frontier was reaching its apex in the late nineteenth and early twentieth centuries, as West Virginia University was growing and beginning to seek out an identity for itself in the landscape of the other land-grant universities with recognizable nicknames, such as the Indiana Hoosiers or the Ohio State Buckeyes. The term *Mountaineers* not only fit into this tradition of adopting a nickname for a state's residents as the university's mascot, it also gave the university a vessel into which it could siphon all of that nostalgia for the state's disappearing history and heritage. But in so doing, it also linked the Mountaineer, for good or ill, to the image of the fussin' and feudin' squatter, soon to be rechristened the "hillbilly."

"Mountain Whites," Mountaineers, and Hillbillies

At the same time that the shifting economic and political landscape of West Virginia was turning the frontiersman into an anachronism, other parts of the United States were experiencing another kind of transformation as immigrants flooded into cities and industrial centers, posing new challenges to the boundaries of whiteness. Irish and eastern and southern European arrivals created a racial dilemma: were such people white? Or were they fundamentally of a different race? While this question may seem ridiculous to us now, they were serious and even scientific concerns in the late nineteenth and early twentieth centuries, as "scientific" theories about race emerged, eventually giving way to the pseudoscience of eugenics. Proponents of this new pseudoscience argued that "Anglo Saxons," those derived from English stock, sat at the top of the racial hierarchy, as could be "proved" by such new measures as cranial measurement and other "scientific" means. And these concerns directly impacted the development of Appalachian identity. As Allen Batteau writes,

> As an ideology, racism was codified during this period. Ideas of racial classification were systematized and their sociological implications developed by persons such as John Fiske, Albert B. Hart, Henry Cabot Lodge, and Nathaniel Shaler. . . . In their conception the Anglo-Saxons were the highest race. . . . Members of the same circle that propounded the ideas of scientific racism were active in the definition of Appalachia . . . because one of the dilemmas posed by the Anglo-Saxon Mountain People was to explain their degraded condition in light of their (possibly) creditable ancestry.[72]

In short, anxiety about the dilution of "real" American stock put some of these theorists straight on the road to Appalachia. Suddenly, the formerly "white trash" rural folk of the region were elevated to racial superiority. Not only were they fully white, their perceived geographic isolation ensured that they remained more purely and "authentically" white than people in other parts of the nation.

This is, crucially, also the period in which the term *Mountaineer* became attached to Appalachians specifically. And perhaps no two men are more responsible for this shift in terminology and its implicit connection to whiteness than Berea College president William Goodell Frost and writer John Fox Jr. Both men were Harvard graduates and contemporaries of their fellow alums, Henry Cabot Lodge and Theodore Roosevelt, both influential theorists about "scientific racism."[73] Frost and Fox played integral roles in promoting the mythos that Appalachia's geographic isolation had rendered its people racially "pure," if backwards. Fox's romanticized fictions about ignorant but noble Appalachians portrayed them as teetering on the boundary between doom and civilization. They only needed to be redeemed by outside forces, after which they could, in turn, redeem and reinvigorate all of white America through their virile connection to nature and freedom.[74] Though he lived in Kentucky himself, Fox was in constant contact with eastern elites. Fox and Roosevelt were particular friends, and Stoll claims that Fox "shap[ed] their conception of an aggressive and inscrutable white mountaineer" and "interpreted Appalachia to the painters Frederick Remington and George Luks, the writers Owen Wister and Richard Harding Davis, and influential publishers, including Charles Scribner and William Dean Howells."[75] In short, Fox's fictional portrayals of mountain culture pervaded virtually every mode of artistic production in late nineteenth-century America.

Even more influential, however, was William Goodell Frost, president of Kentucky's Berea College from 1892 until 1920. During his tenure, Frost essentially "invented Appalachia as a named social entity"[76] and invented a rhetoric about Appalachia that continues to be invoked, however erroneously, today. Frost, too, was connected to the Harvard-based race theorists, and much of his writing functioned to establish "mountain whites" as a racial body distinct from "white trash": "We hear of the 'mountain whites' (they scorn that appellation as we would scorn the term 'Northern whites') as illiterates, moonshiners, homicides, and even yet the Mountaineers are scarcely distinguished in our thought from the 'poor white trash.'"[77] Frost argued that Mountaineers—unlike "poor white trash"—had not been "degraded by actual competition with slave labor"; rather, because mountain whites "had little contact with slavery, [they] retained that independent spirit which everywhere belongs to the owners of the land."[78]

Frost's fashioning white identity in terms of a group's historical involvement (or lack of involvement) with slavery was not new. What was unusual was how Frost's position as president of Berea College compelled him to make policy decisions that directly reflected this belief. Berea College was the only interracial college in Kentucky, and one of the few in the country. Founded in the 1850s by abolitionists, Berea walked its talk: during its first decade of operation, 60 percent of the students were African American, and college regulations did not keep the races separate, allowing for integrated housing and interracial dating.[79] The school's board of trustees included African American members until 1914. Needless to say, these policies were remarkably progressive for their day in any context, much less in the former slave state of Kentucky.

For much of his early tenure as president, Frost supported the school's original philosophy of integration. When he took the helm in 1892, Frost had ambitious plans to increase enrollment and enlarge the college's endowment. He was able to do so, "rais[ing] the value of Berea's plant and endowment from $200 thousand to $12 million" by the time he stepped down in 1920.[80] However, accomplishing these ends required one major sacrifice: he had to throw the college's interracial mission under the bus. After the *Plessy v. Ferguson* ruling in 1896, which made racial segregation legal and ushered in Jim Crow laws, Berea's policies came under greater scrutiny by outside forces. Frost faced a dilemma: his definition of "mountain whites" was rooted in the notion that because the mountainous parts of Kentucky were largely left out of the slave economy, mountain whites were free of the taint of slavery and thus a different "breed" from whites who had owned slaves. But the shifting political landscape after *Plessy v. Ferguson* made it difficult for Frost both to claim that mountain whites were "exceptional" and to support the college's interracial policies.

In "The Black South and White Appalachia," James C. Klotter demonstrates how similarly mountain people and African Americans were described in the late nineteenth century. According to the idea of "cultural evolution" that dominated the emerging fields of anthropology and folklore at the time, both mountain whites and African Americans were regarded as contemporary "survivals" of savage or barbaric cultures. In other words, they were living examples of the less civilized stages of cultural development that white elites believed they had long since evolved out of. This made both mountain whites and African Americans academically interesting, but politically problematic. Klotter argues that as Reconstruction failed and floods of new immigrants posed an additional threat to larger ideas about whiteness, progressives and philanthropists deliberately turned away from African American concerns and focused instead on helping the poor white Other in their midst. This crucible of events is what gave birth to two of the most pervasive myths about Appalachia: that its isolation made it a living survival of eighteenth-century America and that its isolation made it a microcosm of Elizabethan England, as evidenced by the region's language and folk customs.

Both explanations of Appalachian backwardness made its "barbaric" people a more palatable beneficiary of resources and reform efforts. These were people who simply needed to be brought into modernity; they were not recalcitrant or threatening newcomers (immigrants), or representatives of an ugly, complex history that refused to go away (African Americans). Klotter writes that "as large numbers of Eastern European immigrants settled in the United States, old-stock Americans, fearing the influx, saw the Appalachian area as a haven of refuge and a place of hope."[81] Not only were Appalachians largely descended from British stock, but they were Protestants, not Catholics, as were many immigrants of the era. And "the condition and needs of white Americans in Appalachia were presented to the nation at an appropriate time for those disillusioned with black progress. Efforts previously devoted solely to blacks now could be partially redirected to mountain whites."[82]

This is the philanthropic sea change that William Goodell Frost latched onto. As such, Frost's romantic gushing about Appalachian culture and his fund-raising to aid Berea's mountain white students may have had more to do with opportunism than genuine concern. Did he actually believe the myths about mountain people and mountain culture that he was selling, or were they just that: a sales pitch to bring resources to Berea College? It's an important question since Frost wrote about Appalachian culture for some of the most popular magazines of the day, including *Ladies Home Companion* and *Atlantic Monthly*. Frost's cause gained the support of his fellow Harvard alumnus and future US president Woodrow Wilson; in 1899, then Princeton professor Wilson told "a New York audience that Berea College would teach 'self-mastery' to the Appalachian people."[83]

In many ways, Frost seemed to subscribe wholeheartedly to the Appalachians-as-Anglo Saxons/American pioneers theory, as evidenced in his deeply influential essay "Our Contemporary Ancestors in the Southern Mountains," which appeared in the March 1899 issue of *Atlantic Monthly*. In it, Frost lays out a deeply romanticized and stereotyped portrait of Appalachian people and their lives. Traveling to eastern Kentucky, he writes, is "a longer journey . . . than from America to Europe; for one day's ride brings us into the eighteenth century."[84] Once there, the traveler is greeted by "a contemporary survival of that pioneer life which has been such a striking feature in American history" which is also somehow a contemporary survival of Olde England: "Along with these Saxon arts [spinning, weaving, and the like] we shall find startling survivals of Saxon speech. The rude dialect of the mountains is far less a degradation than a survival. . . . Quite a vocabulary of Chaucer's words which have been dropped by polite lips, but which linger in these solitudes."[85] Eastern Kentucky at the turn of the twentieth century was, apparently, a veritable historic theme park.

In the "Contemporary Ancestors" essay, Frost also addresses the anxieties that outsiders tuned into the "feud news" might have about the region: "The reverse side of family affection is the blood feud, which still survives in full vigor. . . . As an institution, it has its roots deep in Old World traditions. It is made possible by the simple fact that the people of this region have not yet grasped the decidedly modern notion of the sacredness of life. Mountain homicides are not committed for purposes of robbery. They are almost universally performed in the spirit of an Homeric chieftain, and the motive is some 'point of honor.'"[86] The language here is remarkable; in a few short sentences, Frost manages to connect Appalachians to the Old World, classical Greece, and Scottish clans. It's a trifecta of cultural legitimization.

But Frost's real aim in this essay is to contrast Appalachians indirectly with "poor white trash" and African Americans, as he does in noting how mountain whites differ from both groups by not having the taint of slavery in their history. More directly, he contrasts mountain whites with new immigrants by casting the former as the living embodiment of America's founding ideals, claiming that "as Appalachian America has received no foreign immigration, it now contains a larger proportion of 'Sons' and 'Daughters' of the Revolution than any other part of our country."[87] As we know by now, this claim wasn't new: Joseph Doddridge had described the backwoodsman as "the father of his country" some seventy-five years earlier. And ultimately, Frost's revisionist take on history is wrong on all counts: Kentucky was a slave state, and European immigrants had been in Appalachia, working in the timber, coal, and other industries for decades by this time.[88]

Frost ends his essay with a call to arms to the would-be saviors of these "pathetically belated" people, saying that "there could not be a clearer call for the intervention of intelligent, *patriotic* assistance."[89] Supporting the cause not only benefits Appalachians, Frost implies, but the entire South, since "when once enlightened[,] this highland stock may reinforce the whole circle of Southern States." In other words, educated mountain whites might offset a racial crisis. Frost's call also invokes the growing pseudoscience of eugenics, as he claims that "while in more elegant circles American families have ceased to be prolific, the mountain American is still rearing vigorous children in numbers that would satisfy the patriarchs. The possible value of such a population is sufficiently evident."[90] Frost is a bit coy here, leaving it to his readers to deduce how such a breeding plan would be valuable, but the implication is that producing larger numbers of these "contemporary ancestors" and raising them up to be "intelligent without making them sophisticated" might offset the cultural and religious threats of European immigrants.[91]

At Berea, this focus on helping mountain whites meant that Frost had to deliberately dismantle the college's long history of racial equality. First, he "overturned the resolution approving interracial dating. He also discouraged social contacts between the races. Seeking a limited black enrollment approximating the state's overall black-white ratio, he succeeded, for by 1903 only 157 of the 961 students were black. As Frost said later, 'We frankly shifted emphasis, appealing more for the Mountaineers.'"[92] In 1904 the Kentucky legislature passed a law that outlawed biracial education in Kentucky public schools. Although Frost rallied mightily against the bill, arguing that Berea's model could be scaled back further to be less radical, eventually he conceded that "public school segregation [was] the 'best arrangement' for Kentucky at the present time."[93] The myth of "separate but equal" won the day. Berea would not admit black students again until 1950.

The racialization of Appalachian identity, however, continued. In fact, by 1914, the label *mountain whites* was perceived as being so redundant that Samuel Wilson, a Presbyterian missionary in the region, suggested a return to the term *Mountaineer* instead, since—in his view—there were "no mountain blacks, or browns, or yellows."[94] Again, this is a patently untrue statement, but one that underscores the desire in the early twentieth century to create a conflated sense of whiteness as shared, normative, and uncontested. As race became an increasingly contentious public issue in the first decades of the twentieth century, Appalachians offered two interdependent benefits to the developing definition of a uniform and unifying sense of whiteness: on the one hand, the myth of Appalachians as isolated survivals of an otherwise long-diluted British past supported the fantasy of racial purity; on the other, constructing Appalachians as a white Other continued to reinforce a class barrier between them and wealthier northern whites.

This embrace of the white Other led to regional interventions and ideas that had a lasting impact on Appalachian culture. While Progressive Era reformers in northern cities were busily setting up settlement houses for recent immigrants, others left ethnically diversifying urban areas for Appalachia to set up similar institutions to help a population that was now seen as "the purest Anglo-Saxon stock in the United States," as anthropologist Ellen Churchill Semple describes it in a 1901 article in the *Geographical Journal*. Notably, Semple's claim coincides with the first print appearance of the word *hill billie* in the 1900 *New York Journal*. There, the hillbilly was described as "a free and untrammeled white citizen of Alabama, who lives in the hills, has no means to speak of, dresses as he can, talks as he pleases, drinks whiskey when he gets it, and fires off his revolver as the fancy takes him."[95] It is interesting that the *New York Journal* article specifically describes the hillbilly as white, since—in succeeding years—the term came to be synonymous with whiteness, just as *Mountaineer* had replaced the allegedly redundant term *mountain white*.

The hillbilly era had begun, and it set off a craze that would reach its peak in the 1930s and 1940s but would continue in other forms for decades afterward. Notably, both terms—*Mountaineer* and *hillbilly*—gained cultural currency in the early twentieth century at precisely the time students at WVU adopted the nickname of the Mountaineers. And by the time the university decided to choose an official Mountaineer mascot in the late

1930s, the hillbilly craze was in full swing. Thus, to understand the full range of the Mountaineer's emerging significance—and also to understand the battles that were waged over what the Mountaineer should look like, and how he (and occasionally she) should behave, we need to look at the hillbilly phenomenon more closely. Because for good or ill, the foundations of the University's mascot were created both in the likeness of, and in opposition to, the pop-culture icon of the hillbilly.

From Slouch Hat to Coonskin Cap

CHAPTER 2

JAKE

THE HILLBILLY MOUNTAINEER VERSUS THE FRONTIERSMAN

THE USUAL YEAR given for the birth of the WVU Mountaineer is 1934, when Mountain Honorary—a service organization founded at WVU in 1904[1]—selected the university's first official Mountaineer, Lawson Hill.[2] In 1937 Mountain developed an annual selection process (the basis for the current process), which resulted in the selection of Boyd "Slim" Arnold, who served as the WVU Mountaineer for three years from 1937 to 1939. (The only other person to serve as the Mountaineer for three years was Rock Wilson, who served from 1991 to 1993.) However, Hill (fig. 2.1) and Arnold (fig. 2.2) were far from the first people to dress up like Mountaineers; that tradition had existed for many years before Mountain stepped in to regulate the selection process. Prior to 1934, individuals at WVU donned flannel shirts, overalls, and fur vests to dress as Mountaineers.[3]

But the label *Mountaineer* was, as we have seen, attached to residents of western Virginia—later West Virginia—for decades

Figure 2.1. WVU's first official Mountaineer, Lawson Hill, 1934.

prior to statehood in 1863, and the founding of the university in 1867. However, the moniker was not officially attached to WVU until 1915.[4] The earliest West Virginia football team was formed in 1891 by students Melville Davisson Post and Billy Meyer, and early teams were known as the Snakers.[5] Once adopted, however, the Mountaineer moniker proved immediately popular with fans. A souvenir program for the 1933 football game between WVU and West Virginia Wesleyan includes the following cheer, which the program dates to 1915:

> It's West Virginia, It's West Virginia
> The pride of every Mountaineer.
> Come on you old grads, join with us young lads
> It's West Virginia now we cheer.

The souvenir program also includes a cheer dated 1923 and attributed to Fred Schroeder, which may well be the origin of the ubiquitous "Let's Go, Mountaineers" cheer:

> West Virginia—Mountaineers,
> West Virginia—Mountaineers,
> West Virginia—Mountaineers,
> Let's Go—Let's Go!
> LET'S GO!!![6]

The fact that Schroeder's cheer is titled "Split Yell" further suggests that this cheer followed the same sort of call-and-response structure as today's "Let's Go, Mountaineers" cheer.

It is likely not a coincidence that WVU adopted the nickname *Mountaineers* in 1915, given the fact that—as noted in chapter 1—around this time the term *Mountaineer* had been suggested as a better term for residents of the Appalachian region than the previous common terminology, *mountain whites*.[7] The decades on either side of 1900 were ones of intense outside interest in Appalachia: part of this was due to lingering public fascination with the feuds that the media had covered with such relish in the 1880s, and part of it had to do with the emerging myth that

Figure 2.2. Mountaineer Boyd "Slim" Arnold, 1938.

mountain whites were the living embodiment of Elizabethan England (or eighteenth-century America, depending on your preference). Although the Elizabethan myth was generated largely from within Appalachia, it, too, was a narrative crafted for outsiders.

Mountain whites, or Mountaineers, were presented as a distinct and more authentic category of Americans. They were held up as being the purest Anglo-Saxon stock in the country, and—as William Goodell Frost, Ellen Semple, and others suggested at the time—the antithesis of "white trash." Defenders of Appalachia, like Berea College's William Goodell Frost, built up the school's endowment by preaching the gospel that mountain whites came from pure Anglo-Saxon stock, untainted by the corruption of slavery, as Southern "white trash" had been. This was an unusual detour from the prior trajectory of racial categorization: previously, the whiteness of mountain people had been measured against Native Americans when the region was still the frontier, and against African Americans before and particularly after the Civil War. By the late nineteenth and early twentieth centuries, however, mountain whites were contrasted with both the "white trash" who had been ruined—so the logic went—by being tied up with slavery, and with the wave of new immigrants from eastern and southern Europe who were entering the country and challenging racial categories.

In the late nineteenth and early twentieth centuries, whiteness was hoarded as an entitlement that would be diminished if extended to newcomers. At this time, an intriguing and important shift happened. White Appalachians had once been the yardstick against which eastern elites bolstered their sense of racial superiority—recall Cornelia Jefferson's reaction to the "half civiliz'd" proto-hillbillies she encountered in Natural Bridge, Virginia, in 1817. By the late nineteenth century, though, the view had flipped: white Appalachians, or Mountaineers, were perceived to be the "purest" of the white race, and immigrant Others were measured against them. In the racial climate of the era—which was deeply shaped by social Darwinism and eugenics—the "uncontaminated," isolated people of the Appalachian mountains emerged as the whitest of whites, their lineage not having been tainted (so the logic went) by the blood of other races or ethnic groups. By 1915 the Mountaineer had become the Romantic embodiment of all that was genuinely American, making it a particularly appealing nickname for the university. But in adopting the name Mountaineers, WVU inadvertently adopted a mascot whose identity would always be tied up with early twentieth-century concerns about race and the nature of whiteness.

The insistence on the "Anglo-Saxonism" of Appalachian peoples ran counter to the reality of growing ethnic diversity in the region at this time. Rudy Abramson and Roberta Campbell explain that "even as writers fashioned the mythical Anglo-Saxon Appalachia in the late 19th and early 20th centuries, Italians, Poles, Hungarians, and other ethnic workers made up as much as forty percent of the workforce in the coalfields, not to mention their presence in urban shops and factories of the nascent Industrial Revolution."[8] Many African Americans worked in these industries as well. So the narrative about the "purity" of mountain whites was a fiction, but one that fund-raisers like William Goodell Frost and eugenicists could use to their advantage.

However, early twentieth-century ideas about race and ethnicity were not the only factors that influenced the emerging image of the WVU Mountaineer. Class consciousness and a sense of being the underdog were equally important influences. Recall the Backwoodsman of Doddridge's 1823 *Dialogue of the Backwoodsman and the Dandy*. After flattening the presumptuous Dandy who dared to call him a "barbarian," the Backwoodsman lectures him about how the Dandy and his fellow "big folk" would be nowhere without the Backwoodsman's labor: they "may freely enjoy the fruits of our hardships; [they] may feast, where we had to starve; and frolic, where we had to fight; but at peril of all of you, give the Backwoodsman none of your slack-jaw."[9] It would be easy to adapt Doddridge's *Dialogue* to working conditions in West Virginia a century later: simply turn the Backwoodsman into a coal miner, logger, or steel worker who is being insulted and taken advantage of by a wealthy outsider industrialist who assumes that he knows what's best for his ignorant employees. The Backwoodsman shows, both verbally and through physical force, just how aware he is of the imbalance of power and demonstrates his resistance to outsiders' elitism. Labor organizers in early twentieth-century West Virginia adopted a similarly resistant attitude. It is little wonder that West Virginia was a powerful crucible for the labor movement. West Virginians already had a potent symbol of grassroots integrity and stubbornness in the figure of the Mountaineer. It is this quality of defensive pride, I believe, that is at the heart of Mountaineer identity and distinguishes the Mountaineer from the early squatter and the later hillbilly.

As the timber, gas, and coal industries occupied ever larger parts of West Virginia's employment sector in the late nineteenth and early twentieth centuries, West Virginians saw most of the wealth from those industries go to out-of-state owners and operators, rather than to the workers. The upsurge of labor activism in the state at this time testifies to growing dissatisfaction with these conditions. But outsiders persisted in casting this resistance in "hillbilly" terms. A notable example is the aforementioned Hatfield-McCoy feud, which historian John Alexander Williams suggests was more likely rooted in economic conflicts than in the innate love of fighting attributed to the Scots-Irish families involved. Williams says that "it is no coincidence that the feud broke out at the turning point from preindustrial to industrial society in this part of West Virginia," noting that this particular feud "dramatized the traditional life of backwoods West Virginia at precisely that time in history when the Mountaineer's way of life was beginning to disappear."[10]

It is not surprising, then, that we begin to see WVU students identifying themselves as Mountaineers in the 1910s and early 1920s; by that point, the aforementioned economic changes had already happened. The Mountaineer was, once again, a nostalgic figure, harkening back to a simpler, more romantic time— though of course, Doddridge's Backwoodsman had served the same purpose nearly a century earlier. But like Doddridge's Backwoodsman, the emerging Mountaineer also had something to prove: he was not the foolish rube who could easily be intimidated by elite outsiders, be they Dandies or wealthy industrialists. The Mountaineer was born self-aware, with an understanding of how outsiders perceived him and a chip on his shoulder to disprove those stereotypes.

However, the flip side of this intense desire to prove others wrong is the equally intense desire to prove one's worth and one's ability to function in the elite world that creates those stereotypes. The WVU Mountaineer was also born out of this kind of anxiety to fit in, to be perceived as "normal." As Williams puts it, "Most West Virginians—particularly the leaders who have acted in their collective behalf—have tried to become part of the mainstream. They have tried in every age to find their way around, over, under, or through the barriers to economic prosperity that the mountains raised."[11] In this context, it was strategic and subversive to describe West Virginia University athletes—and, by extension, students and alumni—as Mountaineers. Whereas the first Mountaineers could only claim a natural intelligence born of experience, now that intelligence could be cultivated and honed by a formal university education. To be a Mountaineer now implied that one was educated, not *un*educated. West Virginia University Mountaineers could stand toe to toe with college-educated citizens of any state.

That anxiety to be seen as part of the mainstream became increasingly important over the twentieth century, as we shall see in this chapter and others: at specific moments in the Mountaineer's history, anxiety about how the Mountaineer looked to outsiders, what it represented about WVU and West Virginians, erupted into full-blown battles about what Mountaineers should look like and how they should behave. It only makes sense that this anxiety would be particularly concentrated at the state's flagship university, which symbolizes the state's connection and conduit to the larger culture outside its borders, and represents the state's (literal) investment in providing the education and experience to prepare its citizens to enter that larger and, some might say, more elite sphere.

Embracing and Resisting
the Cult of the Hillbilly

But of course, just as WVU adopted the nickname *Mountaineers* in the first decade or two of the twentieth century, another term was emerging to describe Appalachians—one that would achieve far broader popular-cultural currency and have a much more lasting impact: *hillbilly*. As mentioned in chapter 1, the word *hill billie* first appeared in print in the 1900 *New York Journal*. There, the hillbilly was described as "a free and untrammeled white citizen of Alabama, who lives in the hills, has no means to speak of, dresses as he can, talks as he pleases, drinks whiskey when he gets it, and fires off his revolver as the fancy takes him."[12] It is interesting that the *New York Journal* article specifically describes the hillbilly as white since—in succeeding years—the term came to be synonymous with whiteness, just as *Mountaineer* had replaced the allegedly redundant term *mountain white*.

The term caught on rapidly. Patrick Gainer notes, "Eight years later, on October 27, 1908, Dr. Leonidas Warren Payne Jr., instructor in English at the University of Texas, finished his first list of dialect and colloquial expressions, which included 'hillbilly.'"[13] By 1934 the term was recognized widely enough to be included in *Webster's New International Dictionary*. What happened between 1900 and 1934 that stoked the term's popularity was the explosion of what we would now label as country music in the intervening years. At the time when country music was first being recorded and then broadcast, there was no uniform label for the new sound, and the term *hillbilly* filled the vacuum. As with the term *Mountaineer*, though, the term *hillbilly*, while seemingly deracialized, was inherently racial. The term appealed to record companies because it distinguished the music it described from white jazz and classical music and also from the other major niche musical genre of the time, dubbed *race music* (or *Sepia* records, to use the term from Cincinnati's King Records advertisement; fig. 2.3). The term *hillbilly* allowed consumers to identify the race of the artists without an explicit label; it also acknowledged the possibility of multiple musical genres for

Figure 2.3. King Records (Cincinnati) advertisement.

white musicians while confining black music to a single category based solely on race. But in counterposing hillbilly and race music, producers, perhaps unwittingly, also drew connections between the two. As Anthony Harkins says, "Although 'hillbilly,' both as a label for a musical genre and for its performers, clearly denoted 'whiteness,' therefore, it constituted a strangely mixed cultural and racial category, simultaneously distinct from and akin to African-American and other nonwhite images."[14]

When WVU adopted the nickname *Mountaineers* in 1915,

it was latching onto the noble side of the figure's family tree, the one descended from the backwoodsman and the frontiersman—and the one that was touted as being authentically white and American. It is probably no coincidence that the term *hillbilly* emerged in the wake of this very romanticized view of mountain people. Depending on who is deploying the term, it could be seen as pejorative (when used by outsiders) or as empowering (when claimed by insiders). Either way, the image of the hillbilly seems to have emerged in part to poke holes in the overinflated ideas about the purity of mountain whites. Harkins's observation that the hillbilly figure represented a "strangely mixed cultural and racial category" further suggests that the hillbilly emerged to challenge false claims about the region's racial purity. Consequently, just as WVU self-identified as Mountaineers, the hillbilly—a newer and more broadly appealing caricature of mountain people—was gaining momentum. And the hillbilly wasn't appealing just to outsiders: WVU students latched onto it, as well, as we shall see. The university would struggle to bring the image of the Mountaineer back to the frontiersman/backwoodsman side of the spectrum for decades.

It's hard to overstate the enormous popularity and staying power of the hillbilly in the early twentieth century. In his comprehensive study of the hillbilly figure, Harkins describes the 1920s and 1930s as the heyday of the hillbilly icon, noting that "by the mid-1930s, the term had become ubiquitous."[15] Its reach extended beyond country music to movies and most notably to comic strips: the year 1934 witnessed the first appearance of Al Capp's comic strip *Li'l Abner*, Paul Webb's *Mountain Boys* (a regular feature in *Esquire*), and the introduction of the character of Snuffy Smith in Billy DeBeck's long-running comic strip *Barney Google*.[16] While we are probably most familiar with *Li'l Abner* and *Snuffy Smith*, Webb's *Mountain Boys* seems to have been more influential at the time. Featuring three interchangeable brothers named Luke, Willy, and Jake, the *Mountain Boys* solidified

Figure 2.4. Paul Webb's *The Mountain Boys* comic strip.

notions of hillbillies as lazy, violent drunkards and inextricably linked them to the moonshine jug, corncob pipe, and shotgun (fig. 2.4). The comic strip ran in *Esquire* until 1948, and in
1938 the *Mountain Boys* was immortalized on film in the movie

Figure 2.5. Movie publicity still for *Kentucky Moonshine* (1938),
with the Ritz Brothers as the cinematic version of
Paul Webb's *The Mountain Boys*.

Kentucky Moonshine (fig. 2.5).[17] As Harkins notes, "The almost
universally favorable review of the film reveals how seemingly
uncontroversial the hillbilly image had become by 1938": while
the Production Code explicitly listed Negro, Italian, Chinese, and
Mexican characters as potentially problematic in film, *Kentucky
Moonshine* was approved with no objections to its portrayal of
mountain people.[18]

In the same year, 1938, West Virginia's second poet laureate,

Roy Lee Harmon, published a book of verse titled *Hillbilly Ballads*, a collection of poems he had written and published in a column of the same name for the Beckley *Post-Herald*, where he also worked as the sports editor. In the book's foreword, Harmon explains why he titled the book as he did:

> On many occasions I have seen West Virginians take offense at the mere mention of the word "Hillbilly."
>
> Frankly, I can't understand why.
>
> To me, that word bears no stigma.
>
> Instead, it is something I wear as a badge of honor.
>
> After all, what is a Hillbilly?
>
> He is a person born and reared among our beloved mountains, where God has spilled nature's beauties in a glorifying heap. Where there is natural wealth that cannot be computed with mere figures and where hardy Anglo-Saxons have built a modern and important commonwealth in what was once a wilderness.[19]

Harmon's use of the term *Anglo-Saxon*, as we know from earlier portraits of Appalachia from the likes of William Goodell Frost, is code for white. By the late 1930s, the term *hillbilly* was financially lucrative, an incentive that Harmon discussed in a 1945 interview with the *National Hillbilly News*. In the interview, Harmon

> tells of an evening, possibly around 1938 or so . . . where he was trying to tune in a good program on the radio. But all he heard was what he called "sad and sobby ballads" from the radio speaker. Supposedly he kicked the radio in disgust and said he could write four of those "sentimental tunes" in an hour. His wife suggested maybe he could make some money that way. He then set out to win a bet that said he had to write a sentimental tune in 15 minutes. In a flash of inspiration, he wrote "Deep in the Hills." He played it on the piano, but seemingly forgot it. He found the manuscript for it years later in his desk and gave it to Judy and Julia Jones, who were appearing on the National Barn Dance on WLS

in Chicago. He forgot about it again until they told him that a Chicago publisher liked it and wanted to publish it.[20]

While we might imagine that only people outside Appalachia were interested in exploiting the hillbilly image for money at this time, clearly that was not the case, although Harmon doesn't appear to have turned much of a profit on any of his hillbilly creations or sentimental tunes.

Harmon's lack of concern about the stigma of the hillbilly image is presumably because by the late 1930s the hillbilly was a recognizable comic type, one that most consumers understood to be the latest incarnation of a long line of "wise fools." The fact that *Li'l Abner*'s Dogpatch, USA, was generic enough to pass, at various times, for Kentucky, Tennessee, Arkansas, Georgia, or Alabama[21] indicates that no one state lay claim to, or felt uniquely oppressed by, the hillbilly moniker. Indeed, as Harmon's foreword suggests, by the late 1930s it was a label to wear as a badge of honor. The figure of the hillbilly had, like the backwoodsman a century earlier, morphed into a folk hero and a trickster figure. An enormous part of the hillbilly's appeal lay in his ability to play the fool and thus outwit his "betters," even if his victories may at times be unintentional.

The hillbilly craze was part and parcel of the spread of mass media throughout the United States in the early twentieth century, as Americans began to have a collective popular culture through radio broadcasts, records, and movies. As these media introduced the hillbilly to people outside of Appalachia, they also introduced the hillbilly to himself: people in the Appalachian region became aware of how others perceived them, just as they had in the early nineteenth century when stories about backwoodsmen gained popularity in the East. A new self-consciousness emerged in this era, and by the 1930s and 1940s, Appalachians either took ownership of the label and wore it proudly, or railed against it.

The battle against the hillbilly image had begun. By 1945

even George Hay of the Grand Ole Opry—who, in the 1920s, had described his own radio broadcast as a "hill billy effort"— declared, "We never use the word [hillbilly] because it was coined in derision. . . . Furthermore, there is no such animal."[22] Hay may have been unhappy with the way the term had evolved over the two decades since he first used it, but by the time he made that statement in 1945, the hillbilly was an entrenched pop-culture figure, one that WVU students actively embraced, as we will later see. But Hay was not the only one who wanted to stop the hillbilly in its tracks: West Virginia's own governor was hot on his trail too.

The Depression and the Mountaineer

Tensions between the frontiersman and hillbilly versions of the Mountaineer escalated through the 1930s, the decade when WVU decided to choose an official Mountaineer mascot. Although a number of students had informally dressed up as the Mountaineer for sporting events as early as 1927 when Clay Crouse volunteered for the position, the first official Mountaineer, selected by Mountain Honorary was Lawson Hill in 1934.[23] Notably, 1934 was the same year that the comic strip characters Li'l Abner, the Mountain Boys, and Snuffy Smith made their debuts. *Kentucky Moonshine*, the big-screen vehicle for the comic strip *Mountain Boys*, would come out in 1938, a year after Mountain formalized its selection process for the Mountaineer. It cannot be coincidence that the university decided to formalize the selection process, duties, and appearance of the Mountaineer during the same decade that the pop-culture hillbilly was at its zenith. The WVU Athletics website notes that "minutes of Mountain meetings from the late 1930s indicate that a donor gave the honorary several deerskins asking that a buckskin costume be made for the Mountaineer. Prior to that the Mountaineer wore overalls, a flannel shirt, coonskin cap, a sheep or bear skin type vest and carried a rifle."[24] The overalls and flannel shirt clearly denote hillbilly; the buckskins, on the other hand, denote the backwoodsman/frontiersman.

This shift in the Mountaineer's kit is significant: by 1934, when the university officially adopted the Mountaineer as its mascot, it is easy to see why the school—and West Virginians generally—might prefer the figure of the backwoodsman to the hillbilly. The state's economy had suffered greatly from the ravages of the Depression; in some counties, unemployment rates were above 80 percent.[25] The Mountaineer would have assumed an even greater symbolic significance to West Virginians during the Depression, since the figure recalled a time when residents had no choice but to be self-sufficient, thrifty, and stalwart. The Mountaineer was, in many ways, a role model for West Virginians who were trying to survive hard economic times while retaining their sense of autonomy and dignity.

This battle to connect West Virginians to their frontier roots and to divorce them from the image of the hillbilly was being waged quite officially by the government; the battlefield in question was the West Virginia branch of the Federal Writers' Project (FWP). The Federal Writers' Project, part of the Works Progress Administration, was developed to employ out-of-work writers to research and write the American Guides series of books, described as "a sort of public Baedeker, which would point out to the curious traveler the points of real travel value in each state and county."[26] The primary goal of the various state and municipal branches of the FWP was to publish guides to each state and its major cities—publications that would list driving routes and destinations for tourists but also serve as portable histories of the places and people they described. The guides sought to capture the intangible cultural heritage of American places and to balance an emphasis on industry and progress with a reverence for the past and for local tradition.

The American Guides' blend of nostalgia and progressiveness proved especially difficult to achieve in West Virginia, primarily due to the near-paranoia of then governor Homer "Rocky" Holt, whose concerns about the West Virginia Guide kept it from being published until after his term ended in 1941. In some ways, the entire agenda of Holt's governorship revolved around issues of cultural representation; one of his major accomplishments was establishing the State Publicity Commission, "a body charged with countering negative publicity and promoting a positive image of the state."[27] West Virginia was a far more rural state eighty years ago than it is now, but nevertheless, radio broadcasts, newspapers, and movies were readily accessible for most of the population, and—given the meteoric rise of hillbilly music, comic strips, and films through the '20s and '30s—mountain people could suddenly see themselves as outsiders saw them or, perhaps more accurately, as outsiders *wished* to see them. All of these factors combined to create a very different conception of the state's identity than had existed previously.

Holt's anxieties about West Virginia's image came to focus on the state guide. Holt maintained absolute veto power over its content. His primary concerns focused on the guide's account of the state's labor history; Holt wanted the entire essay on labor in West Virginia removed from the manuscript, suggesting it was radical propaganda.[28] Holt also objected to the guide's representations of daily life in West Virginia: he wanted to remove a Farm Security Administration photo of a coal miner using a tin washtub because it suggested that West Virginians had no indoor plumbing. He wanted to remove a picture of children being transported to school in an open truck because it suggested that West Virginia children "were herded to school like livestock going to market." He wanted all references to chewing tobacco removed. He objected to a folklore essay describing traditional herbal remedies because it smacked of superstition, and he disliked the old joke about a farmer who plants his corn on a hillside by firing the kernels into the side of the mountain with his shotgun.[29] Taken together, these examples make it apparent that Holt was deeply self-conscious about the ways in which this kind of content would reinforce outsiders' notions of West Virginians as hillbillies. He also objected to the guide's more progressive or critical content, specifically photos and descriptions that countered the notion that West Virginia was an all-white state. Holt called for the removal of details about the contributions of Mexican and Italian immigrants to the state's workforce, references to "black singers with banjo and guitar yodeling mountain ballads on the streets of Charleston," and accounts of "Negro citizens of Charleston being subject to the wiles of ward-heelers."[30] Such inclusions clearly interfered with Holt's explicitly stated notion of West Virginia as "a state proud of its Anglo-Saxon heritage."[31]

As such, Holt was openly determined to maintain the link between Mountaineers and whiteness: his use of the phrase *Anglo-Saxon heritage* explicitly recalled turn-of-the-century ideas about how Appalachians were a more "authentic" and less "tainted" breed of Caucasians, as opposed to the "white trash" of the South. By the time Holt made this statement in the late 1930s, however, this claim to "Anglo-Saxon purity" was outdated and disputed. As Anne Armstrong wrote in a 1935 article titled "The Southern Mountaineers,"

> Much nonsense has been talked and written about the Southern Mountaineers, on whom the Tennessee Valley project, affecting, as it will, the destinies of many of them, has focused fresh attention. Nothing about this primitive folk seems too romantic on the one hand, too grotesque on the other, to be believed. They are referred to as the "Southern hill people," as "our Southern Highlanders"—names equally strange to the Mountaineers themselves; termed our "contemporary ancestors" by psychologists and sociologists, and, along with other varieties of backward Americans, dubbed "hill-billies" by more flippant commentators. But under any and all names they remain a people about whom curiosity is, apparently, inexhaustible, and of whom anyone, it would seem, after even the most casual contact, may venture an interpretation. Visiting poets and novelists write tales about

them, putting into their mouths a jargon which does credit to the author's own inventive powers but which would puzzle any bona fide Mountaineer as deeply as Hindustani.[32]

In just those few sentences, Armstrong neatly punches holes in virtually every stereotype about Appalachians, and also effectively describes the still present "inexhaustible curiosity" that outsiders have about the region and its people.

Holt was late to the "Appalachians as Anglo-Saxons" party. But he may have had a further motive in labeling them as such. Elsewhere in her essay, Armstrong demonstrates how these claims about the racial purity of the region's people were used to exploit their labor. At heart, she argues, the Anglo-Saxon myth is a public-relations move manufactured *by* outsiders to *benefit* outsiders:

> The supreme example of misreading these people has been furnished by the well-known efforts of Northern industrialists, abetted by Southern Chambers of Commerce, to exploit the Mountaineers during the last few years as a source of cheap labor. Here, at last, it was tooted on every side, blazoned on billboards along the highways of the Southern mountain region, were one-hundred-per-cent Anglo-Saxons—workers who could be depended upon, under any and all circumstances, to be loyal, grateful, amenable.[33]

Armstrong's words suggest that Holt may have insisted upon West Virginians' "Anglo-Saxon heritage" for financial, not sentimental, reasons: it was economically beneficial for him to tout that myth to outsiders in order to draw industry and jobs into the state. Holt saw the state guide—as a publication explicitly designed to introduce outsiders to West Virginia and to encourage tourism and business investment—as the ideal vehicle for rehashing that myth for readers. Armstrong's article shows that by the 1930s, the pseudoscientific idea that Appalachians were racially distinct from and racially superior to "white trash" was recognized for what it was: a crock. In her essay, Armstrong also neatly dismisses outsiders' representations of Appalachian dialect and puts the blame for any degradation of Appalachian people and lands squarely on outside exploitation. This is not to say that Armstrong gets everything right; later in her essay she retreads Appalachian stereotypes about moonshining and incest, and waxes romantic when she describes Mountaineers as "a stalwart, raw-boned, untamed race to whom fighting for something, or for nothing at all, constitutes the very breath of life, the quintessence of earthly joy."[34]

What is most intriguing about Armstrong's essay, however, is the way she characterizes the Mountaineer's identity as a "performance," one designed both to cater to and deflect outsiders' stereotypes:

> The Southern Mountaineer, illiterate, "backward," though he be, is not so easy to read. He does not reveal himself to the summer cottager to whom he acts as guide over mountain trails, sells wild berries, home-made hearth brooms, hooked rugs, or even moonshine liquor; far less to scholarly and urbane guests at mountain hotels with whom he may have chance encounters; not at once to the industrialist proposing to build on him as a stable and inexpensive base; and none too fully even to the mountain settlement worker laboring conscientiously in his behalf. Like the Negro, who, through generations of adaptation for protective purposes, has become, in his relation to the white race, a consummate actor, the Mountaineer—though his behavior derives from a different source—masks himself . . . in an almost unbelievably wily fashion.[35]

One is reminded of the African American folklorist and novelist Zora Neale Hurston and her wonderful characterization of how black anthropological subjects deal with white anthropologists:

> The Negro offers a feather bed resistance, that is, we let the probe enter, but it never comes out. It gets smothered under a lot of

laughter and pleasantries. The theory behind our tactics: "The white man is always trying to know into somebody else's business. All right, I'll set something outside the door of my mind for him to play with and handle. He can read my writing but he sho' can't read my mind. I'll put this play toy in his hand, and he will seize it and go away." Then I'll say my say and sing my song.[36]

For "white man," substitute *outsider* or *northerner*, and Hurston's quote could just as easily describe the masking behavior Appalachians adopted to shield themselves from those seeking to exploit or mock them. The wiliness of both African Americans and Mountaineers in the face of outsiders reminds us that being a trickster isn't simply about being a clown: it is far more about survival and resistance.

Armstrong's description is significant on multiple levels. First, although she returns to the old pattern of measuring whiteness against other racial groups—here, African Americans—she does so in a wholly different way. Her goal in comparing the "Negro's" performance of identity with the Mountaineer's performance of identity is not to establish a racial hierarchy, as was the case historically, but instead to link the two groups. The connection she creates is cultural rather than biological, and the shared behavior she describes is protective: both the "Negroes" and the Mountaineers don masks to buffer themselves against outsiders, because both groups—for very different reasons—have reason to suspect that outsiders mean to do them harm. The mask allows for the kind of "feather bed" interaction that Hurston describes: it gives the outsider a sense of having gained something while having only touched the surface. The trickster has deflected a potential threat to his community, and the outsider goes away thinking he understands the Other.

Armstrong's description of the Mountaineer's "mask" is especially significant given that at the same time her essay appeared—in the mid-1930s—WVU chose the Mountaineer as its official mascot and decided that the person portraying the figure would not wear a mask. The WVU Mountaineer was and is one of the few college sports mascots who is an identifiable individual rather than an anonymous person in a costume. However, there is still an element of masking at play in the figure of the Mountaineer. Although the former WVU Mountaineers I've interviewed frequently told me that they did not think of themselves as a mascot and did not think of the buckskins as a costume, they often did describe how putting on the buckskins was a transformational experience, one that lifted them out of their everyday identity and into a larger, more transcendent identity. Even though the WVU Mountaineer is exceptional for its lack of a literal mask, WVU Mountaineers still don a figurative mask when they put on the kit and transform into the mythical figure of the Mountaineer.

Armstrong's description of how Mountaineers perform their identity "in an almost unbelievably wily fashion" might also describe the ways in which WVU students were informally playing with Mountaineer identity during the 1930s and into the 1940s. Although the university officially endorsed the Mountaineer mascot in 1934 and regulated the Mountaineer's customary dress in 1937, this only happened years after students had already been taking on the role themselves. It is important to remember that the official WVU Mountaineer emerged from the informal, spontaneous performance of students who took it upon themselves to play the Mountaineer years before the university's decision to formally appoint one. And students continued to play the Mountaineer well after the selection process was formalized. This play included all the elements of tricksterism: by dressing up as a Mountaineer, students could indulge in behavior that would otherwise be condemned. They could carry a gun and a moonshine jug, yell, and insult the other team all in the name of supporting their own community. In many ways, it's the same license to misbehave that current fans and students deploy on game days now. So what did students get out of playing the Mountaineer in the 1930s and 1940s, after the university decided to designate an official Mountaineer? And how did their performances of the WVU Mountaineer change after World War II?

Donning the Mountaineer Mask after World War II

The enormous popularity of the hillbilly image in the 1930s offered both a model and a target for West Virginia University students as they considered what it meant to be a Mountaineer on a much broader and more complex cultural stage. Harkins notes that the hillbilly image "reached its zenith in the mid- to late 1930s and held sway through the end of World War II, riding the . . . crest of glorification of the common folk and fascination with regional life and culture" that popularized the FWP guides.[37] During World War II, in fact, servicemen were mailed a free paperback collection of Webb's *Mountain Boys* comics, and jug bands were a popular form of entertainment among troops.[38] As veterans returned to campus immersed in the pop-culture iconography of the hillbilly and fresh from experiences abroad that enabled them to think about their cultural heritage in a larger context, the postwar period was ripe for the reinvention of WVU's Mountaineer. At the same time, the GI Bill complicated the traditional associations of the WVU Mountaineer with "whiteness," as it allowed men from underrepresented ethnic groups and working-class families to attend college for the first time. These changes brought new energy to the class consciousness bubbling beneath the surface of the Mountaineer image, and they also challenged the assumption that the Mountaineer is necessarily, to borrow Governor Holt's phrase, of "Anglo-Saxon heritage."

Upon its founding, West Virginia University admitted only white men. The first women were enrolled in 1889, and the first woman to receive a bachelor's degree graduated in 1891. African Americans only were admitted after a 1938 US Supreme Court ruling that required colleges to admit African American students to "any graduate courses that were not available at the state institutions for African-Americans."[39] Thus, the only African Americans on WVU's campus after World War II were graduate students; African Americans were not able to enroll as undergraduates until after the *Brown v. Board of Education* ruling in 1954.

Consequently, postwar West Virginia University was still predominantly white, although the definition of whiteness was expanding rapidly to include members of immigrant and ethnic groups who would not have been grouped under that umbrella even a decade or two earlier—people of Italian and Eastern European descent. And postwar WVU was exponentially larger than it had been before and during the war. In the fall of 1946, when the GI Bill kicked in, "enrollment skyrocketed to a record high of 6,010,"[40] and 60 percent of the incoming class were veterans.[41] By the fall of 1948, enrollment was up to eight thousand students.[42] To meet the heavy demand for both housing and classroom space, "Classes met from 8 a.m. to 10 p.m. and on Saturday. . . . Students crowded into apartments and residence halls, government-surplus barracks and trailers, and homes of Morgantown families; five veterans lived on the second floor of the president's house with the family of President Irvin Stewart."[43]

Among those six thousand students who enrolled at WVU in fall 1946 was my father, David Barr Hathaway, a native of Calhoun County, who had recently been discharged from the army after serving in the infantry in North Africa and Italy. Like the other returning vets, he scrambled to find housing and eventually got a reference from a friend to live in Trinity Hall, a rooming house owned and managed by the Episcopal Church "for indigent Episcopal men." My father was neither indigent nor an Episcopalian, and neither were most of the men who lived on the three floors of the house. Trinity Hall had, in fact, been condemned and was slated to be razed but was allowed to remain open temporarily to address the housing shortage. My father

Figure 2.6. David B. Hathaway in Trinity Hall, fall 1946, with "We're Hillbillies and Damned Proud of It!" sign in background.

lived there for four years, until the building was finally demolished around 1950. And, as a photo of him in his room at Trinity Hall indicates (fig. 2.6), he self-identified as a hillbilly and was "damned proud of it."

As noted previously, the term *hillbilly* was both ubiquitous and contentious. As with other cultural labels, some members of the group tagged as hillbillies rejected it, while others embraced it in an act of cultural reappropriation. In a 1949 essay in *Rayburn's Ozark Guide*, writer Elsie Upton explains the process as follows:

> If I meet you with an extended hand and say, "I'm a hillbilly," I bring the good neighbor policy to your door. I extend friendliness embodied through years of contact with people who seek to help their fellow man. I bring courage instilled by forefathers who battled obstacles to lift their faces above poverty. I bring integrity wrought by nobleness in a way of life.
>
> But if, perchance, I hear some one degradingly using the term, the exalted rank of "hillbilly" is no more and, there being no distinction between the hillbilly that I am myself and the hillbilly that is uncouth and nasty, ignorant and impoverished, I dare to say—
>
> It's all right, up and above board, for one to assert himself a hillbilly, but the common run of folk like to do their own asserting—for by so doing the light of respect is thrown in for good measure.[44]

Upton's description neatly encapsulates the emotional and rhetorical difference between someone being called a hillbilly by a cultural outsider and calling oneself a hillbilly. She also succinctly describes the difference between the two: to outsiders, a hillbilly is nasty, poor, and ignorant; to insiders, he is friendly, courageous, and noble.

What Upton doesn't note, however, is that the *hillbilly* label allows both versions to coexist in the same figure. Certainly, my father's claim to be a hillbilly and "damned proud of it" had as much, if not more, to do with being uncouth and "free" as it did with being a good neighbor (though Upton deserves credit for linking the hillbilly to the nation's Good Neighbor policy with Latin America). More specifically, though, my father's claiming of a hillbilly identity was his way of rejecting and declaring his independence from the traditional Greek culture that dominated campus social life. That was a sentiment shared by all the men living in Trinity Hall, who prided themselves on being GDIs, or goddamned independents, and not members of a fraternity. The fact is that many of the men living in Trinity Hall would not have been admitted to any fraternity at that time since many of them were from Italian, Armenian, Polish, and other ethnic communities, sons of immigrants who worked in West Virginia's coal mines, steel mills, and glass factories. Many of these immigrant groups were still only marginally considered white, and Morgantown itself had segregated neighborhoods for its large working-class Italian American community. Many of the Trinity Hall residents were also first-generation college students from industrial cities like Wheeling or from poor rural counties. Most were veterans of World War II and were determined to take full advantage of the opportunities offered by the GI Bill. By virtue of its composition, Trinity Hall in the postwar years makes a useful case study for examining the shifting notions of the Mountaineer at this time.

Trinity Hall was decidedly not a fraternity, but it did identify itself as an official house in the campus community. In fact, the description of the house in the 1948 *Monticola* yearbook (fig. 2.7) illustrates how consciously Trinity Hall tried to position itself within the campus community and in contrast to the fraternities. The text on the Trinity Hall page of the yearbook notes that "Trinity is one of the outstanding houses of the campus" and that "it has been first in scholastic rating for several years."[45] Even more notable is the description of the hall's residents as coming from "every walk of life," making Trinity Hall "one of the more representative bodies on campus."[46] Trinity Hall clearly understood that its own ethnic and class diversity made it unusual and exceptional as an off-campus residential space. Nonetheless, it actively participated in the formal and informal competitions in the Greek and larger university communities. So while residents might have wanted to distinguish themselves from the class elitism of the fraternities, they also wanted to actively compete with

Figure 2.7. Yearbook page for Trinity Hall in the 1948
WVU yearbook, the *Monticola*.

the Greek community, both in formal ways, through homecoming decorations and other contests, and in informal ways. For while Trinity Hall boasted about having the highest average GPA of any residential house on campus, it also prided itself on its *Animal House*–like atmosphere. It was a houseful of tricksters.

Interviews conducted with former residents in 2007 began with a discussion of the recipe for the "passion punch" that was often available in the hall ("throw in whatever bottles you've got, including the labels"). A letter written to one of the former residents in anticipation of the 2007 reunion related a story about the hall's unsavory appearance: apparently, a father brought his son, a prospective resident, into Trinity Hall to scope it out as a possible place for the son to live while attending WVU. After just a few minutes, they came back downstairs, and the father was heard to say, "You're not going to stay in *this* dirty hall! Hell, I'll build a fraternity house for you before you step in here again!"[47] The key to Trinity Hall residents' sense of identity relied on the seeming paradox of being smart *and* rebellious, often in the same gesture. They could party as hard as anyone else, but still be "first in scholastic rating," as noted on their yearbook page.

The freshman class of 1946 was radically different from previous classes, not only at West Virginia University but across the United States. The majority of men enrolling were returning vets, older than the average college freshman, and with much more worldly experience. My father often told stories about the anxieties the university had about admitting so many vets, with administrators afraid that the war would have made students more aggressive and prone to violence. The reality was that most were just eager to get back to a normal life. The only stories about vets beating up other students had to do with returned servicemen physically resisting efforts to make them wear the previously mandatory freshman beanies.

The 1947 *Monticola* reflects this landmark change in the student body on several levels. The opening pages set up the theme, with their army-like font spelling out the message "Welcome back . . . back to school . . . back to work . . . back to play . . . and best of all . . . back to West Virginia University": a message designed to integrate vets into domestic and campus life (fig. 2.8).[48] The '47 yearbook is notable in other ways as well. The yearbook hadn't been produced since 1943, due to paper shortages during the war, and appears only to have been financially possible during the 1946–47 academic year due to the generosity of Weirton Steel, which subsidized its production and featured itself on several pages, including a full-color page (fig. 2.9).[49] The narrative of

Figure 2.8. Image from the opening pages of the 1947 *Monticola* yearbook welcoming servicemen back to campus after World War II.

masculinity is potent throughout this publication: men returning from war, industrial might, and the resumption of college football, which had also been suspended during the war.

What is also significant about the 1947 and 1948 yearbooks, though, is that the graphics for both prominently feature a hillbilly-esque Mountaineer. The images are not those of the hypermasculine frontiersman but those of the stereotypical poorly dressed, rifle-toting, moonshine-swilling bumpkin (fig. 2.10). Even more notable is the tacit endorsement this image receives from the university by allowing these images to appear in an official publication, something that would never happen today. Although the official Mountaineer mascot had been in place—and clad in buckskins—for a decade by the time these yearbooks were published, the numerous and inconsistent images

Figure 2.9. Full-color, full-page ad for Weirton Steel from the 1947
Monticola yearbook. The company underwrote the cost of
the 1947 yearbook, which had not been published during the war.

of the hillbilly Mountaineer indicate that an official image had
not yet formed. The official WVU Mountaineer may have looked
like a frontiersman, but the unofficial hillbilly Mountaineer was
the far more popular version on the postwar WVU campus. The
campus humor magazine *Moonshine*—with both its title and its

Figure 2.10. The 1947 yearbook included several variants of this hillbilly Mountaineer caricature, which threaded through the entire publication.

artwork—suggests that the hillbilly image was, in fact, preferred over the frontiersman image, at least in terms of its potential for humor and play (fig. 2.11).

Notably, this image of the Mountaineer was not exclusive to WVU at this time. Appalachian State University's hillbilly-like mascot, Yosef, came into being at exactly the same time, and through a similar process. Yosef was initially a figure designed for the 1942 issue of Appalachian State's yearbook, *The Rhododendron*, but really caught on in the postwar years of 1946–49, when

> Yosef served as a guest editorial writer in the student newspaper (*The Appalachian*). He wrote using mountain colloquialism with a penchant for misspelled words.

Figure 2.11. A hillbilly image that appeared regularly in issues of the WVU humor magazine *Moonshine* in the late 1940s and early 1950s.

Yoseff dropped the second "f" and became Yosef in January of 1947. On Nov. 22, 1947, the University sponsored a Mr. and Mrs. Yosef contest. Skills needed for the titles included hog and chicken calling.

The first mention of Yosef as the mascot of the Mountaineers is a picture in the March 12, 1948 edition of *The Appalachian*. The photo tabbed him as a perennial freshman.

In 1949, John Geffrich, a 48-year-old World War II veteran, was one of the first Yosef mascots. Geffrich helped establish a lineage of male undergraduates portraying a bearded man with coveralls, a pipe and a straw hat.[50]

Clearly, Appalachian State Mountaineers, like WVU Mountaineers, were enjoying playing with the stereotypical hillbilly persona in the years immediately after World War II.

Unlike Yosef, though, the WVU Mountaineer had been clad in buckskins for a decade by the late 1940s. The veterans flooding WVU's campus at that time were eager to play Mountaineer, but they opted for a look more like Yosef's hillbilly version, dressing in overalls, flannel shirts, and slouch hats. This getup was closely associated with larger pop-culture images of the hillbilly, and the image was replicated not only in the WVU yearbooks of the era but in other forms as well. Floats and fraternity-house decorations for homecoming weekend in both fall 1946 and fall 1947 featured the hillbilly Mountaineer. But it wasn't just the Greeks who were competing to show that they could fashion the cleverest display of hillbilly identity. Trinity Hall's GDIs were determined to compete on a level playing field with their more privileged counterparts to win the prize for best homecoming decorations.

And they succeeded: Trinity Hall won second place for its 1947 homecoming decorations, which featured a giant Mountaineer face, mounted to the exterior of the house, that talked, smoked a pipe, and spit tobacco intermittently (fig. 2.12). The fact that many of the Trinity Hall residents were engineering majors, or had had technical experience with machinery during the war, allowed them to create an elaborate design that they planned out meticulously in a set of specs that detailed the materials needed as well as steps for the construction and operation of the Mountaineer face.

Sixty years later, former Trinity Hall residents were still immensely proud of this achievement. At the 2007 reunion, a group of them told the backstory about how their award-winning display came to be.

David Hathaway (DH): Hank Hinshelwood . . . he went down to Charleston, and he drew all this up. He and Bob Riggs. And they . . . they did this very detailed plan, of this picture of a Mountaineer above the front porch, with a smoking corncob pipe, and a dialogue that we'd recorded and played on loudspeakers, and then every so often, he'd clear his throat and he'd *spit*. We had a guy who would sit in the upstairs hall, just covered with water, and a *rope* that was tied onto a spring-loaded faucet up there, you know, and he'd—when he'd hear "spit" he'd pull down the handle, spit out into the front yard a big stream of water.

But we needed a big frame . . . to build, to hold that Mountaineer up. And decided it was gonna be about twenty feet in each direction. So, you've seen the pictures. And Tom Ferris . . . [to Tom] now you correct me if I'm wrong on this Tom—

Tom Ferris (TF): The Bureau of Mines furnished the pipe.

[Laughter]

DH: Tom, Tom Ferris worked down by the Field House, at the US Bureau of Mines. And he said, "Well, we've got plenty of pipe stacked up down there in the yard . . . inch-and-a-half pipe, and we can get it down there." . . . Tom says, well, he knows the watchman down there, and . . . before the shift changes, Tom says he always takes a shower. So, he's in there in the shower for about ten minutes after eleven o'clock, so we got Jim Thoms's car, he's the one with this big sedan convertible, and we drove that down on Beechurst Avenue, next to the old Field House, and parked right in front of the Bureau of Mines place.

And Tom got out . . . and the guy who owned the car . . . he was just really *worried* about it. With good reason, I suppose. 'Cause this is going to be a large-scale *heist*! [Laughter]

DH: Tom went up and . . . roll[s] this big gate back, y'know, and went in and hit this big switch and turned on all the *floodlights*!

[Laughter]

DH: [Laughing] Well, the guy that owned the car begun to gun the engine, he's gonna leave right now. And Ferris says, "No, if they see us moving around there in the dark it'll be *suspicious*! Y'know, cops come by and see we got all the floodlights on, carrying pipe around, they're not going to think anything of it!"[51]

It is clear that winning a prize for these decorations of dubious origin was a moment of pure triumph for the postwar Trinity Hall

Figure 2.12. The prize-winning spitting Mountaineer homecoming decoration at Trinity Hall, fall 1947.

residents, proving that they could not only compete with, but they could best the Greeks with their intelligence and mechanical know-how. In many ways, by *constructing* the stereotypical Mountaineer, the Trinity Hall men *became* Mountaineers, both in terms of fully belonging to the University community, and also in terms of asserting their Mountaineer values of independence, caginess, and survival skills.

They attempted to repeat this feat for homecoming 1948, when they produced a giant mechanical Mountaineer that simulated chopping the head off of a gamecock, since the homecoming game was against South Carolina (fig. 2.13). Behind these figures, they painted a mural of a rural scene on bedsheets, which covered the entire front porch, with an outhouse painted above the front steps; to get into Trinity Hall, you had to enter through the outhouse.

At their 2007 reunion, they recalled the engineering wizardry required to accomplish this:

> David Hathaway (DH): I recall that . . . the engine that ran that whole thing was 220 volts. We didn't have that in Trinity Hall, and . . . they went in with big alligator clips down in the basement, hooked it up to the line on the city side of the power meter—
>
> Howard Atkinson (HA): And they got 220 out there free! At no cost—
>
> DH: At no cost, to run that.
>
> HA: That thing went on forever. And we were talkin' about the other day, if you remember, there was somebody designated to be on guard all the time. Night and day, around that, because there's a lot of people . . . that were jealous of that thing, or just ornery enough to wanna tear it—
>
> Nello Antonucci: It was the fraternities—they always won the prizes.
>
> DH: Yeah, that's right. And we, we upset the apple cart the year we won . . . a prize.[52]

We see, once again, the theme of the Trinity Hall men defining themselves in opposition to (and in active competition with) the fraternities, and positioning themselves as superior due to their native intelligence and willingness to skirt the law. In this way, their stories fall in line with the long tradition of trickster stories and, in particular, those popular stories about backwoodsmen getting a leg up on those who attempt to demean them. Like Doddridge's Backwoodsman, the residents of Trinity Hall landed a punch squarely in the face of the fraternity dandies and followed that punch up with a reminder that they not only understood but resented, and would actively resist, being put down on the basis of social class. Only this time, the drama was being played out on campus—and with a more conscious purpose of defining what it meant to be a Mountaineer.

Figure 2.13. The chopping Mountaineer homecoming
decoration at Trinity Hall, fall 1948.

It wasn't just the men of Trinity Hall who were invested in defining the Mountaineer image for themselves at this time, however. The postwar years witnessed very active and dynamic efforts on the part of WVU students to play with the image of the Mountaineer, even though—or perhaps because—the university had formalized and conscribed that image a decade earlier. After homecoming in 1947, a group of students decided that the following game day would be Mountaineer Day. A photo from the 1948 *Monticola* shows clearly the influence of Webb's *Mountain Boys* comic strip (fig. 2.14); the men are dressed up specifically to emulate that very specific incarnation of the hillbilly image, reinforced by the caption of "Mountain Boys" beneath it.[53] The irony, of course, is that today we might view the picture as being stereotypical and degrading, but, in fact, by dressing up as the Mountain Boys, these men were demonstrating their cultural sophistication. *Esquire* positioned itself as a relatively high-brow men's publication at the time (though its photos of scantily clad women might cast doubt on such an appraisal), and only those familiar with the magazine's regular features, including Webb's *Mountain Boys* comic strip, would be in on the joke of this getup. Far from simply buying into and reflecting the larger cultural notion of hillbillies, these men were actively contesting it: their costumes reveal their literacy and their cultural sophistication, allowing them to stake a claim to the *Mountain Boys* identity that is more valid than the claim of the average *Esquire* reader.

On the first Mountaineer Day in 1947, male students were encouraged to dress like hillbillies in order to rally student support for the team (women, of course, were still required to wear skirts, stockings, and heels). Apparently, this effort was quite a success, and most of the jugs the Mountain Boys carried were not only filled with real booze but were all drained during and after the game, as a spirit of misrule took hold of the campus. In some ways, the administration's greatest fears about the returning vets' lack of control were realized on that first Mountaineer

Figure 2.14. WVU's own Mountain Boys at the first
Mountaineer Day, fall 1947.

Day. My father enjoyed telling a story about one of his professors'
reactions to the event:

> At the time I was enrolled in an American Literature class taught
> by James Paul Brawner . . . Head of the English Department. . . .
> On the Monday following Mountaineer Day he came to the class
> visually disturbed. He gave us a dissertation for about fifteen
> minutes on the "thin veneer of civilization." He felt that what he
> had observed on Saturday might set university life back several
> decades. . . . Needless to say, the event was a great success for the
> student body.[54]

In fact, Mountaineer Day became an unofficial, student-
organized event during the fall of every year after 1947, and was

eventually co-opted by the university and reborn as what is now celebrated as Mountaineer Week. According to WVU's *official* history of the event, Mountaineer Day "was conceived in 1947 as an event to arouse more school spirit. The initial weekend started with a thuse [pep rally] on the old athletic field the night before the WVU versus Kentucky football game. Following the game, a dance requiring Mountaineer garb was held with awards given for the costumes most representative of a true Mountaineer."[55] Clearly, the official history has sanitized its account of the first Mountaineer Day. As my father dryly remarked about this depiction, "The online history of the week is very interesting but misses the experience of the initial celebration."

The "initial celebration" had all the elements of Mikhail Bakhtin's carnivalesque—a space where people can engage, temporarily, in subversive and even grotesque behavior.[56] In a carnivalesque atmosphere, the usual social rules are not merely abandoned but sometimes inverted: everyone is required to engage in the kinds of behavior that are normally prohibited. Such was obviously the case with the first Mountaineer Day, which has all the elements of a more recognizable form of carnival, like the New Orleans Mardi Gras: outrageous costumes, heavy drinking, and overall bad behavior. As my father's email suggests, the fact that the administration clamped down afterward is the clearest measure of the event's success. Had Dr. Brawner read Bakhtin, he would have understood—at least theoretically—that by temporarily abandoning social norms, the carnivalesque functions to reinforce those same social norms. Once the day of misrule is over, participants are expected once again to toe the line, just as an observant Catholic follows up Mardi Gras with the solemn rites of Ash Wednesday and Lent.

Despite—or likely because of—the administration's censure of the first Mountaineer Day, it became an annual tradition. In 1949 a Morgantown journalist claimed to be "not altogether satisfied that the undergraduates are showing as much originality and resourcefulness as they possess in characterizing the mountaineer as 'poor white trash' who apparently spends all his time carrying a catalog to the outhouse."[57] Apparently this writer missed the deep play going on in student performances of Mountaineer identity. The June 1951 edition of the *West Virginia University Bulletin* describes Mountaineer Weekend (it had now extended beyond one day) as a celebration "set aside by students for self-entertainment."[58] Both the photo and the caption in the bulletin suggest that four years later, the tradition had stabilized and shifted. Mountaineer Weekend was an established event, but the text points to the university's ongoing wish to distance itself from it: this is a student-generated event designed for "self-entertainment," a description that reflects the administration's distaste for it as an immature, indulgent activity. The fact the university still continues the tradition more than seventy years later indicates that eventually the administration recognized that there was something potentially productive in an event that celebrates "Mountaineer" identity—but *they* wanted to be the ones who defined that identity, and to ensure that it was as disconnected from the image of the hillbilly as possible.

The yearbook photo of the first Mountaineer Day points to this shifting image of the WVU Mountaineer (fig. 2.15). While there are still a few men in this picture dressed in the *Mountain Boys* style, we also see the more frontiersman-like figure with his buckskins and coonskin cap. Reimagining and impersonating the Mountaineer seems to have functioned as a way for postwar students, and returning vets in particular, to reinsert themselves into college life and into local culture. This seems especially true for some of the residents of Trinity Hall, who previously would have been excluded from identifying as Mountaineers because of their ethnic and class backgrounds. Depicting the Mountaineer as a caricature, an exaggeration, opens up space for Others to take on the role; depicting it as a muscle-bound frontiersman does not. In many ways, this class struggle continues to underlie debates about who and what the WVU Mountaineer should be, and what his or her duties are in representing the state. There are

Figure 2.15. Hillbilly and frontiersman Mountaineers
take the field for Mountaineer Weekend, 1951.

those who feel that the Mountaineer represents the freethinking, iconoclastic hillbilly—an individual who takes great pleasure in talking back to, if not undermining, the authorities that oppress him. On the other side are those who see the Mountaineer as the naturally genteel backwoodsman, someone whose common sense and intelligence, both born out of hard experience, elevate him as a leader and a role model for his rougher fellow citizens.

If this debate sounds familiar, it should: the struggle between the hillbilly and frontiersman Mountaineer in the mid-twentieth century in many ways echoes the squatter/back-woodsman debate of the early nineteenth century. We are back to Andrew Jackson and Davy Crockett, with the hillbilly on the Jackson end of the spectrum and the frontiersman on the Davy Crockett end. The connections and the distinctions between these two figures become ever more important as the decade of the 1950s wears on.

Death of the Hillbilly Mountaineer

Over the course of the 1950s, the hillbilly version of the WVU Mountaineer was extinguished, and the frontiersman Mountaineer became the officially sanctioned and, some might say, tamed version. The shift echoes George Hay's rejection of the term *hillbilly* to describe the Grand Ole Opry in the 1940s and Governor Holt's desire to micromanage West Virginia's image away from hillbilly stereotypes. But another even greater force was responsible for the death of the hillbilly Mountaineer: Walt Disney Studios, whose wildly popular television series, *Davy Crockett, Indian Fighter*, provided an iconic pop-culture version of the rugged frontiersman that proved irresistible (fig. 2.16). As Allen Barra writes,

> It is not true that Davy Crockett was forgotten until Disney Studio's *Davy Crockett, Indian Fighter* aired on ABC (which coproduced the episodes with Disney) late in 1954. But the old bear hunter turned congressman turned cracker-barrel philosopher had slid into something of a down period. He had been the subject of perhaps two dozen feature films before Disney, but most of them had been made in the silent era. The closest thing to a recent major movie had been *Davy Crockett, Indian Scout*, with George Montgomery, in 1950.
>
> In his 1954 book, *The Forgotten Pioneer: The Life of Davy Crockett*, Marion Michael Null touched a nerve by sounding a lament

for the supposed loss of innocence represented by the passing of Crockett's frontier. Almost as if in response to Null, Disney's first three installments, ending with "Davy Crockett at the Alamo" early in 1955, didn't merely rejuvenate Crockett but turned him into television's first major merchandising fad.[59]

Disney's Crockett stories, aired as part of its weekly *Disneyland* anthology show, started what Margaret J. King refers to as the "Crockett Craze."[60] The television show not only garnered huge audiences, but its theme song—"The Ballad of Davy Crockett," recorded by Bill Hayes—was on the Billboard charts for twenty weeks, including five weeks as the number one song in the country.[61] As Sean Griffin notes, "Numerous other artists (including Tennessee Ernie Ford, Eddy Arnold, Burl Ives, Mitch Miller, and even good ol' Fess Parker himself [the actor who played Davy Crockett in the Disney episodes]) recorded their own versions. . . . In six months, the combined record sales of all the versions was close to 7 million albums."[62]

Although the coonskin cap that the WVU Mountaineer wears became part of the mascot's official garb in 1937, its importance was cemented by the "Crockett Craze." Never mind that many contemporary accounts and histories suggest that, in fact, Crockett likely never wore a coonskin cap. Sales of imitation coonskin caps exploded in the months following the broadcast of the Crockett episodes on *Disneyland*.[63] Also prominent in Disney's representation were the buckskins, moccasins, and rifle, which remain part of the standard kit of the WVU Mountaineer.

Numerous scholars have speculated about why Crockett emerged as the prototypical frontiersman at this juncture in history, displacing the previously better-known and better-regarded Daniel Boone.[64] King believes that "Disney's Crockett, the common man with dignity—congenial, neighborly, civic-minded, and upwardly mobile, or, in short, other-directed—made him a most fitting ideal for the 1950s,"[65] while Alan Nadel speculates that "like the parents of his chief audience, [Crockett] was a recent war veteran (the Indian Wars), and like their president he had moved into a political career." Nadel further suggests that Disney's representation of Crockett's death at the Alamo "constructed Crockett's memory in the image of the cold warrior, drawn to foreign soil by the cause of 'freedom.'"[66]

In his seminal 1940 article about Crockett's enduring legend, "Six Davy Crocketts," Walter Blair describes six distinct variants of Crockett's persona that were popularized and mined for political gain during and after Crockett's lifetime, most of which bore little resemblance to "Crockett the First," the man himself.[67] Blair describes the qualities that came to be attached to later incarnations of Crockett: he is a rustic who—while short on book learning—is long on horse sense; a backwoodsman who is "not only stupid and clownish but also vicious"; a staunchly independent "homespun oracle"; the "improvident child who fled instinctively from civilization"; and "the incipient poor white . . . with the elements of decay in him."[68] In many ways, then, Davy Crockett both provided the template for the hillbilly Mountaineer and offered the perfect antidote to him in the form of the noble frontiersman.

Thus, it was perhaps inevitable that the hillbilly version of the WVU Mountaineer would meet its demise just a few years after the Crockett craze. The hillbilly Mountaineer was finally and formally "outlawed" in mid-May 1957, when student-body president Roger Tompkins wrote to WVU president Irvin Stewart announcing the following resolution from the student government executive council. Tompkins's description of the ideal Mountaineer here is clearly drawn from Disney's Davy Crockett:

Whereas, Executive Council feels the true spirit of the Mountaineer is exemplified by the coonskin cap and buckskin uniform, and whereas, we feel that there is a definite need for pride in, and respect for the Mountaineer spirit and tradition, We hereby resolve, that the sale of all emblems, symbols, and figures pertaining to, or

Figure 2.16. Fess Parker in Disney's *Davy Crockett,*
King of the Wild Frontier (1955).

suggesting an interpretation of the Mountaineer as a "hillbilly,"
i.e., with jug, felt hat, bare feet and ragged clothes, should cease,
since the use of such, provokes an unsavory and degrading conno-
tation of our Mountaineer spirit and tradition.[69]

Stewart enthusiastically agreed, replying to Tompkins's letter by saying, "In my opinion, this is a very desirable step. I hope that you and your associates will seek to enlist the support of all student organizations in carrying into effect the spirit of this resolution."[70] He immediately wrote to Boris Belpuliti at the campus center (the Mountainlair) and to Ruth Robinson at the campus bookstore asking their cooperation in "bring[ing] to an end the representation of the Mountaineer as a 'hillbilly.'"[71] Stewart further asked that "the sale of items interpreting the Mountaineer as a 'hillbilly'" be stopped immediately,[72] which prompted a rather aggrieved reply from Robinson, who noted that while she would comply, "I checked our inventory of comic Mountaineer imprinted merchandise and find that we are taking a loss in excess of $300."[73] Clearly, the death of the hillbilly Mountaineer had a commercial as well as a cultural impact.

The irony is that the students, and Stewart, were really only substituting one mass-mediated image of Appalachian identity with another: the comic hillbilly version of Paul Webb's *Mountain Boys* was displaced by Disney's Davy Crockett. And the frontiersman Mountaineer was more narrowly defined, leaving far less room for play and subversion than the hillbilly Mountaineer. The hillbilly and the frontiersman do share the traits of independence and rebelliousness, however. As Griffin notes, Disney's Crockett is not the first version to be portrayed as a perpetually childlike, easily bored adventurer; rather, this image of Crockett "as a free-roaming, fun-loving upstart reaches further back than these television episodes," going back to the comic Crockett almanacs of the 1830s, '40s, and '50s.[74] Those almanacs depicted Crockett as an "autonomous, free-roaming adolescent" who is "loose, liminal, and wild."[75] Substituting the frontiersman for the hillbilly, then, gave the frontiersman Mountaineer respectability, while still allowing the freedom of occasional wild behavior.[76] But substituting the Davy Crockett frontiersman for the hillbilly perpetuated the notion that the Mountaineer must be white. It is perhaps not coincidental that the Crockett craze of 1954–55 exploded just a few months after the Supreme Court's ruling in the *Brown v. the Board of Education* case.[77] The Crockett craze may have been fueled, in part, by anxiety that whiteness was no longer synonymous with American identity, allowing white viewers to reconnect with a frontier past allegedly untroubled by racial tensions and reinscribing a white supremacist version of American history.

By the late 1950s, this nostalgia for a vanishing and vanished frontier past was itself a long tradition, dating back—as we have seen previously—to Doddridge's *Dialogue of a Backwoodsman and a Dandy*, on through the Jacksonian era, and into the late nineteenth and early twentieth centuries, when Appalachian advocates begged outsiders to preserve and protect the culture of mountain whites before it was irreversibly tainted by modernity. As the 1950s transitioned into the turbulent 1960s, this nostalgia would become even more intense, and also more complex. As the United States entered the Vietnam conflict, and as the war became increasingly unpopular, the image of a young man armed with a rifle shifted from being nostalgic to being eerily evocative of the present. Was this armed Mountaineer a patriot, fighting for his country? Or an angry and dangerous young man? The twin roots of the Mountaineer's identity would come into conflict—figuratively and literally—during this era.

CHAPTER 3

The Rifle and the Beard

THE WVU MOUNTAINEER IN THE 1960S

THE UNIVERSITY'S MOVE to enshrine the Davy Crockett-esque WVU Mountaineer in the late 1950s was a complete success: more than sixty years later, very little has changed in the Mountaineer's appearance or kit. The hillbilly version—at least in terms of outward appearance—has never shown his face again, although his influence lingers on in the form of unbridled, outrageous behavior, as will be addressed in chapter 5.

In many ways, this shift in the Mountaineer's appearance and kit is exemplified in artwork created in the late 1960s by Thomas Haines, a developmentally disabled young man from Charleston, West Virginia, who was a client at the city's Faith Workshop. Haines was a talented self-taught artist, and in 1967, the Faith Workshop, in conjunction with the Kanawha County Association for Retarded Children (now the Arc of the Three Rivers), published a booklet of Haines's work with the unfortunate title *West Virginia as Seen by Man Child-Tom*. It appears to have been created to sell as a fund-raiser.[1] The book's preface notes that Haines's "interest in illustrating a book for West Virginia about 'Their Proud State' promoted [*sic*] this classic. The staff . . . have enjoyed his work and wish to show it."[2]

Haines's illustrations sum up the distinctions between the hillbilly and frontiersman versions of the Mountaineer figure far more succinctly and clearly than I am likely doing. According to Haines, "Hillbillys grow beards and shoot guns" (fig. 3.1). The West Virginia frontiersman also carries a rifle, but this figure wears the buckskins and the coonskin cap, and is presumably clean-shaven (fig. 3.2). Case closed.

Haines's 1967 illustrations capture the range of iterations that the WVU Mountaineer assumed over the course of the 1960s, a decade that saw the Mountaineer's rifle taken away but that also welcomed one of the first bearded Mountaineers at its close. While those aspects of the WVU Mountaineer's image continued to be fluid during this era, others became solidified, quite literally, in the drive to commission and erect a statue of the Mountaineer on campus. This effort officially began in 1950, but the solicitation of designs and fund-raising efforts continued throughout the next two decades, culminating with the unveiling of the iconic statue in front of the Mountainlair in October 1971 (fig. 3.3).[3]

The process was a long and contentious one, as former assistant vice president of Student Affairs Gordon Thorn recounts in his book *The Mountaineer Statue.* Thorn, who was the most important force in bringing the statue project to fruition, notes that by the late 1950s, the project was bogged down in questions about the sculpture's design and location, but one thing that "was agreed upon was the idea presented by President Stewart that the statue help to erase West Virginia's 'hillbilly' image."[4] Not only had the hillbilly Mountaineer been expunged from the campus bookstore's stock, now a frontiersman Mountaineer would be erected to ensure that the hillbilly was well and truly banished.

The process of bringing the statue to life stretched all the way through the 1960s, a decade of tremendous change, both

Figure 3.1. Thomas Haines's drawing of a hillbilly, circa 1967.

in the world at large and at WVU. While putting up a statue of a young man with a rifle may have seemed uncontroversial in the 1950s, by the time the statue was actually unveiled in 1971, the sight of a young man with a rifle carried a very different array of associations, as the Vietnam conflict escalated through the 1960s and as the compulsory draft—and resistance to it—was reinstated. Prospective designs seem to have included the rifle from the earliest stages of the process. Donald DeLue, the sculptor whose design was eventually chosen and who would create the iconic statue, described the mountain man of his model as a "hard rugged type" who "keeps faith with the rugged honest virtues of his own character"—virtues that include "imagination, courage, integrity, and faith."[5] By the 1960s, DeLue's list of adjectives echoed 150 years of historical descriptions of backwoodsmen, frontiersmen, and Mountaineers, starting with Joseph Doddridge and continuing right through the Crockett craze of the 1950s.

Figure 3.2. Thomas Haines's drawing of a West Virginia
frontiersman, circa 1967.

Figure 3.3. Governor Arch Moore unveils the Mountaineer statue
at the Mountainlair, 1971.

Thorn's book about the statue's history describes the many
controversies that held up the statue's progress during the
1960s—controversies largely about where the final statue would
be placed and how much money would be needed to complete the
job.[6] Yet there appears to have been no controversy at all about
the presence of the rifle, even though efforts to get the statue's
design and creation secured were taking place as the US military
presence in Vietnam was escalating rapidly, from nine thousand
troops in the country in 1962 to five hundred thousand in 1969,
and as the draft became broader, putting real rifles in the hands

of ever younger men—including many from West Virginia.[7] It may be my suburban upbringing that makes it seem strange that no one ever questioned the wisdom of depicting a young man with a gun during a decade when young men with guns were dying daily in Vietnam, when political assassinations rocked the nation, and when many Americans were suddenly fearful of their own rebellious children.

The fact that the inclusion of the rifle was never questioned suggests that the figure was more a symbol of the state's lost and lamented past, not a reflection of the far messier present. To be sure, sculptor DeLue wanted the Mountaineer statue to inspire viewers to strive to better themselves by reminding them of their ancestors' frontier grit. Noting that the Mountaineer "stands on the pinnacle with all the World below," the sculptor hoped that the statue would remind viewers of this lofty figure's virtues, the previously mentioned "imagination, courage, [and] integrity." Notably, though, DeLue couched these virtues in opposition to the chaos of the present, writing, "These are the virtues we hope to recall to mind in this day of ours when so many flounder in the valleys."[8] DeLue expressed these sentiments in a letter written to Mountain Honorary in December 1967, after a year that saw uprisings in the ghettoes of many US cities, large-scale protests against the Vietnam War, and the Summer of Love in San Francisco, where hippies flocked to heed Timothy Leary's advice to "turn on, tune in, drop out." These recent events surely represented the "valleys" that DeLue saw "so many flounder[ing] in."

DeLue's words cast the Mountaineer statue not only in a nostalgic light but in a reactionary one: the Davy Crockett-esque Mountaineer recalls the virtues DeLue listed but also make evident that the Mountaineer has a rifle and he's not afraid to use it. I don't mean to suggest that DeLue or the university administration intended the Mountaineer statue to be a threatening figure. But the decision to move forward with DeLue's design does seem to have been influenced by a sense that young people needed a visible reminder of "true" Mountaineer virtues, and of "better" times, when the world was (allegedly) simpler.

WVU and Vietnam

By the time the Mountaineer statue was unveiled in 1971, however, West Virginia and WVU had been deeply affected by the Vietnam conflict. In fact, the first WVU Mountaineer of the decade—William McPherson, the Mountaineer in 1960—entered the army after graduation and was killed in Vietnam in December 1965 (fig. 3.4).[9] McPherson's cousin, Robert R. Richards, remembers him as "a free spirit. He didn't seem to have any inhibitions; in fact it seemed like the more mischief he could get into, the better. . . . Bill was an extrovert and creative to the point of considering rules to just be opportunities to make an exception"— the philosophy of many a WVU Mountaineer before and since McPherson's time in the role. Richards writes in an online memorial that McPherson's mischievous persona made him an unlikely soldier: "What a surprise it was to learn, when he graduated, that he had gone through ROTC, been commissioned, and intended to make the Army a career! A creative, extroverted, rule-breaker like Bill in the military?! It seemed like a recipe for disaster." But in fact, as Richards later learned from a ROTC professor who knew McPherson, "Bill had developed into a creative, extroverted leader."[10] McPherson's ability to be both a trickster and a stalwart leader should not come as a surprise by this point, since we have seen that the figure of the Mountaineer routinely embodies these seemingly paradoxical qualities.

That the very first Mountaineer of the decade would become a casualty of that decade's most defining and divisive conflict is certainly tragic. But it is also, sadly, not terribly surprising, given the tremendous loss of life that young West Virginians suffered in the war at large. West Virginia had the highest death rate per capita of any state during the Vietnam conflict: 1,182 West

Figure 3.4. William McPherson, the 1960 Mountaineer, who was killed in Vietnam in December 1965.

Virginia natives were killed, a per-capita rate of 8.41 per 10,000 residents in the state, versus the national average of 5.89 per 10,000 residents in other states.[11] The conflict touched everyone. Perhaps for this reason, antiwar sentiment on the WVU campus was muted until late in the decade, when events in Vietnam and on the home front, such as revelations about the My Lai Massacre and the National Guard shootings at Kent State, led even the staunchest supporters to question whether the US involvement was worth all the death and turmoil it created. When the Mountaineer statue went up in 1971, the sight of a young man with a rifle evoked images of both soldiers and of antiwar protesters. Was this clean-cut frontiersman a patriot or a rebel? The roots of the Mountaineer set him up to be perceived in both ways.

The 1960s were historically significant for West Virginians in other ways as well: once again, Appalachia was "discovered" by outsiders eager to help (and exploit) the region's poor. John F. Kennedy made a big push to win voters in West Virginia and Appalachia during the 1960 election; journalist Charles Kuralt exposed the hardships of the rural poor with his "Christmas in Appalachia" television special in 1965; and Lyndon Johnson's War on Poverty brought many young volunteers to the region through a national service program, Volunteers in Service to America (VISTA), designed to fight poverty.

None of these interventions was particularly new. In many ways, these efforts mirrored those of the 1930s: Kuralt's televised coverage of poverty was akin to the photos of Appalachian poverty from the Depression-era Farm Security Administration program, and the VISTA volunteers paralleled the missionary work done by outsiders at the Appalachian settlement schools in the early twentieth century.[12] But just as radio broadcasts, movies, and comic strips had shown Appalachians what outsiders thought of them a generation earlier, in the 1960s Appalachians were able to witness these outside perceptions through television, both via documentaries like Kuralt's and via hugely popular sitcoms featuring stereotypical rural rubes like *The Beverly Hillbillies*, *The*

Andy Griffith Show, *Petticoat Junction*, and *Green Acres*. Once again, the hillbilly was everywhere, a figure to be laughed at or pitied, depending on the context.

Johnson's War on Poverty deliberately encompassed Appalachia to assure his detractors that the effort was not merely focused on urban (read African American) poverty.[13] Johnson knew that in order to accomplish his larger goals regarding civil rights, he needed to show that the federal government was aware of and actively working to uplift rural whites as well as urban blacks. One of the outcomes of this effort was the creation of the Appalachian Regional Commission (ARC) in 1965 and, in turn, the creation of Appalachia as an identifiable and unified (at least in federal terms) place. In many ways, Appalachia didn't exist until the ARC defined it, and the region's boundaries are still fluid today. Determining which states and which counties within those states fall under the ARC's definition of Appalachia is based not solely on geography but on an array of socioeconomic factors.[14] A positive outcome of this attention was an entirely new academic field: Appalachian studies, which brings together scholars from a huge range of disciplines (history, literature, sociology, geography, biology, medicine, education, and many others), all of whom are interested in addressing the particular concerns and needs of the region. Finally, after two centuries of being defined largely by outsiders, Appalachians had a forum for talking back to stereotypes and constructing their own ideas about Appalachian identities.

Antiwar Activism on the WVU Campus

While the 1960s have been immortalized as the decade of "sex, drugs, and rock and roll," the scene was a little different in Appalachia and at West Virginia University. That is not to say that the popular culture of the era, as well as its politics, weren't part of student life at WVU. When I started researching the Mountaineer during this era, I was told that West Virginia was not deeply affected by the cultural and political movements of the 1960s. Many echoed the sentiments of Mary Beth Bingman, who, writing about the anti–strip mining movements of the 1970s, notes that "the models we had in 1972—the civil rights movement, the anti-war movement, international revolutionary struggles—did not fit the Appalachian context historically, culturally, or ideologically."[15]

All of that turns out to be overstated. The very fact that the first Mountaineer of the decade, William McPherson, was killed in Vietnam tells us that WVU students were very much affected by the war. Undoubtedly, many young men attending the university in the 1960s went there specifically to take advantage of college deferments. Many other young West Virginia men undoubtedly joined up voluntarily, since the military—then and now—offered one of the few readily available routes out of poverty. If you couldn't afford to go to college, the military was a solid post-secondary option, and military service was regarded by many West Virginians as a family tradition. And if you *could* afford college, then you were expected to appreciate the opportunity. As Bob Cassell, a Korean War veteran who attended Marshall University in the late 1960s put it, at that time, West Virginia college students held to the mantra that "you go to school, you keep your nose clean, you get an education, you do better than your parents did." Belief in the university as an important site for free and open debate was a luxury that "intruded on education as understood by students at that time."[16]

Consequently, the history of West Virginia University during the Vietnam era is a complicated one. But there was antiwar activity on campus, and it reached its apex in Morgantown after the US invasion of Cambodia and the Kent State shootings in late April and early May 1970. The university also had a branch of the controversial Students for a Democratic Society (SDS), whose membership—though never very large, and certainly never very influential—was monitored by the FBI.[17] And women and African

Americans on campus organized and lobbied for their rights, reflecting the larger civil rights and women's movements in the nation.

If the 1940s and 1950s witnessed a shift in the Mountaineer identity from the upstart hillbilly to the rugged frontiersman, the late 1960s and early 1970s witnessed yet another shift in the Mountaineer's identity. The WVU Mountaineer's inherently rebellious and antiauthoritarian nature made him an ideal model for student activists in the 1960s. And of course, the bearded and barefoot version of the Mountaineer can easily be reenvisioned as a hippie. Just a few years after the university quashed the hillbilly Mountaineer and replaced him with the noble frontiersman, it was confronted with an entirely different kind of rabble-rousing student in the form of protesters and hippies.

Across the United States, the social upheavals of the 1960s fundamentally changed the college experience. At West Virginia University, as elsewhere, students challenged the long-established tradition that the university acted *in loco parentis*—literally, in place of parents—in its relationship to students. Student Mountaineers were beginning to realize that they weren't always free: the university curtailed their freedoms under the auspices of *in loco parentis*. A flier with the clever heading "DADMINISTRA-TION" put out by WVU's nascent chapter of SDS challenges *in loco parentis* directly:

> You have come to the University thinking that you are going to become part of an adult community of students and scholars. . . . We are going to raise some fundamental questions about the way the University is being run. You may decide for yourself whether the answers are close to your vision of what a University should be.
>
> Why has the University adopted a policy of in loco parentis? Is this the proper relationship of a university to its students? How is responsibility acquired? By being controlled? By controlling your own life?[18]

The flier then goes on to question some of the university's specific *in loco parentis* policies: barring students from visiting students of the opposite sex in residence halls and in off-campus housing; requiring female students to live in the dorms longer than male students; and not serving beer in the Mountainlair, despite a student referendum in which 80 percent of students voted in favor of doing so.

While these examples might suggest that students were just seeking permission to drink and have sex, the flier also raises important points about the purposes and efficacy of student government and consumer issues—"Why should the state-run University Bookstore charge higher prices for student supplies than others?" It concludes by framing all of these issues in a much larger context of power and democracy, not just on campus but in the United States in general:

> There is a group of students at the University concerned with these problems and interested in trying to bring about a new university where academic and personal freedom will not be threatened by administrative bureaucracy. Where students become responsible citizens by exercising control of their destinies at the University and participating in the governing of the University. We are the WVU chapter of Students for a Democratic Society. We are interested in bringing about changes in the university community and in contemporary American society that will advance the freedom and welfare of all.[19]

Perhaps most significant during the Vietnam era are the flier's questions about the Reserve Officer Training Corps (ROTC) on campus: "Why is ROTC on campus? What does military training have to do with the pursuit of knowledge and wisdom? Is it not the teaching of unquestioned obedience rather than open questioning, free inquiry?"[20]

It was these sorts of questions that put SDS chapters on campuses across the country on the FBI's watchlist. Scott Bills, a student activist while he was at WVU in the late 1960s (fig. 3.5), went on to become a history professor and donated his collection of antiwar and other protest materials to the West Virginia and Regional History Collection. Included in the collection are FBI

Figure 3.5. Student activist Scott Bills portrayed as the motorcyclist in *Easy Rider* in *The Greek Letter* newspaper, 1970.

reports about Bills's involvement with the WVU chapter of SDS and the subsequent Mountaineer Freedom Party that he formed on campus. Bills obtained these records under the Freedom of Information Act, and though the FBI seems eventually to have decided he posed no danger, the fact that he was monitored indicates how seriously the federal government took the potential threat of student activists.[21]

The SDS was active elsewhere in West Virginia too: Marshall University student activist Al Miller announced his intention to establish a Marshall SDS chapter in 1965, but the group wasn't officially founded until the fall of 1968, at which point it sought to become recognized as an official campus organization. Both conservative students and community members opposed this effort, but Marshall's brand-new president, Roland

Nelson—while not personally supportive of SDS—could not see
any way to deny the group's legitimacy without violating their
right to free speech. Local anticommunists flooded the local
press with concerns about a "reds on campus crisis" in order to
"rally their supporters to the dangers of subversive currents" at
Marshall. Their efforts appear to have had a paradoxical effect,
leading some previously unconcerned students to support SDS,
putting further pressure on the university's administration. In
March 1969 Nelson approved the group's request, saying that
he "acted on the basic principle that the university is a seat
of knowledge and investigation, a place where opposing ideas
can be presented and studied openly." The debate at Marshall
attracted the concern of none other than West Virginia senator
Robert Byrd, who wrote an article for the *Huntington Advertiser*
expressing his opposition to the group. Byrd claimed that SDS
had "a blueprint for the destruction of the entire American
educational system." Byrd wrote of his concern that after successfully infiltrating not just college campuses but high schools,
SDS would "use [schools] as a means to revolutionize American
society according to Marxist precepts."[22]

Far from revolutionizing anything, the WVU chapter of
SDS never gained much momentum. In fact, by the time the
Marshall SDS gained official recognition in the spring of 1969,
WVU's floundering chapter had disbanded. In his detailed history
of WVU student activism and dissent during the Vietnam era,
Jeffrey Drobney notes that "according to FBI records, [the WVU
SDS chapter] had no more than ten to fifteen active members
and ceased to be operational after 1968."[23] In a *Morgantown Post*
article from October 1, 1969, Bills said "SDS failed because of
'clichéism' and bad image."[24]

After the SDS chapter collapsed, Bills and other activists
took a "think globally, act locally" approach and started a student-government party and activist organization called the
Mountaineer Freedom Party. The organization's materials illustrate how it carried on many of the fundamental goals of WVU's

SDS chapter—a brochure titled "Join MFP" says the "doctrine of *in loco parentis* is outdated" and calls for recognition of "the full constitutional rights of all students, faculty, and employees."[25] The brochure touches on many of the same local concerns raised in SDS's "Dadministration" flier, notably those about the bookstore's prices and more meaningful student involvement with university governance. However, the "Join MFP" brochure expresses broader concerns than the "Dadministration" flier had, including "end[ing] the war in Indochina," "sponsoring picket lines in support of the Grape Boycott," and "participat[ing] in the Environmental Teach-In of April 22, [1970]" the first Earth Day. The MFP also made a significant commitment to local concerns, not just on campus but in West Virginia at large; the brochure notes the organization's involvement in seeking "adequate Black Lung legislation" and in "provid[ing] poll watchers for the United Mine Workers election in December of 1969."[26]

These local concerns went beyond the political, however. A full panel of the "Join MFP" brochure is devoted to a call for WVU to expand its Appalachian Center and to create a department of Appalachian studies (fig. 3.6). Although these requests are framed in the organization's overarching rhetoric of democracy, arguing that these efforts would help "tackle the problems resulting from the region's colonial economy," what precedes that specific claim is far more about community, cultural pride, and a rebellious attitude:

> At one time the land known as Appalachia was inhabited by a sturdy people with a sense of community spirit. When a neighbor was building a new barn, people from near and far came to lend a hand. Entertainment was provided by community square dances, quilting bees and church socials. And the hills echoed the sounds of fiddle and banjo.
>
> Little remains today of that proud culture. The politics of assimilation and the attitudes of a broken and exploited people have all but exterminated the Appalachia of the past.[27]

PRESERVE OUR APPALACHIAN CULTURE

At one time the land known as Appalachia was inhabited by a sturdy people with a sense of community spirit. When a neighbor was building a new barn, peo-

montani semper liberi!

ple from near and far came to lend a hand. Entertainment was provided by community square dances, quilting bees and church socials. And the hills echoed the sounds of the fiddle and banjo.

Little remains today of that proud culture. The politics of assimilation and the attitudes of a broken and exploited people have all but exterminated the Appalachia of the past.

The time has come for all residents of Appalachia to resist the destruction of our common identity. We must be proud of our Mountain culture and seek to revive it.

The Appalachian Center should be greatly expanded, including a Department of Appalachian Studies. We must begin to tackle the problems resulting from the region's colonial economy. West Virginia University is not doing its part. We must see that it does.

Figure 3.6. The Mountaineer Freedom Party's brochure, highlighting interest in Appalachian culture and issues.

It's an overblown and romantic view of Appalachia, to be sure, and one that both pre- and postdates this moment in history: the grief about a "proud culture" having been turned into "a broken and exploited people" brings us right back to Doddridge's Backwoodsman and his railing against the Dandies and "big folks" who "freely enjoy the fruits of our hardships" and "feast, where we had to starve."[28]

What's especially fascinating is that the brochure's call for a renewed Mountaineer identity is placed, literally, alongside the larger and more familiar goal of student activists at the time, ending the war in Vietnam. Furthermore, the call to "Preserve Our Appalachian Culture" gets far more space in the brochure than any other single topic. The illustration that accompanies the text features the state motto, *Montani semper liberi!* (complete with exclamation point), alongside drawings of a banjo, a cabin, a miner's pick, and an image of a Davy Crockett-esque Mountaineer in profile.

The very name *Mountaineer Freedom Party* was presumably coined to link student freedoms to the state motto and its claim that Mountaineers are always free. Visually and rhetorically, the brochure suggests that immediate student concerns and national concerns are equal to, and perhaps grounded in, regional concerns, while the text further suggests that reclaiming the resilient, communal spirit of one's Appalachian ancestors is the first step toward becoming a vigorous activist for contemporary issues of all kinds.

Bills's own campaign posters for his bid to become student-government president explicitly evoked the "noble frontiersman-turned-statesman" trope: the signs claimed that he, like Abe Lincoln, had been "born in a log cabin" (fig. 3.7). In a moment of foresight that only a historian could have, Bills also thought to rescue and eventually archive a vandalized version of his campaign sign (fig. 3.8). This one, which he describes as a "poster with graffiti, from Woodburn Hall (I think)," includes the vandal's addition of the phrase *without a father*, so that the updated slogan reads "Scott was born without a father in a log cabin." I like to imagine that Bills saw the humor in this addition, the way it turned the noble frontiersman of his original poster into a degenerate hillbilly of questionable heritage.[29]

The Mountaineer Freedom Party, both in name and in agenda, explicitly set out to reclaim the upstart, squatter/hillbilly aspect of Mountaineer identity. Despite the image of the frontiersman Mountaineer in its recruitment materials, the MFP clearly linked the Mountaineer spirit to activism and dissent, reviving the notion of the WVU Mountaineer not as an armed

SCOTT **Was** **Born** **In** **A** **Log** **Cabin**

He **Cares**

Vote **Bills/Pyles**

VOTE **MFP**

Without a father

SCOTT **Was** **Born** **In** **A** **Log** **Cabin**

He **Cares**

Vote **Bills/Pyles**

VOTE **MFP**

Figure 3.7 (*top*). Scott Bills's student government campaign
poster and its Abe Lincoln allusion.
Figure 3.8 (*bottom*). The graffitied version of Scott Bills's
campaign poster with a hillbilly addendum.

pioneer/patriot but as a freethinking rebel. Even though the Mountaineer statue and the MFP used frontiersman imagery to represent their version of the Mountaineer, the ideology behind each could not be more different. The statue, as DeLue's words suggest, is designed to rein in rebellion and remind viewers of a more noble frontier past, whose values we should try to recapture. The MFP's Mountaineer is also linked to past values, but these are values of political engagement and resistance. Same Davy Crockett image, very different connotations.

And those were, indeed, the two competing ideas about the WVU Mountaineer's identity operating on campus in the late 1960s and early 1970s. The next section explores these competing ideas about the Mountaineer through the experiences of two men who served as the WVU Mountaineer during this time, Doug Townshend (1969–70) and Robert Lowe (1970–71).

Four Dead in Ohio and
Six Expelled at WVU

In late April 1970, things were heating up on college campuses throughout the United States, including WVU. Places like the University of California at Berkeley, the University of Wisconsin, and other traditional liberal bastions had been sites of antiwar and other student protests for years by then, but as the Vietnam War dragged on and politicians became increasingly tone deaf to the antiwar movement and to youths in general (this is the moment when President Nixon famously referred to student activists as "bums"), student protests occurred at many more campuses throughout the country. In early April 1970, California governor Ronald Reagan responded to a question about protesters on his state's campuses by saying, "If it takes a bloodbath, let's get it over with."[30] Tensions escalated on April 30, 1970, when Nixon ordered US troops to invade Cambodia, something he had previously claimed he would not do. In fact, in the weeks leading up to the Cambodian invasion, Nixon had proposed a gradual withdrawal of US troops from the region in an apparent effort to make good on a campaign promise to end the war.

Immediately after the Cambodian invasion, college students throughout the country took to the streets to protest, even at previously quiet institutions. Confrontations between students and campus police and local law enforcement were common, and the use of tear gas, rubber bullets, and tactics to disperse crowds of protesters was widespread. In Ohio, student protests were particularly vigorous at Ohio State University in Columbus and at another state campus further north: Kent State University. On May 2, 1970, Ohio governor James Rhodes said of the protesters at Kent State, "They're worse than the brown shirts and the communist element and also the night riders and the vigilantes. They're the worst kind of people we harbor in America. I think that we're up against the strongest, well-trained, militant revolutionary group that has ever assembled in America. . . . We're going to eradicate the problem, we're not going to treat the symptoms."[31] True to his word, two days later, Rhodes ordered the Ohio National Guard to the Kent State campus, where they fired on unarmed protesters and bystanders, killing four and wounding nine others.

Campuses everywhere exploded after Kent State, including many in Appalachia: in addition to protests at WVU, students demonstrated at the University of Kentucky at Lexington, where the Air Force ROTC building was burned down; at Ohio University in Athens, where two firebombs were lobbed at the ROTC office on campus; at the University of Tennessee in Knoxville, where over 75 percent of the students were reportedly on strike; and at numerous other campuses throughout the region, including Madison College in Harrisonburg, Virginia; Carlow University, Chatham University, and Carnegie Mellon University in Pittsburgh; Marietta College in Ohio;

and Davidson, Livingston, and Greensboro Colleges in North Carolina.[32] Students who may have felt insulated from the war in Asia could no longer ignore the war at home. Within a couple of weeks, more than two hundred campuses across the country had shut down, sending students home before the spring semester ended. WVU's academic calendar was a few weeks ahead of many other schools, so the week of the Kent State shootings—which happened on a Monday—was also final exam week at WVU, meaning that students were nearly done with the semester. It is probably this more than student apathy that kept WVU's response to the Kent State shootings relatively tame. Nevertheless, there *was* a response.

Before I did any formal research into the history of these events at WVU, however, I heard two very different first-person accounts of them from two former Mountaineer mascots of that era whom I interviewed in 2015. The first account came from Doug Townshend, who served as the WVU Mountaineer from spring semester 1969 through spring semester 1970 (fig. 3.9). When I first heard Townshend's story, I wasn't aware that the events he described were a specific response to the Kent State shootings; I'd asked him more generally what the WVU campus was like when he was the Mountaineer, since it was such a tumultuous time on campuses across the United States. Townshend replied that

At the time, we had what we call "hippies." . . . And then . . . the freedom movement, if you will, and I can remember when we had the riots—student riots in Morgantown, and the State Police marched up . . . was it—Oglebay Circle there? In front of the Mountainlair? And they had all their riot gear on. And, and I was—we were there watching, and again, I—in the position I was in [as the official Mountaineer] was not to partake in anything. I was just interested in observing. And it was—they were throwing water balloons at each other. I mean, basically it was the Greeks versus the . . . "hippies."[33]

Figure 3.9. Doug Townshend, the Mountaineer of 1969–70.

Townshend followed this story up with the comment that "they were worried about what had happened at Kent State," which was my first indication of when this event took place. Initially, Townshend's account confirmed what I suspected about WVU: that it had been no hotbed of student activism in the Vietnam War era, but rather a place where a springtime water-balloon fight got exaggerated in the retelling to become a full-blown "student riot."

A few weeks later, I interviewed Bob Lowe, the Mountaineer who followed Townshend, serving in the 1970–71 school year (fig. 3.10). In May 1970 Lowe was completing his junior year at

WVU, where he was a varsity basketball player, and had recently been selected as the following year's Mountaineer. After we'd been discussing his experiences for a while, I asked Lowe about the climate on campus during in the late '60s and early '70s. Notably, Lowe's daughter was present during the interview. She had just graduated from college a few months earlier, and before he started telling the following story, Lowe looked at her and asked, quite seriously, "Remember the story?"—signaling that this was an oft-told and important narrative for him:

> It was right after Kent State. . . . There was a group of students who took over Grumbein's Island for three days, asking the then University President [James Harlow] . . . to issue a statement on behalf of the student body of West Virginia University that we . . . abhorred . . . the senseless killings at Kent State. . . . Our coaches had told us, anybody who's involved in any antiwar protest will have their scholarship taken away, will be kicked off the basketball team, [but] I'm out there, anyway, because I really believed strongly [in the antiwar movement]. But on the morning of the third day [of the protest], you hear the bullhorns saying, "You need to leave the area immediately. We are about to give you tear gas." And you look up—one road coming down was the West Virginia State Police in riot gear. Coming from down where the library and where the law school used to be is the city police, and coming from the old Mountaineer Field is the National Guard and they're in riot gear. And the tear gas canisters come in and I was out of there in a heartbeat.[34]

This, clearly, is a different account of the same event: while Townshend acknowledged that the state police had broken up the protest, he did not mention that they threw tear gas. In fact, his words and his tone both suggest that he felt that the state police had seriously overreacted to what he characterized as a water-balloon fight.

Later in my conversation with Lowe, after I'd turned off

Figure 3.10. Bob Lowe, the Mountaineer of 1970–71.

the recorder (of course!), he added another chilling detail to his account of the demonstration: that the counterprotesters on the steps of the student center threw water balloons *filled with ammonia* at the antiwar demonstrators. Suddenly, the motif that made Townshend's story seem so funny was transformed into a far more sinister one; the balloons were no longer playthings but weapons.

After hearing Lowe's story, I realized that I needed to do some archival research to find out what was on record as having happened at WVU in May 1970. What I discovered was that there had indeed been significant demonstrations in Morgantown, both on campus and at the county courthouse. Photographs from the university's historical photos archive and articles in the Morgantown newspapers and the *Daily Athenaeum* confirm that police in riot gear were called to break up the protest and that they had thrown tear gas canisters at the demonstrators (figs. 3.11 and 3.12). A letter to the Morgantown *Dominion News* from Lynne D. Boomer, an instructor in the WVU department of English, confirms Lowe's account of the ammonia-filled balloons. Describing the actions of the counterprotesters on the Mountainlair steps, Boomer writes that the group "threw eggs and rocks down on students protesting the war. And, although I can understand emotions running high in this kind of situation, I have a hard time dealing with the mentality that calculatingly fills balloons with ammonia to throw at peace protesters."[35] Boomer also notes that some counterprotesters yelled, "We ought to shoot all these hippies."[36]

The disjunctions between Townshend's and Lowe's stories can, of course, be attributed to many factors, including the vagaries of memory, which parts of the multiday protest each man witnessed, and the difference in the men's political leanings. But I was most struck by the differences in their performances of these narratives: Townshend was casual and lighthearted about his account, and we laughed together at several points, chiefly over the notion of the state police overreacting to a tension-relieving, end-of-semester water-balloon fight among college kids. Lowe's narration was serious, compounded by his daughter's presence: this wasn't a casual trip down memory lane—this was an important piece of personal and national history. That serious tone was underscored by the fact that he followed up his account by saying that a few weeks later he attended a Neil Young concert in Baltimore where Young played "Four Dead in Ohio" for the first time. Lowe also described a phone conversation he had with his father the night before the infamous draft lottery of December 1, 1969: his father, a career military man—an active officer who was a veteran of World War II and Korea—asked Lowe what he planned to do if he got a low draft number. Lowe said he told his dad he wasn't sure, and his father simply replied, "Let me know if you need a ride to Canada."[37]

I followed up with both men after I'd done my additional research, sending them copies of the newspaper articles describing the events and Boomer's letter. Lowe confirmed that all of this

Figure 3.11. Students teargassed during a protest of the
Kent State shootings, May 1970.

jibed with his memories. Townshend said that he "just recall[ed] it being nothing else more than a shouting match and throwing some water balloons."[38] At this point, a historian would likely question which man's account was the more true or accurate. And that is, indeed, an intriguing question, but perhaps an irrelevant one. As a folklorist, I know that both reality and storytelling are far more complex than simple notions of truth encompass. Each man's perception of the original events was deeply shaped by his own experiences and beliefs as well as when and where each was physically present.

After all, the demonstrations went on for three days, and the conflict escalated until the police and the National Guard cleared the area with tear gas. It's likely that early on the demonstrations were less heated and more playful and only later turned ugly. And, of course, time changes our narration of events dra-

Figure 3.12. National Guardsman in riot gear on University Avenue during a protest of the Kent State shootings, May 1970.

matically: how Townshend and Lowe described their experiences right after the events occurred was likely very different from the way they related them to me forty-five years later; the benefit of hindsight and decades of life experience would certainly shape their memories. The fact that Lowe had told this story before to his daughter and the way he framed it with other events of the time—his father's offer to help him get to Canada and Neil Young's performance of "Four Dead in Ohio"—indicate that, for Lowe, the story is about history: his own personal history as well as the nation's history. For Townshend, the story is about college antics that got out of hand. As different as they are, both versions are absolutely true, as are the uncollected accounts of the thousand or more others who were there.

Townshend's and Lowe's stories are important, though, in the ways that they underscore the deep divisions in the United States at the time and the ways in which one's political views shaped and colored one's perception of events. And for me, it was an important lesson in not assuming that everyone who was a college student in the late 1960s and early 1970s participated in the antiwar movement. While that is the lasting stereotype about students of the era, it is just that: a stereotype. Then, as now, campuses are populated by individuals with a full spectrum of political beliefs and values. What is more remarkable is that both men—one who was the current WVU Mountaineer and the other who would become the WVU Mountaineer the following year— were firsthand witnesses to this seminal event in WVU's history of campus activism. Equally remarkable is the fact that two young men who stood on very different sides of the debate about the Vietnam War could both serve as the university's official representative during that same tumultuous year of 1970. Townshend and Lowe's consecutive service as the WVU Mountaineer underscores the fluidity of Mountaineer identity at this time.

Notably, in photos from their years of service, Townshend is clean-shaven and Lowe is bearded. In fact, Lowe told me that he'd been wanting to grow a beard for some time, but as a varsity athlete, he was prohibited from doing so. One of the pluses of being the Mountaineer was that he had an official reason for growing one. As he told me in an interview, the "basketball coaches wouldn't allow you to have facial hair or long hair, so the last game of my senior year, I arrived with three day's growth for the last game." He added that he has only shaved once since that time, and that when he did, his "daughters looked at [him] and said, 'No Dad, put that back on.'" Lowe's daughter, Bethany, who was present for the interview, added, "We didn't recognize him."[39]

The question of facial hair at this point in American history is a critical one. In his excellent book *Of Beards and Men: The Revealing History of Facial Hair*, Christopher Oldstone-Moore explains that a clean-shaven face had been a sign of conformity for most of the twentieth century, making it "almost inevitable that critics of the status quo would . . . choose facial hair as a sign of protest."[40] Having long hair or a beard was a political statement in mid-century America. In previous decades, beards had been worn primarily by "scholars, ecclesiastics, artists, bums, musicians, and frontiersmen," as Eleanor Page, the society editor of the *Chicago Tribune* wrote in a 1958 article titled "Does a Beard Add to Manly Charm?" But when Page's article appeared in the late 1950s, that group of beard-wearing social outcasts was being "joined by increasing numbers of young men."[41] And, of course, by the end of the 1960s, facial hair was almost required to prove a young man's commitment to the antiwar cause. As the legendary antiwar activist Jerry Rubin said, "Rebellion begins on your face. . . . Our hair is our picket sign and our Molotov cocktail. Our hair hurts/offends [the establishment] more than anything we can say or do."[42] A 1968 issue of *Newsweek* declared that "today, hair power is second only to black power as a driving force of American life."[43]

In our current era, when facial hair is part of mainstream male fashion and even a trendy look for hipsters and professional athletes, it may be difficult to understand just how radical having a beard was in mid-century America—and how much danger a beard both communicated and invited. Travel writer Richard Atcheson captured the risks of beard wearing well when he wrote, "I have been up the Zambesi without a paddle; I have flapped through the sky in a disabled helicopter over the Great Barrier Reef; I have been menaced by slitty-eyed pimps of Tijuana . . . but I have never been as scared in distant places as I was while traveling in my own country, in the summer of 1970, while wearing long hair and a beard."[44] In the summer of 1970, after the Kent State shootings, every young man with long hair and a beard was suddenly a potential threat to the status quo. Bob Lowe's decision to grow a beard that summer was risky, indeed, even if he did have the perfect excuse to do so.

Eleanor Page's roster of beard wearers in her *Chicago Tribune* article lists familiar names, including the final entry: frontiersmen. This seems an odd figure to include in a list of beard wearers since the most recognizable frontiersman, Disney's Davy Crockett, played by Fess Parker, was clean-shaven. Even if frontiersmen were typically imagined to be bearded, as Page's article suggests, television producers certainly didn't want to depict them with beards, given the beard's increasing connection with radical politics over the course of the 1960s. The pop-culture frontiersman needed to be clean-shaven so that the audience would see him as a defender of the status quo, not an opponent of it. Presumably, DeLue's Mountaineer statue reflects this cleaned-up beardless version of the frontiersman, popularized by both television series. By the time DeLue submitted his design in 1967, putting a beard on the Mountaineer statue would have broadcast a political message that no university would agree to pay for and display.

And yet, the growing popularity of beards in the late 1960s eventually led to much wider social acceptance of male facial hair in general, and it certainly marked an important turning point in the WVU Mountaineer's appearance. As facial hair became less stigmatized and even fashionable, men serving as the WVU Mountaineer increasingly wore beards as part of their kit. Looking at photos of Mountaineers prior to the 1970s, very few wore beards; after 1970, the vast majority of male Mountaineers are bearded.[45] This shift is a clear reflection of how facial hair became more mainstream as its association with leftist political views or poor grooming diminished. But the expectation that the WVU Mountaineer should have a beard would also lead to problems down the road, when Natalie Tennant became the first woman to serve as the Mountaineer, as will be discussed in the next chapter. Just as outlawing the hillbilly Mountaineer to enshrine the frontiersman Mountaineer had unintended negative consequences for the university, so too did the unofficial expectation that the Mountaineer should be bearded.

But back to the beardless WVU Mountaineer of 1969–70,

Doug Townshend, and the bearded WVU Mountaineer of 1970–71, Bob Lowe: having a clean-shaven Mountaineer followed just a year later by a bearded one seems to mark the beginning of this cultural shift, and it also reminds us that despite the university's management of the Mountaineer image, there were still two very different ideas of the WVU Mountaineer that coexisted at this time. The clean-shaven Mountaineer stood for the Davy Crockett version—the rugged, all-American frontiersman, ready to fight for his land. The bearded Mountaineer, on the other hand, stood for the rebellious version—the man who is always free, who speaks his mind and challenges authority—and who wears a beard when that is the clearest visible manifestation of his antiauthoritarian views. These were also the warring images of what it meant to be an American at the time: was one's loyalty measured by one's willingness to defend the country by taking up arms, or by one's commitment to the principles of free speech and dissent upon which the country was founded? This debate played out in a physical way in the shift between Townshend's clean-shaven Mountaineer and Lowe's bearded one.

The demonstration at WVU in protest of the Kent State shootings was not just a significant memory for Townshend and Lowe; it also marked a turning point in student/administration relations and in student activism at WVU. In June 1970 six students, including Scott Bills, were ordered to a disciplinary hearing for allegedly vandalizing Woodburn Hall during the May demonstrations. The so-called "Morgantown Six" were accused of "tearing down two bulletin boards . . . damaging both boards and wall, as well as breaking a window and destroying certain teaching materials," causing approximately five hundred dollars in damage.[46] The letter claimed that a larger group of thirty-five students had entered Woodburn Hall, and that when others were identified, they too would be brought before the disciplinary committee. However, that never happened, and, in fact, it appears as if the university targeted these six young men because they were known student activists. If the university thought that conducting this hearing during the summer would keep it quiet and rid the university of agitators, they were mistaken: four of the six accused hired attorney Herb Rogers, who in turn consulted with the defense attorney for the Chicago Seven, William Kunstler, who agreed to attend the disciplinary hearing as co-attorney with Rogers. A *Daily Athenaeum* article says that Rogers and Kunstler were "working on a federal suit to dismiss disciplinary proceedings" on the grounds that the university had no official student rules and regulations, although state law requires that the university file such rules through the state board of regents.[47]

The hearing, initially scheduled for June 24, was postponed until August 19, and then indefinitely; ultimately, the hearing never happened, and the university seems to have decided to let the episode pass as quietly as possible.[48] This was perhaps due to the fact that far from quelling campus unrest, the administration's response instead stoked student action, even during the low season of summer term. The Scott Bills collection includes three fliers that list phone numbers for students to call to get involved in "the political issues of this campus and this nation . . . before it's the Morgantown 14,000 instead of the Morgantown Six."[49] The fliers, which were distributed on campus in the summer of 1970, include considerably more militant rhetoric than those urging students to become more active. One flier directly invokes the memory of Kent State in its appeal: "Remember Kent State and remember that by protecting the Morgantown 6 now you are actually protecting yourself from future repression!"[50]

On June 24, the day the hearing was supposed to take place, students instead organized a rally for the Morgantown Six and called for student solidarity more broadly.[51] A group of about 175 people came together in Woodburn Circle to discuss the case of the Morgantown Six. "Call it Woodburnstock," quipped a student in the crowd.[52] Speakers included William Haymond, a philosophy professor who lost his position as chair of the philosophy department after participating in the May demonstrations and "stay[ing] in the streets with the demonstrators because [he] felt they had legitimate complaints."[53] As with the May demonstrations—and, indeed, at Woodstock—the group at Woodburnstock had a variety of reasons for attending: some were there to find out more about the Morgantown Six case, some were there to "listen to music," and one used the occasion to urge others to "heed the knocking of Christ on the doors of their hearts." Participants interviewed were also divided in their response to the university's disciplinary actions. One said the university was right to hold the students accountable for the (alleged) damage they caused, while another asked, "Is it just them on trial, or is it all of us?" Another student—living up to his billing as a "public relations senior"—praised the event for "open[ing] meaningful intercourse between the two polarized groups, freaks and straights."[54]

Woodburnstock was just one incident of student action over the summer following the May demonstrations. *Daily Athenaeum* articles and documents in the Scott Bills collection describe additional action that took place in the Mountainlair during freshman orientation sessions over the summer of 1970. In late July, several bomb threats were made on campus, two to the Mountainlair and one to the Towers dormitory complex.[55] These threats coincided with freshman orientation, which was taking place at both of those locations, and appear to have been called in specifically to disrupt the orientation activities. On all three occasions, the Lair and the Towers complex were evacuated. After these false alarms, however, university administrators continued to clear the Lair of students, even though no further threats were received. The *Daily Athenaeum* reports that at 3 p.m. on Wednesday, July 22, an intercom announcement told students to leave the Lair "for security reasons"; however, "freshman orientation participants were allowed to remain in the Building."[56] Students who refused to leave were photographed and asked to give their names and student numbers to a Lair employee, and one was arrested "on a charge of indecent gesture."[57] When the building reopened, anyone wanting to enter was required to show a faculty card or a student fee receipt card, proving they were a current student. These kinds of surveillance tactics upset some students, so they circulated a petition asking for the resignation of Edwin Reynolds, director of the Mountainlair, for "his flagrant disregard of student rights and needs."[58]

Documents in the Bills collection continue the story. A multi-page booklet titled "Sunrise at WVU: To the People, By the People" opens with a press release from "Woodstock Nation" explaining that "the enclosed booklet is one of 20,000 copies distributed to the students of West Virginia University during registration."[59] "Sunrise at WVU" neatly catches its readers up on the eventful few months since the end of spring semester, and it lays the groundwork for fall-semester activism, saying "There has been many and varied rumors about what will happen on the campuses this fall. This publication should clarify all doubts." The booklet then lists its contents:

- an explanation of the issue (issues) surrounding the case of the MORGANTOWN 6.
- a correspondence specifically welcoming/informing freshmen.
- a complimentary re-cap sheet about the LIBERATION of the 'Lair.
- a cultural sheet containing a little of everything: new shops in town, new groups formed, sources of information, etc.
- a critique of the new mandatory student code of conduct.
- the text of the NORTH BEND STATEMENT!
- and a final "call to arms" suggesting possible means of converting frustration and militancy into an effective political weapon![60]

The booklet includes a one-page flier that "was distributed to incoming freshmen during orientation ceremonies in the Mountainlair," describing orientation as an "indoctrination ceremony" designed to "program you into the passive type of student THEY want you to be" and encouraging students to "get involved" and "work to change this University into a viable community where free exchange of intellectual ideas is a reality instead of a slogan."[61] It suggests that freshmen get involved in "concerts, rallies, demonstrations, love-ins, live-ins, and sensitivity groups," all "legal and beautiful ways of communicating to each other our ideas."[62]

It was the distribution of this flier, apparently, that led the administration to evacuate the Mountainlair and close it to all but incoming freshmen during orientation sessions; keeping the freshmen isolated prevented older student agitators from communicating with them. As the "Sunrise" booklet goes on to explain, "During these ceremonies, someone called in a bomb threat," which led to the evacuation, and "the 'Lair administrators immediately and arbitrarily assumed that the group distributing the leaflet was responsible." Administrators searched the evacuated building and then brought the orientation groups back in "before every freshman assembly during the two week program."[63] According to "Sunrise," the incident on July 22 came after several routine afternoon evictions, when "150–200 students mounted a sign, 'Hell No; We Won't Go!' in the snack bar and calmly informed the administration that they were not leaving." A Mountainlair official told them that the evacuation was "ordered by the fire marshal," which "the fire marshal later denied." The following day, students burned an effigy of the Mountainlair official. In response, the real-life model for the effigy showed up, doused the flames, and challenged the protesters to a fist fight.[64] No one—neither student nor administrator—comes out looking good in the booklet's description of the events at the Mountainlair in the summer of 1970. Clearly, the administration's hope that the campus would quiet down over the summer when most students were away was not realized. And the students seemed to have made effective use of the less crowded summer schedule to get organized and to plan and carry out more pointed demonstrations. The "bomb" turned out to be a symbolic one, and the administration seems to have decided that the only way to defuse it was to censor it. But in so doing, they merely added fuel to the fire.

However, the university and the state government were working on other tactics to defuse tensions in the summer of 1970. For example, West Virginia joined forty-one other states in introducing legislation designed to prevent campus protests and to clarify punishment for protesters. In West Virginia, this took the form of an amendment made to the Riot Act of 1849, a law that went into effect when West Virginia was still part of the state of Virginia. In brief, the amendment enabled "anyone refusing to be deputized by an authorized official of the law . . . [to] be considered a rioter." In other words, anyone refusing to help law enforcement would be violating the Riot Act and subject to jail and fines. The amendment also declared that a law enforcement officer who shoots a rioter shall "be held guiltless" and that police officers had the "the right to enter private dwellings without a search warrant while chasing rioters." The legislation also made destruction of a building punishable with a one- to ten-year jail sentence.[65] Other states passed legislation that even more clearly limited students' free-speech rights: in California, students could lose their state financial aid "if convicted of taking part in a campus disorder," and in Ohio, students and faculty members could be immediately dismissed from their universities for participating in a campus disorder.[66]

West Virginia University also doubled down on its own rules. As previously noted, the primary reason the administration couldn't make its case stick against the Morgantown Six was because it did not have an official student code of conduct on file, although the university was required by law to have one. Articles in the *Daily Athenaeum* suggest that the university had been dragging its feet to develop a student code of conduct for nearly two years,[67] but unsurprisingly, getting one completed and approved jumped to the top of the administration's list of priorities in the summer of 1970. As a flier titled the *North Bend Statement* dated August 9, 1970, indicates, the state board of regents quickly developed and formalized a student conduct code in the months after the May demonstrations. From the beginning, student participation in creating the code was limited,[68] but the *North Bend Statement* suggests that students were explicitly left out of the process of finalizing the code: "The Board of Regents . . . have consistently refused to open their meetings to public scrutiny. And now, in complete secrecy they have arrogantly decreed a code of conduct without consulting any students, because they 'did not choose to consult any.'"[69] The *North Bend Statement* concludes by likening the board's decision to the Dred Scott case, and ends by declaring that "the students of West Virginia will not stand idly by while their rights are trampled on. INCREASED REPRESSION WILL ONLY BRING INCREASED RESISTANCE."[70] Just as the administration hoped its efforts to deal with the Morgantown Six case during the quiet summer term would stem further student protests, the university rushed to put an official student code of conduct in place over the summer and without student participation. This effort not only failed to quell student dissent; it actually stoked it.

In the meantime, some Morgantown citizens were voicing their own concerns about the May protests and the political climate on campus. Throughout the summer of 1970, a group calling itself the Concerned Citizens Committee circulated a so-called Petition to the West Virginia Board of Regents for the Ouster of Radical Faculty Activists, which stated that the undersigned were "alarmed and concerned at the increasing anti-American radicalism on the campus of West Virginia University" and asked that any faculty who "aided, abetted, and encouraged such activities by demonstrating in Morgantown, May 5–7, 1970, be summarily dismissed from . . . service."[71] According to an article in the Morgantown *Dominion News*, the group was formed in response to an article published in the paper on June 21 by Frank Bucca, father of Daniel Bucca, one of the Morgantown Six.[72] In his article, the elder Bucca claimed that "his son Daniel . . . has become a 'parasite,' a 'radical,' and a 'traitor,' largely because of the influence of philosophy teachers at WVU."[73] One of the members of the citizens' group, C. E. Messenger, explained that the group was asking for the removal of radical faculty rather than radical students because "these kids are blameless; they're at the age they can be influenced."[74] However, Daniel Bucca, the "radical traitor parasite" himself, rejected such claims, saying, "I haven't been influenced to any extent by faculty members. If anything, today many instructors are being influenced by the kids," adding, "Actually I have never had a teacher at WVU who I would consider liberal. . . . There are not really any 'radical faculty activists' here at all."[75] Bucca further implied that this was a family conflict that had no relation to the larger issues, saying that his father's charges "distort the real issues at hand. What he considers to be my 'deterioration' is my political ideals. It's a matter of issues and not personalities; that's what everyone should be concerned with."[76] The Bucca family feud may have played out very publicly, but it certainly reflects the generational divide that pitted many conservative parents against their antiwar children. And all of it reflects the larger move at this time away from the doctrine of *in loco parentis*.

In a larger sense, the parents' and the administration's reaction to student dissent shows, again, how difficult it was for the university to define and limit what it meant for student Mountaineers to be "free" during the Vietnam era. The administration's crackdown on students after the May demonstrations parallels professor James Brawner's response to the first Mountaineer Day celebration in 1947: it's fine to have fun and blow off some steam, but the "thin veneer of civilization" must be maintained, and if it is eroded, then the grownups will step in and put an end to the play. Of course, the first Mountaineer Day participants were in it purely for the fun, even if a great deal of their pleasure came from violating normal boundaries. As Townshend's and Lowe's accounts illustrate, participants in the May demonstrations had complex and sometimes contradictory reasons for being there. Some were there to voice genuine political concerns; some were there to taunt those who seemed to be taking themselves too seriously; some were there hoping to provoke a physical fight; and many others, undoubtedly, were just there to observe the spectacle so they could say they were part of it.

The student protests and riots during the Vietnam War era were, in many ways, festive activities that had a serious motive and tangible, real-world outcomes. While some activities might look like play, they often serve larger, more transformational purposes, however lighthearted and unfocused they may seem. A recent illustration of this dynamic can be seen in the Women's March on Washington after Donald Trump's inauguration in January 2017: many participants wore "pussy hats" (which looked remarkably like medieval fools' caps), carried jokey signs, and chanted funny slogans. The very playfulness of the event highlighted its serious purpose. Playing the fool to make a point is at the heart of Mountaineer identity: David Crockett, Andrew Jackson, and Doddridge's and Twain's backwoodsmen all knew how to string their audience along, allowing the audience to believe they were witnessing an ignoramus's buffoonery, only to be fooled by the fool in the end, as the audience discovers that they're the ones who have been duped and schooled.

And that is exactly what happened when the administration refused to address the student protesters' concerns: the administration's attempts to expel the Morgantown Six and shut down future protests backfired. Like the dandies in Doddridge's and Twain's narratives, the students dealt a serious blow to the administration by hiring William Kunstler to argue their case. Over the course of that summer, students continued to fight back and assert their intelligence and independence in ways both serious and comical, advocating to be full participants in the creation of a student code of conduct through written materials that were peppered with jokes and biting wit. While the students who called in bomb threats to the Mountainlair undoubtedly enjoyed the chaos they created, others recognized that their eventual success depended on more reasoned actions—but actions, nonetheless, that reminded the administration that they weren't fools and that treating them as such might yield unpleasant consequences.

Mountaineers without Guns

———

By the time the Mountaineer statue was unveiled during Mountaineer Weekend in October 1971, more than a year had passed since the tumultuous events of May 1970, but the Vietnam conflict dragged on. The sight of the long-dreamed of bronze frontiersman in front of the Mountainlair may well have seemed like a 1950s throwback to the students of the early 1970s. Certainly it was ironic that just as the smooth-faced Mountaineer statue became an official symbol of the university, the real-life Mountaineer mascot and many male students were far more likely to be bearded. The hillbilly Mountaineer may have given way to the frontiersman Mountaineer, but the person assuming the official role of Mountaineer looked more and more like the hippies that many conservative students, administrators, and parents feared just a few years earlier.

And although it is only coincidental, even as the new statue held a rifle, the official Mountaineer was disarmed. Part of the story of the Mountaineer of the late '60s that's left untold has to do with why Doug Townshend's tenure as Mountaineer encompassed eighteen months rather than a full year (or two). In the fall of 1968, the then Mountaineer, Gil Reel, suffered an unfortunate accident at the football game against Virginia Tech: while checking to see if the rifle was loaded, it accidentally discharged, and Reel "lost his right index finger" and "was taken by ambulance to a Norfolk, Va. hospital where he remained for several days." Reel told a *Daily Athenaeum* reporter that he hated being in the hospital—"I'm an outdoorsman, anyhow"—and was concerned about returning to classes, since he knew he would "have some trouble writing."[77] But the following weekend was WVU's homecoming, and there was no alternate Mountaineer then, as there is now. So Mountain scrambled to find a temporary substitute, tapping junior Steven Hite for the job.

Hite had applied to be the Mountaineer the previous spring, but Reel was selected for the job. Hite must have made an impression on the interviewers, though, because after Reel's accident, he says,

> I got a call . . . I don't even know who it was . . . said, "You're going to be the Mountaineer next week." I said, "Really?" They said, "Yeah. Gil Reel got hurt." I said, "Oh," I don't know what I said. They said, "We're going to bring the uniform by—where do you live?" This is the way I remember it. I was standing in the living room and whoever it was came up to the door and just threw it [the uniform] in and it just landed on the floor. No instructions.[78]

Surprisingly, given the reason why a substitute was needed in the first place, Hite was allowed to fire the musket at the game, even though he had never fired one before. "I must have had some instructions . . . [because] I didn't know how to fill a musket," he said. He did know enough not to put his finger over the top of the muzzle, however, and remembers that he "did shoot at the . . . other mascot . . . at a distance."[79]

Of course, as Hite noted, it was the homecoming game, and "they had their minds on other things, I guess."[80] Hite only served as Mountaineer at homecoming and at the last home game of the 1968 season. By the time Doug Townshend took over the position of Mountaineer in the winter of 1969, the university had apparently had time to ponder Reel's accident and decided to disarm the Mountaineer. Hite figures that he may have been the last Mountaineer to fire the rifle until the move to Milan Puskar Stadium in 1980. Consequently, Townshend and future Mountaineers for the next decade were allowed to carry the rifle but not to fire it.[81] Feeling the need to have *some* kind of noisemaker, Townshend borrowed a professor's hound dog—which had an incredibly loud howl—and brought it to games instead.[82] Today, both the Mountaineer and the alternate Mountaineer are required to pass the West Virginia hunters' safety course by the time of the spring football game.[83] Thus, for the Mountaineer, the turbulent decade of the 1960s ended with a bang *and* a hound dog's whimper.

A year and a half after the Kent State demonstrations, the Mountaineer statue went up with sculptor DeLue's hope that it would remind students of "the virtues we hope to recall to mind in this day of ours when so many flounder in the valleys." But while the antiwar movement and other cultural shifts in the 1960s may have altered the Mountaineer's appearance, neither the civil rights nor the feminist movements made much of an impact: the role of the Mountaineer would continue to be filled by white, male students for nearly another twenty years. Meanwhile, WVU basketball games featured a new attraction during the 1973–74 season—the "Buckskin Babes," "four lovely co-eds . . . attired, naturally, in buckskin outfits for a Mountaineer image." As the *Dominion Post* article announcing the "latest and most attractive addition to the West Virginia University basketball program" explained, "the two-piece outfit consists of hot pants and a halter top."[84] It was more or less the "buckskin bikini" that both future women Mountaineers, Natalie Tennant and Rebecca Durst, were later taunted about. With the selection of both women, the gendered nature of the figure of the Mountaineer would become crystal clear.

Policing the Student Body

CHAPTER 4

"MOUNTAIN DEARS" AND (SEXY) GIRLS WITH GUNS

IF EVER THERE WERE an icon for women Mountaineers, "Mad" Anne Bailey was it. An English immigrant, she lived on the Virginia frontier in the late eighteenth century, and after her husband was killed at the Battle of Point Pleasant in 1774, she vowed to avenge his death by teaching herself to shoot a rifle and becoming a scout. She relayed messages between frontier forts in western Virginia until the Treaty of Greenville ended the border wars in 1795. After that, she carried mail and drove livestock through the region.[1] West Virginia poet Louise McNeill's "Ballad of Mad Ann [sic] Bailey" (1939) describes her as wearing "a wamus shirt / And britches made of a red buck's skin / Instead of a linsey skirt," as well as a "coon tail cap . . . ringed with dust." To complete the picture, McNeill's Ann also carries a rifle and a "jug of rum."[2]

The WVU Mountaineer has its own female forebear in the figure of Leila Jesse Frazier (fig. 4.1). One of the first women to attend WVU's School of Law, Frazier arrived in Morgantown in

1898 on horseback, "wearing a . . . 'divided skirt,' riding 'man fashion,' [and] carrying 'a brace of revolvers.'"[3] Frazier, a native of England, went on to serve as president of the Women's League of WVU, the university's first organization for female students. After her graduation in 1899, she practiced law in Morgantown with her husband, James Frazier. Smart, independent, and comfortable with both controversy and firearms, Leila Jesse Frazier set a high bar for female Mountaineers to follow. Yet it would be nearly a century before a woman would serve as the official WVU Mountaineer.

Despite Frazier's dramatic arrival on campus, the initial integration of women at WVU, like the later integration of African American students, happened quietly and in response to an external situation: on April 23, 1889, the Morgantown Female Seminary burned to the ground. In response to this event, the university's board of regents voted in June to admit women to all departments when the fall term began. During the 1889–90 school year, ten women enrolled, including Harriet Lyon, the first woman to receive a WVU degree, graduating at the top of her class in 1891.[4] Women had attended classes informally since 1883, and Ohio County senator Nathan B. Scott successfully passed legislation allowing women to be fully admitted to WVU in the summer of 1885, but the house of delegates tabled a similar bill because of the conflict between women's exemption from military training and the fact that all WVU students were required to serve three years in the Cadet Corps.[5]

Even after the quiet admission of women in 1889, the state legislature still balked at the idea of making the university fully coeducational, with one legislator arguing that without dedicated housing for women (and careful supervision of female students), the university would not attract "the class of young girls you would like to see . . . but only those whose parents do not care especially to watch over them."[6] Despite such concerns, the number of female students at WVU continued to grow, and when the university officially allowed women to be admitted to all departments except the military department in 1897, there were 112 women, a number that more than doubled to 240 during the 1899–1900 academic year.[7] The university's law school also

Figure 4.1. Leila Jesse Frazier, WVU Law student, straddling her horse in "man fashion" on campus in the late 1890s.

opened admissions to women at this time, graduating its first female lawyer, Agnes J. Morrison, in 1895, three years before Frazier's dramatic ride into Morgantown.

Traditional ideas and images of the Mountaineer have always constructed the figure as a man, and many of the Mountaineer's most vaunted characteristics are ones also frequently associated with American masculinity: an iconoclastic spirit, a resistance to authority, and the ability and willingness to fight for one's honor. These links between Mountaineers and masculinity were strengthened by the establishment of the frontier Mountaineer as the university's officially sanctioned image in the 1950s and 1960s. In its efforts to banish the hillbilly Mountaineer and replace it with the Davy Crockett-esque Mountaineer, however, the university unwittingly solved one problem and created another. The frontiersman Mountaineer that the university authorized in the late 1950s was unquestionably male, a reality made tangible with the erection of the Mountaineer statue, whose image then became a licensed logo of the university. The frontiersman WVU Mountaineer might have functioned to liberate the figure from hillbilly stereotypes, but eventually it, too, would prove to be limited and limiting in its own ways.

In the spring of 1990, WVU student Natalie Tennant decided, since she hadn't been elected president of her sorority, to try out for the position of Mountaineer. And her choice was, in part, driven by the Mountaineer statue. She told *USA Today* in an interview after her selection that she had served as North Marion High School's mascot, Super Dog, but when she arrived at WVU as a freshman, she "wasn't sure a woman could be selected [to be WVU's mascot]. Most of the Mountaineers I'd seen had beards." Then "she noticed that the statue of the Mountaineer sitting in front of the student union didn't have a beard" and "decided to go for it."[8] Of course, the fact that the statue was of a male figure was, in turn, used by Tennant's detractors as an argument against her selection, and one prankster went so far as to put a bra on the Mountaineer statue—whether in protest or support is unclear.[9] A similar dynamic played out in 2009, when Rebecca Durst became the second woman to serve as the Mountaineer, and the statue was again cited by detractors as evidence that a woman could not be the WVU Mountaineer. Like Tennant before her, Durst noted that "the Mountaineer doesn't have a beard—not even the statue does."[10]

The Tennant and Durst years mark another moment of profound change for the image of the WVU Mountaineer: the two women's candidacies challenged the long-held assumption that only a man could serve as the WVU Mountaineer. In some ways, having a woman as WVU Mountaineer opened the figure to the kind of playful reinterpretation that students enjoyed in the post–World War II period. Tennant and Durst exposed the limitations of the university's institutionalization of the Davy Crockett/Daniel Boone image of the Mountaineer in the late 1950s. Simply by virtue of their gender, Tennant and Durst tapped back into the figure's potential for play and transformation. In so doing, however, they were met by opposition from some whose rigid sense of tradition declared that women could not possibly serve as the WVU Mountaineer. But these two remarkably strong women channeled their inner Anne Bailey and Leila Jesse Frazier to deal with the harassment they endured during their years of service.

The First Woman WVU Mountaineer: Not Your "Mountain Dear"

When Natalie Tennant (fig. 4.2) applied to become the Mountaineer mascot in early 1990, she told the student newspaper, "When people first hear of a lady Mountaineer, they think 'Oh, no.' But the reason I applied was not to prove any point, but to show my enthusiasm."[11] Her roommate, Renee Ziemianski, told the student newspaper that Tennant was not "doing it to be the first woman mascot."[12] Regardless of intent, barriers can never be broken quietly or without opposition. Not only was Tennant the first woman to be a finalist for the position the year that she applied, but she and another female student were the first women ever to have applied to become the Mountaineer, period. Although the position is open to the entire student body, 1990 "was the first year that any women applied," according to Marilyn McClure, who was then president of WVU's Mountain Honorary, the organization that selected the WVU Mountaineer

Figure 4.2. Natalie Tennant, the first woman to serve as
Mountaineer, 1990–91.

(now a committee selects the Mountaineer).[13] In fact, Mountain
itself had only admitted women for about eight years at that
point: the honorary was all-male until 1982 and initially voted

down a motion to induct women, only agreeing to admit them after the university revoked its sponsorship of the group.[14]

The selection process for the WVU Mountaineer is extensive. Applicants must submit a written application, including several essays, and be interviewed by the honorary's membership. The finalists then participate in a "cheer-off," traditionally at the last home basketball game of the season. The finalists appear in the Mountaineer kit and lead the crowd in cheers. Members of the Mountaineer selection committee observe to see which candidate is the most enthusiastic and the most successful at getting the crowd fired up.

Fired up is certainly a phrase that can describe some fans' reactions to Tennant's appearance at the cheer-off. The student paper reported that some fans booed her, while Tennant herself reported that she heard comments ranging from "Go back to the kitchen and make babies" to questions about where her beard was.[15] "I didn't want them to yell 'Go back to the kitchen,'" Tennant said afterward, because "It's come down to the gender issue, which I never wanted it to become."[16] *Daily Athenaeum* sports writer Kirk Bridges piled on to blame the victim by saying that Tennant "motivated the crowd to yell things like 'Go back to the kitchen,' and she enthused people so much that those people felt inclined to insult her."[17] According to student Carrie Webster, however, these "large groups of hecklers organized beforehand so they could be there to boo [Tennant] off the floor."[18]

Bridges went on to speculate that Tennant's competitor, Doug McClung, was a victim of reverse discrimination, and ominously asked, "What happens next year when a woman tries out and loses? The honorary will be said to have discriminated on the basis of the woman's gender."[19] Better, apparently, not to allow women to compete at all than to risk accusations of discrimination against them, or—worse still—to commit reverse discrimination against men.

As the spring semester of 1990 went on, the editorial pages of the *Daily Athenaeum* regularly featured letters opposing

Tennant's selection: sometimes these were openly sexist, arguing that a woman simply should not be the WVU Mountaineer,
while others tried to moderate their views by masking them in
the rhetoric of tradition or by criticizing the selection process
itself, usually carefully noting that they were not questioning
Tennant herself but rather Mountain's method of choosing her.

One particularly logically challenged letter from a WVU graduate argued that Tennant should step aside so as to not bring
further bad press to the already maligned state of West Virginia:

> Novelty once again has taken precedence over reason. She [Ten-
> nant] won and the University will lose. Her tenure will last a year.
> But for those involved, from alumni and students to potential
> students coast to coast, as well as the University, negative impli-
> cations will affect the rest of their lives. . . .
>
> The gender jokes, such as references to the "Mountainettes"
> have already made their way to North Carolina. Like many uni-
> versity faithful my roommate, Carl Fochler, and I have heard our
> share of cheap shots taken at our state, and more specifically at
> our school. In all past cases, we have been ready, willing and able
> to defend all involved. However, in the case of the new Mountain-
> eer, I find myself neither ready nor willing, much less able to fend
> off the idiosyncratic onslaught. . . .
>
> Natalie Tennant, you are to be admired for your ambition, your
> focus, and your follow through. Yet, I sincerely feel that you have
> chosen the wrong arena in which to display such talents. The same
> school you represent distinguishes between its athletes by refer-
> ring to them as Mountaineers and Lady Mountaineers, respec-
> tively. Perhaps that alone suggests that a lady should not be "The"
> Mountaineer.[20]

The writer, Derek Fawley, a 1988 graduate in journalism, implies
here that the hillbilly jokes he's been subjected to will only be
exacerbated by the selection of a woman as WVU Mountaineer;
he believes that ending a previously unquestioned, sex-based

entitlement makes West Virginia appear *more* backward, not less so.

The "tradition" argument shows up in sports writer Kirk Bridges's editorial, in which he asks readers to "imagine football games next season. A female Mountaineer running up and down the steps, shooting the gun off and raising hell with the Nittany Lion and the panther. NO!"[21] Mark Lambert, a graduate student in civil engineering, appeals to a sense of tradition as well in an April letter to the editor that asks, "What is so wrong with allowing tradition to rule so that the Mountaineer is a man? What is a great University without great traditions? . . . Should we stop yelling 'Eat Shit, Pitt' because it contains a vulgarity? . . . great traditions aren't easily dismissed, but one of the University's finest traditions is now gone forever."[22]

All of the *Daily Athenaeum* letters opposing Tennant's selection during the spring semester of 1990 appear to have been written by men (judging by first names), while only one man wrote to support Tennant. All the other letters of support in the spring semester came from writers with female first names, many of them turning the arguments cited by the opposition around. Monica Gaudio, a sophomore majoring in biology, addresses Lambert's concerns about tradition directly, writing, "To answer Mark Lambert's question . . . what is so wrong with allowing tradition to rule so that the Mountaineer is a man? It is wrong because it is a sexist and chauvinistic attitude. It is wrong because it says that a woman cannot be a 'mountaineer.'"[23] Many of the letters supporting Tennant invert the rhetoric of tradition to instead engage in what I call hillbilly shaming, suggesting that those who oppose Tennant are reinforcing stereotypes about West Virginia as a provincial place. Gaudio says that "the people who have been whining about Natalie Tennant have just been proving what West Virginian hicks they truly are,"[24] and Jayne Armstrong writes that "Outsiders label West Virginia and its people as being backward. We have always denounced those views as unjust, but now I must wonder. Recent actions of some individuals in our student body actually promote this stereotype."[25] An editorial in the *Daily Athenaeum* after the cheer-off echoes these sentiments, noting that the fans who booed Tennant's performance offered "a first-hand look at one of the reasons West Virginians are plagued by a reputation of ignorance."[26] When Tennant began her official service as the WVU Mountaineer in the fall semester, more males began to show their support, again often via the rhetoric of hillbilly shaming. For example, Tim Wilson, a 1984 alumnus, urges boorish fans to "grow up," because "this is precisely the backward, socially impoverished image that we West Virginians have been struggling to cast off for decades."[27]

Hillbilly shaming was countered by expressions of hillbilly pride, sometimes in the same column or letter, as writers sought to assert the presence and importance of women throughout the state's history. In the same editorial that decried West Virginians' "reputation of ignorance," the writer notes that "One would think from all of this that the mountain men who walked the West Virginia hills hundreds of years ago must have reproduced asexually."[28] In another editorial in the same issue, *Daily Athenaeum* city editor Dawn Miller cites Sacajawea and Confederate spy (and Martinsburg native) Belle Boyd as examples of strong frontierswomen, and then she goes on to describe her own mother taking a rifle to the family rooster when it started attacking a new brood of chicks.[29] Gordon Thorn, Mountain's faculty advisor, said, "I'm sure the women had just as much pioneer spirit as the men did to get through those days."[30]

In response to an article that appeared in the *Wall Street Journal* in the fall of 1990, Frank Betz cites the example of Elizabeth Zane, the frontierswoman who, in September 1782, stole out of Wheeling's Fort Henry to successfully retrieve gunpowder from a cabin sixty yards outside the fort (fig. 4.3). Betz suggests that Zane's actions in this final battle of the Revolutionary War should be credited for ending the war and asks, "Is Elizabeth Zane to have served in vain and all the frontier memories to be reserved for the Daniel Boones and the Davy

Crocketts? Here's to Mountaineer mascot Natalie Tennant and the memory of Elizabeth Zane and the women of the frontier. . . . Wake up and attend WV History 101."[31]

Despite such efforts to reinscribe women into the historical sense of the term *mountaineer*, the campaign to reify the WVU Mountaineer as an exclusively male icon continued through the spring of 1990. A petition circulated to have Tennant ousted, and bumper stickers and buttons reading "We don't want a Mountaindear, Give us back our Mountaineer" appeared.[32] Tennant found the "Mountaindear" slogan amusing, even at the time:

I saw a ["Mountaindear"] bumper sticker, and I saw a pin. And I had . . . a bumper sticker. I was at the sorority house . . . and . . . I'd left it on the coffee table and fallen asleep . . . and when I woke up it was gone. And I think that [my sorority sisters] had taken it to protect me, not to have to see it. But I really wanted it! And then, that fall [of 1990], there was a woman who . . . particularly did not like me, and . . . I made it a point to go past her row and see her every game then. And one game she showed me this button that said "We don't want a Mountaindear, Give us back our Mountaineer." I'm like, "Oh, that's kind of cool!" And she said [Tennant holds her hand out to imitate the woman offering the button], "Here, you want it?" And I said, "Yeah, yeah, I do." And she's like, "No. You can't have it." [Tennant pulls hand back to indicate how the woman snatched the button away.] She would have given it to me if I *didn't* want it, but that I wanted it, she didn't give it to me. And so I wanted it for a keepsake. "We don't want a Mountain-dear." . . . I thought that was really clever! It was like, "Man, somebody spent money and time to do this against me—this is really good."[33]

Tennant's sense of humor was fundamental to her success as WVU Mountaineer even before she took on the role officially. Regarding the cheer-off, she said,

As soon as I walked out there you hear booing. And they're booing, they're booing, and . . . they were yelling "Go back to the kitchen," "Go back to the kitchen and go make babies." And so, you know, I had been a mascot before in high school. I was Superdog. But I was covered in fun fur. And I knew how to react to people with gestures and things like that. Well, I couldn't use gestures here, but I can remember saying, "I don't know *how* to cook!" [line delivered in a cutesy, sarcastic voice]. Kind of making the joke, because you . . . have to defuse things with humor, and . . . that's who I am.[34]

That ability to defuse things with humor would serve Tennant well, as she had to draw on it repeatedly over the next year.

Tennant quietly began her official duties in the summer of 1990 and was able to do so without public criticism, as no articles or letters to the editor appear in any of the student newspaper's summer editions. But once fall semester began, the controversy flared up again. Prior to the first football game of the season, the *Daily Athenaeum* ran a front-page article reintroducing Tennant to students. In the article, Tennant describes how she won over a reluctant older alumnus whom she met during the summer and who eventually "said he was her biggest fan, adding, 'If I were younger, I'd marry you.'"[35] The *Wall Street Journal* article reported a similar instance of Tennant charming a similarly crusty naysayer:

> This past summer, attending a pig roast in coal-mining Boone County, [Tennant] was told to avoid a 70-year-old resident called "Ol' Buster." Instead, she marched right up to him, extended her hand and said, "I hear you're my biggest fan."
>
> "The hell I am!" Buster snorted, refusing to shake it.
>
> But Ms. Tennant persisted. She had her rifle; and Buster also carried a muzzle-loader. Bonded by gunpowder, the two of them went to an abandoned field to blast away. "Buster"—Mosie Atkins—was won over. Today he offers her his ultimate compliment for her tomboyish toughness. "Hell, she's worse than a damn boy!" he says in admiration.[36]

The popularity of these stories is intriguing on several levels. First, they resituate the sexist resistance to Tennant's selection onto older, rural men, when the most vocal public opponents

Figure 4.3. Revolutionary War hero Betty Zane carrying gunpowder to Wheeling's Fort Henry.

were male undergraduates, grad students, or recent graduates of the university. Second, they illustrate how the media casts a female WVU Mountaineer as palatable: she's charming and attractive enough to garner marriage proposals from the unlikeliest of suitors, and her ability to shoot a gun is simply "tomboyish toughness," not a threat. Another anecdote in the *Wall Street Journal* article describes a "small blonde-haired boy" running up to Tennant in the football stadium, handing her a quarter, and saying, "Call me." So, the female Mountaineer appeals to children and senior citizens, but not to her male peers.

One of the most prevalent ways the media and fans found to make Tennant's service more acceptable was to fit this lady

Mountaineer into preexisting gender stereotypes. One particularly strange manifestation of this impulse came in a letter to
the *Daily Athenaeum* from James A. Swart of Charleston who
suggested, "Now that Natalie Tennant has embarrassed herself
and the 1990 Mountaineer fans and alumni, let's reason together.
The University should have a Mr. and Ms. Mountaineer. To avoid
the matrimonial perception, they would be brother and sister."[37]
Swart's letter is presumably tongue-in-cheek, but notable in its
insistence that while *sex* should be a factor in choosing both a
male and a female Mountaineer, any implication of sexual *activity*
between the two needs to be ruled out. Were Swart not writing to
oppose Tennant, one imagines his letter might have gone on to
make a tasteless joke about hillbillies and incest.

The *Wall Street Journal* story is particularly interesting in its
stereotypical depiction of West Virginia and West Virginians:
Tennant and Ol' Buster overcome their differences to discover
that at heart they are both hillbillies who love shooting off
guns and a good pig-pickin'. Details such as the fact that Boone
County's main industry is coal mining also serve to remind the
reader that this encounter took place in a sort of present-day
Dogpatch, USA, and therefore we are free to laugh at the backward, sexist antics of the characters. The national press's representation of West Virginians as pathetically out of touch with
the rest of the country was nothing new and continues to be a
standard trope in the twenty-first century, as we shall see in the
next chapter.

However much the *Wall Street Journal* may have indulged in
stereotypes, its description of fans jeering Tennant with shouts
of "Go back to the kitchen" and "No Mountaineer can have PMS"
and pelting her with cups and ice was entirely accurate.[38] The
Daily Athenaeum commended Tennant's ability to endure this
treatment, saying that "she did a great job of ignoring the boos
and heckles from the student section, while refusing to back
down from the narrow-minded students that profanely jeered
and threw cups at her."[39] A number of letters to the editor in the

first weeks of September show that this behavior continued well beyond the first game of the season. Most letter writers called on their fellow students to knock it off, though one Tennant detractor suggested she earned the booing by her lackluster performance, while conceding that perhaps "students and fans (mostly the students) should try to curb the booing to some degree."[40]

Ironically, the day that that letter appeared in the *Daily Athenaeum* was the same day, September 26, that the *Wall Street Journal* article appeared. Its publication unleashed a torrent of letters and editorials denouncing the behavior of those who opposed Tennant not merely for their sexism, but for the ways they reinforced stereotypes about West Virginia. Two days after the *Wall Street Journal* article was published, the *Daily Athenaeum* featured an editorial that began, "It's one thing when people from other states in the country mistakenly stereotype West Virginia as a state full of illiterate, barefoot hillbillies; but it's *another thing* when actual state residents—some of whom are University students—display such prejudice and ignorance in their actions that they help reinforce those prevailing attitudes about our state."[41]

Letters to the editor reflected the same concern. John Morgan, a 1989 WVU graduate, writes, "What the hell? As a loyal alumnus who is consistently enduring, and most often battling, the array of negative West Virginia stereotypes, all I can say is: . . . Um. Gosh-golly-gee . . . it's 1990—even in West Virginia. Girls can be whatever they wish to be, and you know the rest. This is truly embarrassing."[42] Alumnus Glenn H. Gould III expresses a similar concern when he says that "Since graduating from the University's Graduate School in December of 1974, it has been a continuous effort to overcome the stigma and prejudice commonly held against West Virginia and its residents," concluding his letter with the derisive comment that "It would be redundant to invite West Virginia to join the twentieth century since the invitation has been extended on numerous occasions by individuals better prepared than myself."[43]

The *Wall Street Journal* article garnered several letters to the editor of the *Daily Athenaeum* from people outside the state with no affiliation to West Virginia or the university. But interestingly, these letters focus solely on the sexism of the fans' behavior and do not mention anything about how that behavior confirms their beliefs about West Virginia. Heidi Zimmerman of Salt Lake City notes that the *Wall Street Journal* article "boasted that the Mountaineer stood for 'the embodiment of the state's macho frontier past,'" countering that "even in those long forgotten times, women were treated with more respect than they get from some of these 1990s men."[44] Dan McCullough, a resident of Chicago, says the harassment of Tennant is "an insult to the proud tradition of your university" and calls on students and fans to "applaud" Tennant's selection "as a breakthrough for women, rather than derided as a break with tradition."[45] McCullough goes on to note that if the leprechaun mascot of his alma mater, Notre Dame, "were portrayed by a woman, a minority, a homosexual, or another non-traditional student, I would welcome the progressiveness and praise the people who made such a selection as contributing to the cultural diversity of the institution." Leaving aside Notre Dame's own struggles with its Fighting Irish leprechaun mascot, the letter is intriguing in its progressive definition of tradition, emphasizing the need for traditions to be flexible and reflective of contemporary mores, rather than static and rigid.

Back at the *Daily Athenaeum*, though, the editorial focus was squarely on hillbilly shaming. Staff columnists Kevin Silard and Jim McKenzie both published columns responding to the *Wall Street Journal* article in the week after its appearance. Silard writes, "There we were, West Virginia and the University, on the front page of the *Wall Street Journal*. Some of you probably thought, 'Great, we are the laughingstock of the nation.'"[46] Writing a few days later, staff columnist Jim McKenzie chastises "those close-minded individuals who don't show support to this University's mascot and refuse to accept change," suggesting they are "the reason that others in our country see West Virginians as 'backward.'" McKenzie goes on to highlight other recent events he thinks proud West Virginians should be more concerned about: "Within the last two years nearly 20 public officials have been indicted and/or are serving time in a federal prison. . . . In addition to corruption in state politics, West Virginia is ranked lowest or near lowest among all 50 states in almost every statistical study including economic growth, education, and teacher salaries." McKenzie argues that far from "hurting" the image of the university and the state, Tennant is "helping to shed a positive light on a state that holds too many untrue stereotypes."[47]

Despite the national attention, criticism of Tennant continued through the fall semester. She was apparently heckled and harassed as she marched in the homecoming parade a few weeks later,[48] and an alumnus wrote to complain in particular about her "repeated slinging of a rubber chicken to the turf" during a Thanksgiving Day football game against the South Carolina Gamecocks.[49] Those who didn't write to complain about Tennant specifically continued to complain about the selection process for the Mountaineer. The same issue of the *Daily Athenaeum* that described Tennant's treatment during the homecoming parade also included a letter to the editor that once again claimed that Doug McClung had been the victim of reverse discrimination. Notably, this time the editors included a note after the letter saying that "Members of the Mountain Honorary . . . stated last semester that Doug McClung violated rules governing the mascot tryout competition."[50] A follow-up letter then suggests that "the current tradition of the Mountain Honorary selecting the Mountaineer should be done away with," allowing "the students and fans to decide."[51] Interesting how the same folks who felt that a great tradition had ended when a woman was named as the WVU Mountaineer were willing to dispense with other long-standing traditions that they saw as problematic.

It is perhaps not surprising, then, that when an announcement about applying for the position for the 1991–92 school year appeared in the *Daily Athenaeum* in January, it prominently included detailed information about the judging and selection process. In the ad, Tim Bailey, Mountain Honorary chairperson, stressed that the WVU Mountaineer "spends more time representing the University at non-University functions than at University functions" and that the cheer-off is only one criteria for selecting the mascot: "I think that there was a misconception last year that the two candidates came into the cheer-off even. We want everyone this year to understand it's cumulative."[52] A couple of days later, Susan C. Malone, the former managing editor of the *Daily Athenaeum*, wrote a letter to the editor expressing her "hope [that] women will not be discouraged from auditioning for the Mountaineer. Furthermore, I would love to see a racial or ethnic minority (of either sex) represent the University as Mountaineer."[53]

The start of the Gulf War on January 17, 1991, forestalled another semester of debate about the identity of the Mountaineer. Coverage of and debates about the war dominated the *Daily Athenaeum*'s articles and editorials for most of the spring semester. By the time US president George Bush declared that war over in late February, the new mascot—Rock Wilson, a second-year law student—had been selected as the new Mountaineer. Tennant did not apply for the position again (though she was able to), and Mountain reported that no women applied that year at all and that they only received fifteen applications altogether, down from twenty the previous year.[54] Perhaps because of the war, or because of exhaustion about the issue, the *Daily Athenaeum* minimized its coverage of the selection process: the article in the sports section about the basketball game at which the cheer-off occurred makes no mention of the cheer-off and, in fact, notes that the game had the lowest attendance of any during the whole season.[55] The lack of attendance seems a bit surprising, given some students' outrage over feeling that their voices had not been heard at the previous year's cheer-off, though of course this could also be why they did not even bother to show up in 1991. Or perhaps they had received Mountain's message that the cheer-off was not the deciding factor in the competition.

Neither kudos nor critiques about the new Mountaineer appeared in the *Daily Athenaeum* editorial pages following Wilson's selection. The only nod to the change was in the short-lived, student-drawn comic strip *I Don't Get It* on February 19. A single-panel image showed a ponytailed girl in a Boy Scout uniform, giving the Boy Scout salute, with the caption "Natalie Tennant as a little girl." A letter to the editor on February 22 criticized the comic's artist, Jim Dierwechter, saying that "Natalie has gone through enough this year and does not need the whole situation brought out again as she is ready to conclude her term as the Mountaineer."[56] The letter writer, Louis D. Schwartz, adds that "it was unjust to reopen this over-publicized scar" and concludes that it's Dierwechter who "doesn't get it." Notably, *I Don't Get It* ceased to appear in the *Daily Athenaeum* after February 22. Whether this was due to the Tennant cartoon or other factors is never explained in future issues of the paper.

Later in the spring semester, several people wrote in to thank Tennant for her service as the WVU Mountaineer and to applaud her handling of the controversy. And in an interview, the new WVU Mountaineer, Rock Wilson, called the scrutiny Tennant faced "unfair" and said that "no one else could have withstood the pressure so well."[57] Wilson said that during the annual Gold-Blue Spring Game, many fans cheered him loudly, and some made "crude remarks about Tennant" or simply said that "they were glad to have a man back." "It's a bad way to get a good response," he conceded.[58]

Girls with Guns (and Other Weapons)

_____

In my interviews with Tennant and Durst, neither mentioned getting any specific flack about being a woman carrying a rifle—which is rather surprising, given the anxiety some fans felt about having a woman do all the other parts of the WVU Mountaineer's job. One would imagine that those folks would be especially concerned about the thought of that woman brandishing a live firearm. Perhaps there was some trash talk about the gun, but neither Tennant nor Durst minded because both felt comfortable handling the rifle. Both women grew up in rural areas and had been around guns most of their lives, and even though Tennant had not fired a rifle before becoming the Mountaineer, when she was selected, she turned to her brothers for training.[59] Durst had "grown up in a hunting family" and had hunted with her father as a child; even now, she says, she and her father "will go out and just shoot firearms for fun while we're home."[60] Importantly, both women connected their ease with the rifle to a larger sense of Mountaineer identity, with Tennant saying "that's really just farm life" and Durst saying "being out in the woods and learning about nature, and being able to care for yourself out in the wild . . . that makes you feel really empowered, too, and also makes you feel like a true West Virginian."[61]

Like most former WVU Mountaineers, both Tennant and Durst had their own mishaps (and misbehavior) with the musket. Tennant recalled going to a party the night after the first football game of the season during which she was Mountaineer:

After the first game . . . I had gone to a friend's house, and I was still in the Mountaineer outfit, 'cause they were close to the stadium, and I'd walked over to their house. And they're like, "Shoot the gun, Natalie. Shoot the gun!" And I was still [in] the Mountaineer [outfit], so I shot the gun off. And they're like, "Yeah! Yeah! Yeah!" So, that's Saturday.

On Monday, I get a call in, and Herman Moses [dean of students] is sitting here, and Gordon Thorn [the Mountain adviser], and they're like, "How did it go the first game?" . . . You know, they—they didn't know how to handle a girl Mountaineer either. They said, "We got a report that you shot the gun off on city property. Did you shoot the gun after the game?" I was like [in a hangdog, ashamed voice] "Yes, I did." And then so they were like, you know, "Well, one of your friend's neighbors called the police." So, I'm like, "OK." They're like, "Don't do that anymore." I didn't. I think they were surprised that . . . I just came out and said "Yeah, I shot it." You can't say no! And so that was the only discipline—if you want to call that discipline—that I, that I had. Because I shot the gun inside city property.[62]

Durst, similarly, recalled that

After the Pitt game . . . Jarrett Brown was the quarterback, and we had just broken a two-year losing streak to Pitt. So JB came over to me, and we were singing "Country Roads," and he was like, "Can I hold the rifle?" And nobody except the Mountaineer is supposed to hold the rifle. But I let him hold it for . . . that time. It was just a really awesome experience, with everybody out on the field, and he held it, and . . . I loaded it up for him, too, and he fired it, and . . . I thought that was a really cool moment. . . . I asked for forgiveness later, like Brady [Campbell] said. And . . . I was still the Mountaineer! They didn't kick me out![63]

Being comfortable with a rifle undoubtedly lends a lot of ammunition to the argument that frontier *women* were just as tough and capable as frontiersmen, an argument that was used to defend the selection of Tennant and Durst as the Mountaineer. If Elizabeth Zane could run out of a fort under siege to retrieve gunpowder, surely a woman can fire off a musket at a football game.

But being capable with a weapon is, if you'll pardon the pun, a double-edged sword for women. On the one hand, being able to handle a rifle gave both Tennant and Durst a leg up, and some needed street cred, as they took on the role of the Mountaineer. On the other hand, a facility with weapons can brand a woman as unnatural or unfeminine. An incident that Natalie Tennant experienced early in her tenure illustrates this point. After a summer of intense preparation to be the Mountaineer, including running up and down the steps of the stadium, Tennant told those who asked that she was "mentally ready, [and] I can *get* physically ready' . . . with the gun, and everything." Her first official appearance, though, was a sobering taste of the harassment to come and a reminder that the idea of a girl with a gun still posed a threat to some fans:

> One of the first events that you have is the picnic for freshmen. And they have it at Towers. And I can remember driving up . . . and parking right in front of Towers and walking through there and thinking, you know, "It's all blown over, there's not gonna be much grief. These are . . . young freshmen, they don't even know what happened last year 'cause they were in high school." And . . . [I] get out of the car, walk through, outfit on, gun on, and thinking, "This is gonna be a piece of cake. Nobody's going to say anything." And I hear someone yell out the window, "Dyke!" And I was like, "Here we go." [64]

It's somewhat surprising that Tennant didn't get many more comments of this ilk. Perhaps her ability to win over children and old men allowed her to seem gender conforming—or perhaps she, and the *Daily Athenaeum*, chose not to focus on the homophobic responses to her service.

It's important to consider the reactions to Tennant in light of larger responses to empowered women in the early 1990s, which suggest that the reaction to Tennant was not a hillbilly problem but the localized version of a larger national trend. The 1990s saw an increased anxiety about powerful women and eventually about women with weapons. In October 1991, Anita Hill, a prominent attorney and law professor, came forward to charge the Supreme Court nominee, Clarence Thomas, of sexual harassment. Hill contended that Thomas had made sexually provocative statements to her when she worked for him at the US Department of Education and at the Equal Opportunity Employment Commission in the

1980s. Hill's testimony, which lasted three days, turned out to be a surprise television hit: Americans were riveted by the he said/she said debate playing out at the highest levels of government power. Although Thomas's nomination was eventually confirmed, the event exposed the ubiquity of sexual harassment in the workplace and also helped many notice just how white and male the US Senate was. Perhaps unsurprisingly, in 1992, a record number of women ran for public office and won, taking four seats in the Senate and twenty-four seats in the US House of Representatives.[65] And of course, Tennant herself would eventually go on to pursue public office, serving as the West Virginia secretary of state from 2009 to 2017. In fact, she credits her experience as Mountaineer with preparing her for the hard work of running for office: "I can remember . . . in 2003, when I started running for 2004—people were like 'Is she tough enough? Is she tough enough for politics?' 'Oh, yeah—I got that one. I got that one covered.'"[66]

The outrage about Tennant's service as the WVU Mountaineer reflects these larger anxieties about gender and power that were poised to boil over in the early 1990s. Although the Anita Hill/Clarence Thomas controversy erupted the year after Tennant served as the Mountaineer, some fans' rage about her "usurping" what they perceived as a male entitlement mirrors the outrage others felt about Hill's coming out of "nowhere" to threaten Thomas's chances of winning the Supreme Court nomination. In the Hill/Thomas case, the viewing public was riveted by the spectacle of a previously unknown woman being able to nearly derail the career of a powerful man, and that public was deeply divided in its response to Hill's challenge. While many supported her, others vilified and discredited her. These are, of course, the same dynamics that played out in the months after Tennant's selection as Mountaineer, most notably in the early stages, when some students felt that Tennant had "robbed" her male opponent, Doug McClung, of his rightful win.

Other events in the early 1990s also reflect this increased anxiety about powerful women. In 1992 Bill Clinton's election to the presidency was accompanied by anxiety about his wife, Hillary Rodham Clinton, an accomplished attorney in her own right, and the role she might play in her husband's administration. These fears escalated after he took office and Hillary Clinton took on an active role in the health-care debate. But the potential threat of Hillary and other powerful women came to a head in 1993 and 1994, when two more sensational and salacious examples of the dangers of powerful women came to light. In 1993 Lorena Bobbitt was brought to trial for having cut off her husband's penis (after he had raped her on multiple occasions), and in early 1994, champion figure skater Tonya Harding was discovered to have instigated an attack on rival skater Nancy Kerrigan in an attempt to keep Kerrigan out of the US Figure Skating Championships and the 1994 Olympics. Suddenly, powerful, angry, or ambitious women appeared to pose not just a social threat but a physical threat as well. As one of the jokes circulating at the time went, "Who's the most dangerous woman in America? Tonya Rodham Bobbitt."[67]

Such jokes indicate the level of anxiety in the early 1990s about the changing role of women in public life. In this broader context, the prolonged and vehement opposition to Tennant's selection as the Mountaineer seems slightly more in keeping with the times—it was not so much a backward state issue as a backward nation issue. One wonders what the response might have been had a woman been selected as WVU Mountaineer immediately after the incidents with Lorena Bobbitt and Tonya Harding; undoubtedly, the concerns would also have included the danger of giving weapons to women. Anxiety about a woman with a loaded rifle was still visible, however: the sign protesting Tennant that read "No Mountaineer should have PMS" makes concrete this very concern about giving a loaded weapon to a "hormonal" woman.

In light of these larger cultural events, the explosive reaction to Tennant is really a microcosm of shifting sexual politics in the early 1990s. Tennant handled the onslaught with humor and per-severance, seemingly paving a smoother path for future female Mountaineers. But another woman would not be chosen as the WVU Mountaineer for eighteen years.

Objectifying the Student Body: The "Hot Girl Mountaineer"

One would imagine that nearly two decades after Tennant's ser-vice as the WVU Mountaineer, the response to a second woman being chosen would be vastly different. However, when Rebecca Durst was selected to serve as the WVU Mountaineer in the spring of 2009, she faced the same kind of criticism (fig. 4.4). The only significant change had to do with where and how that criticism was expressed: in Tennant's era, the controversy played out on the editorial page of the *Daily Athenaeum*, and in Durst's era, it played out on Facebook and other social-media platforms. The hostility toward Durst did not last as long, nor was it as vir-ulent, but I believe this is not because some audience members recognized the sexism of their negative reaction; rather, I think it was due to a different form of sexism that had come into play in the intervening years. Specifically, it is the sexism that allows women to be powerful, but only via the objectification of their bodies: "hotness" is powerful, and thus, many of Durst's critics were able to overcome their opposition to her by positioning her, instead, as the "hot girl Mountaineer."

Like Tennant, Durst was booed when her selection was announced, and she was asked where her beard was.[68] After the announcement was made, students took not to the editorial pages of the student newspaper, but to Facebook to voice their displea-sure with or their support of the choice. Facebook groups—such as "WVU students against beardless Mountaineers," "If Rebecca Durst can grow and maintain a full beard, I'll fully support her," and, more prosaically, "Screw you Rebecca Durst"—popped up, as did groups for supporters, such as "I fully support Rebecca Durst as the new Mountaineer" and "As long as that musket fires, and fires often" (referring to the Mountaineer's tradition of firing the musket after every WVU score). The largest of these, "WVU students against beardless Mountaineers" and "I fully support Rebecca Durst as the new Mountaineer," each had between 1,700 and 1,800 members by the end of spring semester 2009.[69]

Arguments against Durst's selection followed more or less the same rhetorical pattern as had objections to Tennant's selection nineteen years earlier—objectors claimed that "other schools will make fun of us for having a girl mascot," as student Todd Gutta put it.[70] *Daily Athenaeum* columnist Brannan Lahoda dismissed "the ridiculous, simple-minded, inane arguments . . . that she is not a he, cannot (presumably) grow a beard and that she would have a difficult time doing the traditional pushups every time the football team scores" as well as "the slightly better 'tradition' argument" that bases the insistence that the Mountaineer be male on the fact that the university's official logo features a male Mountaineer.[71]

Lahoda, however, was also a Durst detractor. While he suggests that his objections to Durst's selection will be more sophisticated, his editorial falls back on yet another logical fallacy of the Tennant era: the argument that the selection process was flawed. Lahoda writes that "many people were less than impressed with the level of enthusiasm" of the three candidates who competed against incumbent Mountaineer Michael Squires at the cheer-off, reprising similar critiques of Tennant's cheer-off performance nineteen years earlier. As before, the "flawed process" argument is presented as a gender-neutral critique. And like many of Tennant's critics, Lahoda implies that his unhappiness with Mountain's selection doesn't have anything to do with the fact that Durst is female, but instead with Mountain's failure to use crowd response at the cheer-off as its primary criteria in selecting the next Mountaineer: "The tryout

Figure 4.4. Rebecca Durst, the second woman to serve as
Mountaineer, 2009–10.

was supposed to be a major portion of the selection process—obviously, it was not." The proof that neither of these arguments is truly gender neutral lies in the conclusion of Lahoda's column, where he speculates that

> From the outside it looks as if the committee chose Durst simply because she is a female, solely in an effort to heal the University's dreadful image—which in the past year has included an academic scandal as well as claims of race-based discrimination by a former coach.
>
> Choosing a female for a male-dominated role, albeit as a college mascot, seems like a meager attempt to put a "progressive" spin on the otherwise traditional nature of WVU.
>
> If this was the case, it is a shame and a particular insult to . . . Durst's qualifications.[72]

Lahoda conveniently omits the detail that two of the four finalists who competed in the cheer-off were women: in addition to Durst, junior Rebecca Funk also made the final cut.[73] So the chances were 50/50 that the new Mountaineer would be female. Would Lahoda have said Funk's qualifications had been insulted had she been chosen instead of Durst? And if the other male finalist, senior Brock Burwell, had been selected (as indeed he was in 2010 and 2011), would Lahoda have complained about the choice due to Burwell's lack of enthusiasm?

An interesting shift takes place in the two decades between Tennant and Durst's service: the *Daily Athenaeum* writers and many of the students, male and female, whom they quote in their articles are all very careful to distance themselves from overt sexism, as in Lahoda's labeling of sex-based discrimination as "ridiculous, simple-minded, [and] inane." However, despite such disclaimers, gender bias is still at the root of their opinions. When Lahoda characterizes Durst's win as a "shame" and an "insult," one engineered by the university to look "progressive," he suggests that Durst has no agency of her own: she is merely the naive tool of the university's publicity machine. Furthermore, his suggestion that somehow the ideal of meritocracy has been tarnished by her selection also smacks of sexism. Essentially, Lahoda's is the same reverse-discrimination argument made by some about Natalie Tennant's selection, but in 2009 it is softened by being presented as concern about female *dis*empowerment.

Objections to Durst's selection garnered another round of hillbilly shaming, although this, too, was expressed less overtly than it had been during the controversy around Tennant's appointment. The *Daily Athenaeum*'s editorial about Durst's selection focused more on Mountaineer pride, and called on students and fans to "realize what the mascot represents. It is our fighting spirit, our determination and our character. Our willingness to see past gender only continues to strengthen our character."[74] The message here is not so much "if you don't support her, you make us look bad" as it is "by supporting her—or at least not insulting her—you are a true Mountaineer." Even a letter to the editor of the *Daily Athenaeum* in April 2009 couches its hillbilly shaming in the language of Mountaineer solidarity:

> Those who criticize Rebecca Durst . . . should realize the harm they do, not only to themselves, but to our University.
>
> As West Virginia University students, we are all aware of the negative stereotypes facing our University as well as the state of West Virginia.
>
> Please realize that criticizing our University's mascot on the basis of her gender can only perpetuate these misconceptions and portray WVU as an institution unsupportive of cultural diversity and gender equity. . . .
>
> By ridiculing and criticizing Rebecca Durst, we validate their arguments and do ourselves even greater harm than our rivals are capable of inflicting.[75]

The letter writers conclude by describing the "true Mountaineer" as one who "embodies the values of hard work, poise, acceptance and honor."[76]

Another notable difference between responses to the selection of a female WVU Mountaineer in 1990 and in 2009 has to do with the sex of the students interviewed and of the letter writers. In 1990, as we have seen, objections to Tennant's selection came exclusively from males, and the vast majority of letters supporting her selection came from female writers. The above letter supporting Durst well illustrates the shift from 1990 to 2009: of the five people who signed that letter, only two have recognizably female first names. However, significantly more women openly objected to a female mascot in 2009. After the cheer-off, student Dianne Cerulli expressed her hesitation about the possibility of a woman winning, saying that "because we're in West Virginia, no one is going to respect a female Mountaineer."[77] Cerulli's concern seems like preemptive hillbilly shaming: why select a female Mountaineer when you know the state's backward population will disrespect her? Better to bow to sexism before it has a chance to rear its ugly head. Other female students expressed concern about Durst's inability to grow a beard. In a *Daily Athenaeum* article published after the first football game of the 2009–10 season, freshman Kelsey Jagger said she was "hesitant to support Durst in the position at first because of her gender," but "was impressed by her performance" at the first game, "even though some people were a little put off by the fact that she didn't have a beard."[78]

In an interview, Durst acknowledged the prevalence of opposition from other female students, saying that "the group that I sensed, and experienced . . . the most that wasn't accepting was actually college-aged females, which I thought was very interesting."[79] Durst surmised that this might reflect female students' own anxieties about breaking gender barriers and the possibility of a backlash against them for doing so. She said, "Many females probably don't have the . . . inclination to try out as the Mountaineer, because they think that it's not a role that they can accomplish or perform up to the standards of the University."[80] In her typical positive style, Durst deflects the criticism she received from other women by casting her service as WVU Mountaineer as evidence that women "can really do anything and shouldn't be angry at another female because she's doing something different." Furthermore, she notes, "Now I see a lot of younger girls that were in elementary school when I was the Mountaineer, and they're like, 'I remember when you were the Mountaineer! That was so cool! I want to do that now.'" Durst also expressed hope that it wouldn't be another twenty years before a third woman was chosen as the WVU Mountaineer.[81]

Even though there was significant pushback against Durst's selection, the opposition died down far more quickly than it had when Tennant was selected as the first female Mountaineer in 1990. However, Durst's year as the Mountaineer was not without its own challenges. The question of her physical ability to do the job continued to be a concern for some students and fans, although not to the same degree as it had been during Tennant's service. However, this does not mean that biology and the Mountaineer's body played no role in the controversy this time around. Like Tennant, Durst was subjected to sexist taunts, and like Tennant, she learned to take it "with a grain of salt and a little bit of humor." She explains,

> You know, everybody was always like, "Is she gonna wear a buckskin bikini?" "Is she gonna wear a fake beard?" "She needs to be in the kitchen, doing all the cooking, or barefoot and pregnant." And I just thought that a lot of those comments were really funny. And before I had my initial meeting with the Mountaineer Advisory Board, where they kind of coached me on how . . . interactive with the public I was supposed to be, I actually responded a little bit on some of the message boards and forums. And the fans got a

kick out of that too, and they realized that no matter what they said, I'm not going to respond to it and get angry about it. I'm just gonna laugh at it, and tell you how it is.[82]

As the question about the "buckskin bikini" suggests, however, reactions to a female Mountaineer took on a more overtly sexual tone during Durst's service. In many ways, the body of the female Mountaineer was even more open to criticism and commentary in 2009 than it had been during the controversy over Tennant's selection. Some of this attention focused on Durst's ability to physically perform the Mountaineer's duties. Brian Combs, a member of one of the anti-Durst Facebook groups, apparently changed his mind about Durst's suitability for the job after watching her perform at the Gold-Blue scrimmage in the spring: "She did the pushups and everything, and I was impressed."[83]

But other forms of attention to Durst's body were far more gendered. In a December 2009 article about a typical game day for Durst, reporter Samantha Cossick describes Durst's entrance to the stadium from the Law School steps as follows:

As [Durst] tries to walk down the steps, a traffic jam ensues as people line up to greet her and take pictures, some not as coherent as others, but all demanding her attention. "It must be a nightmare to deal with drunk people," one man in the crowd said.

Durst has gotten used to attention with people yelling and grabbing at her, and tries to see as many people as possible in the amount of time available.

"I'll go to whoever wants to grab me or wants a picture," Durst said.[84]

This depiction of fans' grabbiness, and Durst's apparent resignation to it, is more than a little disturbing. While coverage of Natalie Tennant's interactions with skeptical male fans often implied her ability to win them over with her "feminine wiles" (and her musket), suggestions of her sexual availability were mild. We hear only about the humorous, safe interactions, such as her marriage proposal from the elderly Ol' Buster and the kid who gave her a quarter and urged her to call him. Rebecca Durst seems to have experienced much more aggressive fan overtures; the *Daily Athenaeum* reports fans saying "at least they have a hot girl now" and telling Durst "Give me your number" or "I'll find you on Facebook." Durst herself says that "Tonight, some fans were yelling at me to 'take it off' referring to the buckskins," but attributes this to fans "just getting into the game."[85] It seems that some fans' objections to having a female mascot were outweighed by the potential to be found in sexualizing the Mountaineer.

Durst attributes this attention more to the advent of social media than to her gender:

> That was sort of when Twitter and social media were starting to get big . . . and I had wanted to have like a Mountaineer Twitter [account] but the Mountaineer Advisory Board wasn't super comfortable with it yet. But now the Mountaineer does have a Twitter account and is able to interact with fans that way and I think that's really great. And, you know, people are all into selfies now so they are . . . trying to grab the Mountaineer and do more of that. . . . I would take a lot of pictures and then I felt like I had to refuse a lot of pictures because, you know, you could only stand there for so long and take pictures and that kind of drains the energy that the rest of the crowd deserves to have from the mascot.[86]

Undoubtedly, the crowd's expectations of the Mountaineer have shifted dramatically in the age of the selfie, and Mountaineers spend far more time being photographed with fans than they ever did before. However, the images of fans grabbing Durst and asking her to "take it off" remain distressing evidence that for some, the only way to justify the selection of a female

Mountaineer was to objectify and commodify her body. Because she's "hot," it doesn't matter if she can grow a beard or not. While male Mountaineers, too, have faced criticism for not looking the part (by having a less-than-full beard or not meeting a fan's notion of what the male Mountaineer body should look like), there is a big difference between that sort of body shaming and requests for a female Mountaineer to don a buckskin bikini or to take it off. Catcalling, however, is not flattering or empowering: it's an assertion of power, a reminder that women's bodies are always subject to the male gaze and its judgment.

Conclusion: Erasing the Mountaineer's Body

In the years since Durst's tenure as the second female Mountaineer, a number of women have applied for the position, and two have served as the alternate Mountaineer: Daryn Vucelik in 2013–14 and Savannah Lusk in 2016–17. The controversy that Durst's selection generated and the ways that controversy got subsumed by a focus on her body made it clear that the physical embodiment of the Mountaineer had become problematic. Just as many Americans suddenly saw the US Senate's overwhelming majority of white men for the first time after the Anita Hill hearings, the Durst controversy seems to have brought the university to an awareness that by using the Mountaineer statue as an official logo, it was tacitly promoting a specific and static image of the WVU Mountaineer as white and male.

As such, it doesn't seem coincidental that in the years after Durst's service, the university began the process of redefining its relationship with the icon of the Mountaineer, hiring a public relations agency to analyze and revamp the university's brand. The result was the "Let's Go" brand that rolled out in 2015, whose key change was to restrict the use of the Mountaineer logo to athletics only. No longer would the Mountaineer's image be part of the university's academic branding. Instead, the marketing agency quite skillfully managed to repackage the Mountaineer via a new campaign that draws on the values and qualities associated with the Mountaineer, as discussed in the next chapter. This rebranding shifts Mountaineer identity away from a specific, bodily incarnation and toward a more abstract set of characteristics.

This official shift away from the WVU Mountaineer as depicted in the statue (and the logo based on the statue) is a fascinating maneuver, since it manages to retain the history and heritage of the Mountaineer in the abstract, while eliminating the problematic physical body from the equation. Whether it results in the next female Mountaineer facing less opposition remains to be seen, however.

Inclusion, Exclusion, and the Twenty-First-Century Mountaineer

CHAPTER 5

FOLKLORISTS ARE always on the lookout for patterns in storytelling within groups, and as I interviewed former WVU Mountaineers, one particular narrative came up over and over again as they described their time in the buckskins: they'd tell me about some breach in official protocol they'd committed, whether allowing someone else to fire the rifle or showing up at a party in the uniform, and justify it by concluding that it's "Better to ask forgiveness than permission." I was astonished at how frequently that saying came up, unprompted, until it occurred to me that it's the perfect motto for the Mountaineer in general: act on your own impulses and do what you need to do without concern for rules or social expectations. If you go too far, you can repent later.

This notion of the Mountaineer as a figure who acts first and asks forgiveness later is by now a familiar theme. However, it's also one that has taken on new meaning, both officially and unofficially, in recent years as West Virginia University has rolled out a new branding campaign around Mountaineer identity and the notion that "Mountaineers Go First," and also as the figure of the hillbilly has reappeared in both WVU culture and American culture at large. In the 2010s the term *hillbilly* reemerged, representing both an entertaining character and a political playing card via television shows such as MTV's *Buckwild* and J. D. Vance's best-selling book *Hillbilly Elegy*. Meanwhile, West Virginia University has spent much of the decade fighting its own battle against the hillbilly associations that accompanied the university's designation as one of the country's top party schools and several well-publicized student riots on campus. Also still prevalent is the ongoing tension between West Virginians and the outsiders who benefit from trading in those well-worn stereotypes. As the term *Mountaineer* enters its third century, the battle over what it means to be a Mountaineer shows no signs of abating.

Everything Old Is New Again: Appalachia as Spectacle and Specimen

Old stereotypes about Mountaineers die hard. In 2012 the cable network MTV launched a new reality TV show set in West Virginia called *Buckwild* (fig. 5.1). The series featured fun-loving young hillbillies (my word, not MTV's) doing what twenty-first-century hillbillies do, at least according to MTV: going mudding in four-wheelers and drinking to excess. Even before the show aired it was controversial, prompting West Virginia senator Joe Manchin to send a preemptive letter to MTV executives asking that the show be scrapped and denouncing them for maligning the people of West Virginia: "This show plays to ugly, inaccurate stereotypes about the people of West Virginia. . . . Let me tell you: People have given their all for this great country. They've done the heavy lifting to produce the energy that is needed to produce the steel that builds our factories and cities. . . . The proud veterans of our state have shed more blood and made more sacrifices than most other states to keep America free."[1] Manchin's letter condemns *Buckwild's* negative hillbilly stereotypes by countering them with another by now familiar set of stereotypes: the romantic version that extols the virtues of the state's humble, salt-of-the-earth working people. It's a touching tribute, but needless to say the MTV execs were not moved to cancel the show nor to recast it with miners and veterans.

Buckwild was filmed in Sissonville, West Virginia, just south of Charleston, though the show made it appear as if Sissonville was much more rural than it actually was. MTV hoped *Buckwild* would be a successful replacement for its recently ended *Jersey Shore* series; like *Jersey Shore*, *Buckwild* focused on the crazy antics of a group of twenty-something friends. MTV's gambit worked: according to the network, the show garnered around three million viewers per episode and was "the top-rated original cable show on its respective night in MTV's twelve to thirty-four target age demographic."[2] Its appeal rested largely in its evocation of the same hillbilly image that has been mined so continuously from the era of Sut Lovingood forward: that of the leisure loving, barely civilized white rebel living on the margins of mainstream culture.

The show was canceled in April 2013 after the accidental death of one of its stars, Shain Gandee.[3] Two other cast members had been in trouble with the law, including one who was stockpiling oxycodone and heroin with the intent to sell.[4] Although Gandee's death was tragic and untimely, the show's demise was welcome news to Charleston mayor Danny Jones, who said he was "relieved and happy the show is cancelled, and so is everyone around here. The show does nothing for us and exaggerates every negative stereotype about us."[5] After Gandee's death, Huntington mayor Steve Williams revealed that parts of *Buckwild*'s second season would have been filmed in his city, a decision he felt ambivalent about: "Charleston was portrayed in a very positive light [as] lovely and vibrant. When [the cast] went to Morgantown [in one episode], it was portrayed in

Figure 5.1. The *Buckwild* cast, including Shain Gandee (*far left*).

a similar fashion. We were looking forward to Huntington in a favorable light and [concurrently] worried about the unscripted events."[6]

Some Huntington residents were less inclined to see the benefits: Elsa Littlepage denounced the show's stereotypes, saying that "West Virginians are not rednecks. Many live in the city. They don't drive ATVs in the mud and act uncivilized. . . . Why didn't they go to Arkansas, Tennessee or Mississippi?"— all less "civilized" places where the "real" hillbillies live, apparently.[7] Meanwhile, Joe Murphy, head of Huntington's Office of Film, Theater, and Broadcasting, echoed the resentment earlier generations felt about their exploitation at the hands of outsiders, claiming: "While the film 'carpetbaggers' are making their way to West Virginia to capitalize on America's fascination with the Appalachian man and woman, we are working to be a film friendly city while being good stewards over the people and perception of our city."[8]

Although the *Buckwild* controversy came to an abrupt end with Gandee's death and the network's cancellation of the show, the furor around its representation of West Virginians demonstrated that insiders' anxieties about how outsiders perceived Mountaineers was alive and well in the twenty-first century. Manchin and Littlepage's comments avoid using the term *hillbilly* specifically, but that is the image that both clearly feared *Buckwild* would refresh. And Murphy's comments about carpetbaggers evoked the long and storied history of shady outsiders coming into Appalachia to fleece natives during and after Reconstruction—stories that in their own day recalled the even older tale of the backwoodsman and the dandy.

The *Buckwild* controversy also foreshadowed renewed public interest in Appalachia. During the presidential election of 2016 and its aftermath, media outlets around the world seized on Appalachia as the perfect microcosm of the "forgotten America" that reared up and propelled Donald Trump to victory. In the lead-up to the election, and even more so in the confusing days, weeks, and months following, the media scrambled for explanations of Trump's popularity, seizing on Appalachia as a sort of Mecca for journalists wanting to commune with Trump's "people."

A century after William Goodell Frost declared Appalachia to "contain a larger proportion of 'Sons' and 'Daughters' of the Revolution than any other part of our country," and two centuries after Joseph Doddridge described the Backwoodsman as "the father of his country," Appalachia was once again a barometer for Americanism. The dandies—coastal "elites"—had been metaphorically knocked down by the backwoodsmen, and the media swarmed in to find out how this curious specimen thought and acted.

While some journalists approached the region and its residents with an open mind, others came armed with hillbilly stereotypes that constrained their view and deeply shaped the stories they told.[9] Just as Frost and other advocates of "Appalachian exceptionalism" conveniently overlooked the racial and ethnic diversity of the region in order to garner support from wealthy northern donors, so twenty-first-century journalists overlooked the racial, ethnic, economic, and political diversity of contemporary Appalachia. The stories that emerged after the election suggested that all West Virginians were current or former coal miners and that most were either uneducated, unhealthy hillbillies or else stalwart, long-suffering, salt-of-the-earth frontierspeople. Very few portraits attempted to provide an alternative view of the state and its people.

The cause was not helped by the simultaneous popularity of J. D. Vance's *Hillbilly Elegy: A Memoir of a Family and Culture in Crisis*. Published in June 2016, Vance's book quickly climbed best-seller lists, topping the *New York Times*'s list in August 2016 and January 2017. It was touted by many critics as the explanation for Donald Trump's popularity in the American heartland. In fact, an interview with Vance in the *American Conservative* in late July 2016 drew so much traffic that it briefly crashed the publication's website.[10] The interviewer, Rod Dreher, starts the interview with an anecdote about "a friend who moved to West Virginia a couple of years ago [who] tells me that she's never seen poverty and hopelessness like what's common there. And she says you can drive through the poorest parts of the state, and see nothing but Trump signs. Reading 'Hillbilly Elegy' tells me why."[11] It doesn't matter to Dreher that Vance has no connections to West Virginia at all. Apparently, Vance's childhood visits with family in eastern Kentucky grants him all the "hillbilly cred," as his own cousin described it, that he needs to speak for West Virginians and all Appalachians.[12]

Vance grew up in Middletown, Ohio, but his memoir emphasizes the family's origins in eastern Kentucky—the roots of the hillbilly identity he claims in the title and throughout the text. How Vance is defining the term *hillbilly*, however, is ambiguous and changeable. Curiously, given that Vance is a lawyer, he never fully or precisely explains what he means by *hillbilly*. The early parts of the text connect hillbilly identity specifically with Appalachia and with the resettlement communities in the northern cities that many Appalachians migrated to in the mid-twentieth century. Unfortunately, Vance's characterization of hillbillies regurgitates all the usual stereotypes; he says that "Hillbilly culture at the time (and maybe now) blended a robust sense of honor, devotion to family, and bizarre sexism into a sometimes explosive mix."[13] He further boasts of being kin to "hillbilly royalty" via an ancestor who married into the Hatfield family on his father's side of the family, adding that his mother's ancestors "had a feuding history nearly as illustrious as Papaw's."[14] Vance's hillbillies are violent, and he prides himself on inheriting the "Appalachian honor code"[15] that compels him to fight anyone who insults his family. In one dramatic episode, Vance's grandparents destroy merchandise in a drugstore after the clerk tells a young Vance to leave, an event that Vance concludes with the dubious moral, "That's what Scots-Irish Appalachians do when people mess with your kid."[16] His grandmother, who in many ways turns out to be the heroine of the book, frequently threatens to shoot interlopers and once set fire to her husband.[17] Ever true to stereotype, Vance stresses the Scots-Irish background of his hillbillies, linking their ethnicity to their violent natures.

Vance's notion of who hillbillies are is a mess, a mish-mash of tired clichés based on region, class, and ethnicity. Most disturbing is Vance's insistence that hillbilly identity is inherited—that poverty is not transmitted merely culturally, but biologically. Though his association of hillbilly identity with the Scots-Irish drops off by the end of the book, Vance still concludes with his concerns that he cannot ever escape his hillbilly destiny: "conflict and family breakdown seem like the destiny I can't possibly escape. In my worst moments, I convince myself that there is no exit, and no matter how much I fight old demons, they are as much an inheritance as my blue eyes and brown hair."[18] He even goes so far as to suggest that the only way to escape this destiny is by diversifying the gene pool, noting that "every single person in my family who has built a successful home—Aunt Wee, Lindsay, my cousin Gail—married someone from outside our little culture."[19] The stereotype of hillbilly inbreeding and the legacy of eugenics echoes loudly at the conclusion of Vance's book.

I am certainly not the only critic to note the disturbing echoes of eugenics in Vance's book; Elizabeth Catte analyzes these at some length in *What You Are Getting Wrong about Appalachia*, as does John Thomason in an article titled "Hillbilly Ethnography" for the *New Inquiry*. Both writers suggest that these echoes are far from unintentional on Vance's part, with Catte pointing to an October 2016 interview of Vance by Charles Murray. Murray is coauthor of 1994's controversial book *The Bell Curve*, which uses pseudoscience to claim that African Americans are genetically predisposed to have lower IQs. Murray's more recent book, *Coming Apart: The State of White America, 1960–2010*, was one of the few sources Vance cited in *Hillbilly Elegy*.[20] During their interview, Murray and Vance discussed the white working class, and "over laughs and jokes, the pair discussed their 'pretty clean Scots-Irish blood' while getting to the heart of what 'hillbilly culture' actually is."[21] And while Vance cuts himself slack by claiming that *Hillbilly Elegy* is not an academic book, it is notable that the few sources he cites are those of Murray and "Razib Khan, a

writer who the *New York Times* dropped as a regular science con-
tributor after *Gawker* revealed his 'history with racist, far-right
online publications.'"[22] Thomason says that while "Vance's view
of Appalachian culture feels more opportunistic than sincerely
white nationalistic . . . this opportunism makes the book's racial
determinism all the more insidious: it makes it more palatable to
audiences that might normally be on guard against explicit white
nationalism."[23]

And indeed, *Hillbilly Elegy* has proven to be palatable not
only for those outside Appalachia seeking easy answers about
our region's "peculiar people," it has won over many inside the
region too. A number of WVU faculty who read the book told
me that they thought it "explained a lot about our students" and
that it should be required reading. These are people who, in most
other instances, would claim to be both attuned to and critical
of racial and ethnic stereotyping. To me, that was the most disturbing reaction imaginable to Vance's book: that somehow his
"insights" about hillbilly culture could explain the complexity of
Appalachian history and—for faculty members at WVU—of student behavior.

The fact that *Hillbilly Elegy* was received by so many as an
ethnographic account of Appalachian culture should disturb all
of us, whether we agree with Vance or not. Vance's book renewed
the perception of outsiders that Appalachia is a strange and
backward place, full of ignorant, helpless people who—because
they seem to have rejected progress—can, in turn, be rejected
by progress. Vance is proud of his kinship with "hillbilly royalty"
and waxes romantic about his tough-talking, pistol-packing
grandmother; he admires what he calls "Appalachian justice" even
as he describes how long and difficult a process it has been for
him to realize that "not every perceived slight—from a passing
motorist or a neighbor critical of my dogs—is cause for a blood
feud."[24] He subscribes to the romantic view of the hillbilly as
a rebellious, Scots-Irish upstart bound by honor to defend his
family, while condemning hillbilly culture for its dysfunction. His

book, in short, is a repetition of the same old story that has been told about lubbers, backwoodsmen, squatters, white trash, and Mountaineers for hundreds of years.

A very different version of that story was crafted by West Virginia's public school teachers in the spring of 2018, when years of frustration about low salaries, a floundering health-insurance program, and threats to seniority led to an unprecedented nine-day work stoppage. Teachers and school service personnel in all fifty-five of West Virginia's counties participated, leading to the hashtags #55United and #55strong. But one incident in the middle of the strike seemed to galvanize teachers like no other. During a February 26, 2018, town-hall meeting in Wheeling, a teacher in the audience interrupted Governor Jim Justice, prompting him to tell her that he, too, could be the "town redneck," a response that elicited boos from the audience.[25] Many teachers wondered whether the governor was aware of the historical significance of the term *redneck* in West Virginia's labor history: the term emerged out of the mine wars of the 1920s, when striking coal miners wore red bandanas around their necks to identify themselves. In response, teachers on picket lines and in the state capitol began wearing red bandanas both to talk back to the governor and to connect their movement to the larger history of labor movements in the state.

The teachers were also talking back to J. D. Vance and those outside the state who painted hillbillies as lazy, uncaring, and therefore unworthy. The striking teachers, like Doddridge's Backwoodsman, had finally had enough of the willful misunderstanding and insults of the "dandies" in the capitol, and they punched back. At the same time, they demonstrated the Mountaineer's traditional hospitality and concern, making sure that students who would go hungry without school breakfasts and lunches got fed. Regardless of one's views about the strike, after the 2016 presidential election and the increased attention it brought to Appalachia, it was refreshing to see West Virginia being covered in the national and international news in ways that defied the stereotypes that had been at the heart of so much recent journalism, and to allow Mountaineer voices to speak for themselves.

Riots, Couch Burning, and Rebranding WVU Mountaineer Identity

By the time of the 2016 election, West Virginia University had been trying for several years to craft an alternative vision of Mountaineer identity, an effort that was ratcheted up a few notches in the wake of the election.

In February 2015 the university launched a new public relations and branding campaign whose signature slogan is "Mountaineers Go First." In a letter to the university community announcing the new campaign, WVU president Gordon Gee urged people to "take time to think about what it means to you to be a Mountaineer."[26]

The new campaign seems to have been launched in part to combat WVU's growing reputation as a party school: in 2007, WVU topped the *Princeton Review*'s list of party schools,[27] and in 2013 it topped *Playboy* magazine's list.[28] During the period between and shortly after the two list-topping years, WVU witnessed several riots that tested the administration's and law enforcement's tolerance of student tradition. The circumstances surrounding these riots varied widely. The first notable event took place after Osama Bin Laden was killed on May 2, 2011, when WVU students took to the streets to celebrate. The celebration—which took place during spring semester's finals week, when students were in need of some stress release—escalated to include twenty-two intentionally set fires.[29] In March 2012, Saint Patrick's Day celebrations got out of hand, in part because the YouTube channel "I'm Schmacked" was on campus to film the events. The popularity of the channel's video of the Morgantown

Saint Patrick's Day celebrations was undoubtedly a factor in *Playboy* ranking WVU as its top party school the following year.[30] But the two events that really seemed to test the university's tolerance were the riots that took place after major football wins over the University of Texas in October 2012[31] and over Baylor in October 2014.[32]

I use the term *riot* to describe these events with some trepidation, as it is a loaded word. The summer of 2017 marked the fiftieth anniversary of urban uprisings in cities like Detroit and Newark. While both events were labeled as riots at the time, fifty years on the word *riot* had become so freighted with racist baggage that other labels were used to describe what had happened in Detroit and Newark: they were uprisings, rebellions, demonstrations, or simply unrest. Since 1967, the term *riot* itself has become racially charged, associated primarily with people of color; calling something a riot is a way to demonize participants and discount their legitimate concerns. For example, after Michael Brown, a young, unarmed African American, was fatally shot by a white police officer in Ferguson, Missouri, in August 2014, the black community there and in other places around the country took to the streets to demonstrate against police brutality. When some of these events turned violent (often due to provocation by the police), they were labeled as riots, thus delegitimizing their purpose.

But the word *riot* has a secondary meaning, denoting a kind of chaotic, anarchistic mob mentality, in which people act in ways that, under normal circumstances, they never would. Rioting involves consciously violating understood norms of behavior, either for a specific purpose or for the catharsis of violating those norms. In some ways, rioting can be a festive activity: participants enter a liminal space where normal social rules are suspended and where violating those rules is not only expected but pleasurable. It is this sense of the word *riot* I'm calling on to describe the various events that happened in Morgantown after the two big football wins in 2012 and 2014.

Obviously, the students whose postgame celebrations led to wanton destruction of property in 2012 and 2014 weren't engaging in that activity to make a political point or to express some kind of grievance. These events were a far cry from the post–Kent State protests that took place at WVU in May 1970, another time when police in riot gear teargassed students. Rather, the 2012 and 2014 events were riots in the second sense: the students created a self-sanctioned, temporary rule-free zone where intoxication, violence, and destructive acts were permitted. When the police responded to the 2014 event by teargassing participants, it was an instance in which two groups playing by very different rules came into conflict.

The 2014 riot following the WVU football team's win over Baylor was particularly destructive, causing about forty-five thousand dollars in damage,[33] and the university cracked down hard, expelling three students[34] and demanding a culture change on campus. In a strongly worded and lengthy statement following the Baylor riot, President Gee denounced the actions of "a minority of students [who] diverted the attention from the team's achievement to inexcusable and lawless actions," vowing "zero tolerance for this type of criminal and unruly behavior."[35] Most notably, Gee declared that "This is not how Mountaineers behave."[36]

Or is it? In a newspaper article about the 2014 riots, Morgantown fire chief Mark Caravasos commented that on one level, such events had always been part of college culture, noting that fire department records documented a riot after a WVU football win over Princeton in 1919.[37] In that instance, students apparently burned down the university observatory.[38] And to be sure, pranking and other sorts of rowdy, liminal behavior have been part of college culture from the beginning. The pranks that the men of Trinity Hall enjoyed were their way of showing themselves to be masters of college culture, even though others might consider them—as veterans and first-generation college students—to be outsiders to that culture. And their elaborate pranks were certainly far more clever than the same era's rage for panty raids—in which groups of male students raided women's dorm rooms to steal their underwear—a prank that WVU students participated in eagerly. Of a particularly large panty raid in 1952, WVU vice president Charles Neff wrote, "The fact that the episode was conducted in a spirit of fun does not alter the fact that it was both unimaginative and incredibly stupid."[39] To our contemporary view, a panty raid may seem quaint and harmless, if patently sexist. Even so, we might wish that students would return to that tradition in lieu of setting fires. But in many ways, panty raids and couch fires are part of the same trajectory, and both actions can be rationalized as being part of the rambunctious, lawless behavior of college students generally, and of the hillbilly Mountaineer specifically.

As a folklorist, I was fascinated by the debate about tradition that erupted after the October 2014 riot. I was teaching WVU's American Folklore and Culture class at the time, and when I discussed the events with students, they were divided about whether such activities were traditional and whether labeling something as tradition excuses what would, in another context, be considered violent or criminal behavior. Recall that WVU's 2014 riot took place shortly after the events in Ferguson, Missouri, protesting the fatal shooting of Michael Brown by a white police officer, Darren Wilson. Students were outraged at having been teargassed by police and felt themselves to be victims of police brutality. In the context of what was happening in Ferguson—and in other locations around the country where sister protests had popped up—I had very little sympathy with that feeling, frankly. But the larger question—whether rioting was or should be considered a traditional part of WVU culture—was a more compelling and ambiguous concern.

One aspect of that traditional culture that particularly came under scrutiny between 2007 and 2014 was that of couch burning. Somehow, students had become convinced that this was a tradition unique to WVU, although incidents of couch burning were numerous at other universities. In fact, the city of Boulder, Colorado, had banned upholstered furniture on porches in 2002 after one too many incidents of couch burning by students at the University of Colorado.[40] A *New York Times* article about Boulder's ordinance says that it came in response to more than one hundred couch burnings between 1996 and 2002, and that the city's new ruling "mirrors laws in other campus towns, including Fort Collins, Colo., Normal, Ill., and Blacksburg, Va."[41] Couch burning may have become a broader college tradition in the mid-1990s, but it was certainly not one that was ever unique to WVU.

Nevertheless, the belief that couch burning is a central WVU tradition has been widely accepted and even embraced. After students burned couches to "celebrate" the death of Osama Bin Laden on May 1, 2011, the university and the city of Morgantown started cracking down on intentional fire setting. This crackdown, in turn, inspired students to push back, start-ing a Facebook group called "WVU Couch Burning—Save the Tradition by making it a University Event," which argued exactly that: that the university should make couch burning "official" and monitor the event. A *Daily Athenaeum* editorial published in November 2011 supported this idea, arguing that a sanctioned burning "would show the rebellious montani semper liberi (Mountaineers are always free) spirit that defines Appalachia, but within a more modern and safety-conscious framework." It would also serve to rid the tradition of its hillbilly connotations, by "tak[ing] a blemish on our University and turn[ing] it into a unique characteristic that can be safely added into the fabric of our campus' culture."[42]

It's not only students who regard couch burning as tradition; businesses in the community certainly support the notion by cre-ating merchandise that celebrates it as such. For a few years, the Kroger bakery at Morgantown's Suncrest Towne Centre made and sold "couch-burning cakes" during football season. These confec-tions were constructed and iced to look like couches and came complete with candles so that you could set your own sugary "couch" on fire and eat it too. (These cakes were only available for a couple of years, around 2009–10, and a recent tweet from @westva75 says that "#kroger wouldn't sell us a burning couch cake [because] it 'promotes bad behavior.'")[43] T-shirts available in stores around town repeatedly reference the practice, such as one that read "Where greatness is learned and couches are burned," and another more recent example claiming that "Saturdays are for couch burning" (fig. 5.2).

After the Texas football win in 2012, a *Daily Athenaeum* article asked, "Is the practice of burning couches really a tradition?" The article quotes Morgantown fire marshal Ken Tennant as saying that couch fires are "almost like folklore. . . . People hear stories from their parents when they were here or from other fraternity members." Tennant cites statistics showing that this "tradition" is fairly recent in genesis: "Before 1997, there were never more than 20 street fires a year. In 1997, there were 120. The yearly average since '97 is 113 and peaked at 255 fires in 2003." Rioting and retaliating against police and firefighters at the scene is an even more recent part of the "tradition"; as Tennant puts it, "If you're celebrating a victory, how does that turn into picking up a rock and throwing it at a firefighter or a police officer? I can't make that connection."[44]

For some students, however, even rioting and throwing things at the police have become deeply "traditional" and cherished college experiences. In an article in the *Daily Athenaeum*'s 2015 graduation issue, seniors recall the Saint Patrick's Day 2012 events fondly—one describes it as "one of the best days . . . that has ever occurred in town," a sentiment the *Daily Athenaeum*'s writer, Taylor Jobin, echoes, saying that "it was the greatest [Saint Patrick's Day] anyone has had in a long time." Another student's account of the 2012 riot after the Texas football game suggests that the police's response—to "tear-gas the whole street"—led to the football team's downfall that season: "Sure enough, we lost the next five games after that." Apparently, not only was law enforcement's response overblown, it directly caused the football team's slump. The very title of the *Daily Athenaeum*'s article—"For Better or Worse, Mountaineers Go Hard"—says everything about contemporary notions of Mountaineer identity: a real WVU Mountaineer is all in, regardless of the consequences.[45]

It's difficult to argue with that interpretation of what it means to be a WVU Mountaineer. In some ways, students rioting and burning couches is exactly the kind of antiestablishment behavior we have come to expect of the hillbilly Mountaineer: is it really all that different from the out-of-control thuse, or pep rally, that was the first Mountaineer Day in 1947? Which is the less criminal act: destroying private property during a riot or stealing government property for the purposes of making a homecoming decoration, as the men of Trinity Hall did when they took pipe from the US Bureau of Mines? In many ways, the administration's response to the October 2014 riot was not dissimilar from the response that followed the first Mountaineer Day in 1947: James Brawner's "thin veneer of civilization" had once again been eroded, and students violated the boundary between harmless fun and incivility.

This boundary was again tested in early 2019. In the last few days of January, the East Coast of the United States experienced a polar vortex—an arctic blast that brought subzero temperatures to Morgantown and closed the WVU campus for three days, from midday on Wednesday, January 30, through Friday, February 1. While the initial two days were frigid but sunny, Friday brought slightly warmer temperatures and about six inches of snow. After days of being cooped up inside, students relished a real snow day. At the top of Spruce Street—a steep, hilly road above campus where a number of fraternity houses are situated—several hundred students began sledding, snowboarding, and drinking. In the midafternoon, a city snow plow came along to clear the street; students objected strenuously, blocking the road, and the conflict escalated to the point where a few students were throwing rocks and bottles at the

Figure 5.2. A burning-couch T-shirt in WVU blue and gold, seen at a clothing shop in Morgantown in 2019.

police. The police, in turn, tried to break up the gathering with sonic blasts, pepper balls, and smoke grenades. Sure enough, by the time the local news aired that evening, WVU was again in the spotlight for a student "riot." The *Daily Athenaeum*, however,

titled its story about the event "The Battle of Spruce Street."[46]
The conflict between the rioting hillbilly Mountaineer and the
beleaguered frontiersman Mountaineer was reignited. As it had
after previous "riots," the university again called on students to
behave in ways that "represent our Mountaineer values."[47] But
how those Mountaineer values are defined depends on who you
ask to describe them.

For some students—in 2019, as in 1947's first Mountaineer
Day—those values include rowdy behavior and drunkenness.
And WVU is not alone in that respect: getting drunk and acting
up have been part of college life virtually since the establishment of colleges. However, the perceived status of being officially declared a top party school is a new phenomenon; the
Princeton Review and *Playboy* only began making such rankings
in the late 1980s.[48] WVU's appearance at the top of those lists
creates an odd sort of pressure to stay on top of the lists—once
Mountaineers "go first" in the party-school rankings, don't they
have an obligation to maintain that status? Such rankings may
in fact encourage some students to escalate party behavior to be
perceived as ever more out-of-control and more intense. After
the Baylor riot in October 2014, WVU criminologist Karen
Weiss, author of *Party School: Crime, Campus, and Community*,
noted that universities across the United States were experiencing more destructive behavior and that the minority of students
who engage in such behavior "see that as benefiting the school.
. . . There's just a warped identity with the school as if their
party behavior is actually good for the school."[49] Mountaineers
who "go hard" are real Mountaineers; everyone else is failing at
Mountaineer identity.

After the Baylor riot, President Gee seemed to imply that it
was this false equivalence—the idea that being a Mountaineer
means to "go hard" regardless of consequences—that needed to
be challenged, as reflected in his insistence that this was "not how
Mountaineers behave." The Go First branding campaign, already
in development before the 2014 Baylor victory riot, coincided

nicely with the administration's commitment to changing campus culture, while also urging students to "go hard" and "go first" in more academic and productive ways.

The 2012, 2014, and 2019 riots reignited the old conflict between the wild and crazy hillbilly Mountaineer and the noble frontiersman Mountaineer. While some WVU students relished being in the spotlight for partying too hard, others echoed the administration's pleas to embrace more noble Mountaineer values. Immediately after the 2014 events, students Deonna Gandy and Chris Hickey began using the hashtag #RespectfulMountaineer on social media to indicate that their version of the WVU Mountaineer was not the out-of-control, destructive hillbilly.[50] The 2014 riot also marked an important turning point when outsiders were tagged as the "uncivilized" louts at the root of the problem. At the first Student Government Association (SGA) meeting following the 2014 riot, SGA President Chris Nyden lay the blame for the riots squarely on the shoulders of out-of-state students, saying, "We need to stop letting in students who choose to attend WVU for party reasons rather than academic reasons. This will require the University to increase admission standards for out-of-state students, but it is absolutely necessary. . . . We cannot sacrifice our integrity as an institution in the name of a higher enrollment."[51] Nyden's statement wasn't simply based on rumor but reflected the reality of the event: the Morgantown police reported that "Six of the nine people arrested Saturday night during the riots were WVU students, and eight were from out of state"; the one person arrested who had a permanent West Virginia address was not a WVU student.[52] Similar stories circulated after the 2019 "snow riot": the real perpetrators were alleged to be out-of-state students—and in fact, according to the *Dominion Post*, nine of the eleven students who faced charges after the 2019 event were from out of state, and one of the two West Virginia residents charged, as in the 2014 event, was not a WVU student.[53]

Blaming riots on out-of-state students and outsiders in

general marks an interesting new version of Mountaineer identity: here, the drunken, lawless hillbillies are not West Virginians, but outsiders. This is a fascinating shift, but one that is in keeping with traditional ideas about in-state versus out-of-state students at WVU, with each group making up roughly half the student population.[54] Within the state, WVU is generally held in high esteem (except among Marshall fans, perhaps). For many native West Virginians, attending WVU is a crowning educational achievement. Stereotypically, out-of-state students, especially those from the East Coast, are suspected of having chosen WVU either for its party reputation (as Nyden's comment suggests), or because they didn't have the grades or test scores to get into their own state universities.[55] This belief, which is echoed in Nyden's comments, puts the blame for hillbilly behavior on outsiders, implying that stereotypes about West Virginia may give such students license to misbehave because they imagine that it is an accepted and traditional part of the culture. (Certainly, J. D. Vance's characterization of hillbilly culture would seem to back this up.) The #RespectfulMountaineer hashtag inverts that notion: real Mountaineers do not behave this way. Nyden's comments and the hashtag turn the classic insider/outsider construction of Mountaineer identity on its head. The logic is that if outsiders didn't buy into false stereotypes about West Virginians, the outsiders wouldn't feel free to come here and act this way.

Although the #RespectfulMountaineer hashtag was launched by students, the university quickly picked up on it and began promoting it in a more official way. The hashtag was just one component of a much broader effort to remake the Mountaineer image after the October 2014 riots, however. Just as the university had consciously remade the WVU Mountaineer's image over in the 1950s, outlawing the hillbilly and institutionalizing the frontiersman, it stepped in after the riots and exercised another top-down makeover with the Mountaineers Go First campaign, which was launched just a few months later. Notably, the Mountaineer of the Go First campaign is a different creature from previous incarnations.

The Go First campaign preserves the Mountaineer's innate qualities—a pioneering spirit, resilience, generosity, and fearlessness—while disconnecting those qualities from any particular kind of body. In other words, the campaign extends Mountaineer characteristics to the whole student body, not just white males. The campaign capitalizes on the mythology of the frontiersman Mountaineer while erasing the "man" on the frontier. One of the ways it accomplishes this is by repackaging the rebellious aspects of the Mountaineer's identity into more positive and productive qualities. The university's extensive Brand Center website explicitly defines (and limits) these qualities as six personality traits: pioneering, passionate, innovative, tireless, grounded, and caring, noting that these traits "drive the voice and image of our entire brand."[56] A page describing the brand's identity says that "it is a signature, a stamp of quality and a symbol of pride for all Mountaineers—past, present and future—to rally around."[57] Above all, the Brand Center encourages consistency in its portrayal of Mountaineer identity.

But as we have seen again and again, only part of Mountaineer behavior or identity is tied up in the noble, pioneering spirit that the Go First campaign tries to capture. The other part is allied with the other side of the Mountaineer family tree—that of the rebellious squatter/hillbilly. Repeatedly, we have seen that you can't have one without the other, despite the university's efforts, past and present, to control the uncontrolled and uncontrollable aspects of the figure. When the university stepped in to formalize the selection and management of the WVU Mountaineer in the 1930s, little did they know what they were getting themselves into: as we have seen, the administration and the student body have played a long tug-of-war game with the Mountaineer's image and identity ever since.

Figure 5.3. The unauthorized button made by students affiliated with the WVU LGBTQ+ Center.

The Go First campaign may have the power to officially define who and what the WVU Mountaineer is, but it cannot quash the impulse and, really, the *right* of the university community to interpret the figure in their own ways.

A lovely illustration of this by now familiar impulse is in this unauthorized, unofficial button produced by students affiliated with the university's LGBTQ+ Center, which reads "We're here, we're queer, we're [Mountaineers]" (fig. 5.3). As noted above, use of the Mountaineer logo is strictly regulated and limited under the Go First branding. But the LGBTQ+ students' appropriation of the image is totally in keeping with the long tradition of reinterpreting and extending Mountaineer identity to make it fit those who have been perceived as outside its parameters. The button plays with the Mountaineer image in ways similar to the ways Trinity Hall's motley crew of first-generation college students from immigrant communities played with the Mountaineer image in the late 1940s—and for similar purposes: to claim Mountaineer identity for themselves. Pairing of the Mountaineer logo with a revised version of ACT UP's slogan "We're here, we're queer, get used to it,"[58] the button simultaneously expands the

Mountaineer's identity to include the LGBTQ+ community and portrays the Mountaineer as queer.

The button reminds us again that the informal, student-driven image of the WVU Mountaineer and the university's official ideas about the figure can coexist peacefully. And as we have seen, at other moments the disconnect between those two visions of the WVU Mountaineer has widened, creating conflicts that ended with the university reasserting its authority over the Mountaineer's image, as when President Stewart banished the hillbilly Mountaineer in the 1950s. President Gee and the current administration seem determined to banish the latter-day incarnation of the hillbilly Mountaineer, that of the rioter. Whether those efforts will be successful lies in understanding that the frontiersman Mountaineer and the hillbilly Mountaineer are inextricably linked. Both will find expression one way or another. The language of the Mountaineers Go First brand may encourage students to push past obstacles, but as Gee's statement on the Baylor riots suggests, there are other boundaries that students will not be allowed to cross. Being Mountaineers, though, it's in their nature to try.

Erasing and Rewriting the Mountaineer Body

Significantly, the Go First Mountaineer is grounded in language, not in any particular image or figure. It is a rhetorical construction and an abstract idea rather than a person. The Go First campaign further separated the characteristics of the WVU Mountaineer from the caricature of the Mountaineer itself, phasing out an iconic logo featuring an image of the Mountaineer based on the Mountainlair statue.[59] Eventually, the Mountaineer logo would only be allowed to be used by university athletics. As such, the Go First brand brilliantly separates Mountaineer values from any particular physical body. In the campaign's initial phase, people

pictured in campaign materials were seen only in silhouette, photographed from behind, or portrayed by representative items,
such as the Mountaineer's moccasins. Because the Mountaineer
was not associated with any race or gender, the implication was
that anyone can be a Mountaineer, a goal explicitly stated on the
Brand Center website.[60]

Given the university's efforts to diversify by recruiting and
enrolling more students of color and more international students,
this attempt to disconnect Mountaineer identity from a physical
body—and in particular, from a body that has always been constructed as white and male—is particularly strategic. As we have
seen, from the moment the term *Mountaineer* came into use as a
synonym for residents of western Virginia, it has been a marker
of whiteness and masculinity and has even been used explicitly as
a descriptor for a particular class of whites, as it was at the turn
of the last century by Appalachian advocates like William Goodell
Frost. So in quietly phasing out the Mountaineer logo and introducing the concept-based Go First notion of Mountaineer identity, the university has subtly opened that identity to people of
any race, gender, or nationality.

WVU is not the only institution of higher education to try to
redefine and reinvent its nickname. In April 2018 the University
of Wyoming rolled out its own new marketing campaign, whose
central slogan was "The world needs more cowboys," with cowboys representing students, athletes, and alumni of Wyoming's
flagship university. Opposition was swift, with faculty object-
ing to the "very 1950s" way of "think[ing] that 'boy' somehow
includes 'girl,'" and Native Americans on campus noting that "the
history of cowboys and Native people . . . has not ever been positive." The university's communications director countered that
those very conflicts are exactly "why this campaign works—it's
the dissonance between the term 'cowboy' and the image that
draws attention." That dissonance is highlighted in a promotional
video that shows a diverse range of students engaging in all kinds
of activities, including working in a laboratory and studying, and

also in a flyer that "identif[ies] historical figures such as Galileo, Mary Wollstonecraft, and Martin Luther King Jr. as cowboys." As one critic noted, however, "If you have to . . . show a video of your slogan, and have a one-page explanation of your slogan, you have a bad slogan."[61]

The University of Wyoming appears to be trying to modernize its nickname and its branding in exactly the way WVU has: by reimagining what it means to be a cowboy, just as WVU's Go First campaign reimagines what it means to be a Mountaineer. The fact that WVU's rebranding did not encounter the same kind of pushback that the University of Wyoming did highlights the surprising fluidity of Mountaineer identity. Even though the two women who have served as the official mascot were both told that women couldn't be Mountaineers, there's nothing in the term itself that excludes them, in the way that "cowboy" is gender specific. In many ways, the success of WVU's marketing campaign hinged on that tiny bit of wiggle room.

Nevertheless, the folk response to the university's top-down management of this longstanding cultural icon has been mixed, as one might expect. Can the Mountaineer really exist only in words and ideas? And can the university successfully dissociate the platonic ideal of the Mountaineer as a concept from the physical person of the WVU Mountaineer? And can students and alumni be broadminded enough about who can serve in that position to allow someone who doesn't look like the Mountaineer to be the Mountaineer? Or would another woman, or a person of color, still be challenged on the authenticity of their portrayal?

It seems that even the university is struggling to decouple its high concept from the physical body. Although the rebranding campaign attempts to dissociate Mountaineer identity from ideas about race and ethnicity, an enormous sign on the front of the Mountainlair shows that there's still an element of essentialism to this new configuration of Mountaineer identity: it reads, in part, "At West Virginia University, we are determined to go first. It's in our blood. It's in our sweat. And it's in our nature" (fig. 5.4).

Figure 5.4. The giant Go First sign on the Mountainlair exterior,
with the contentious "It's in our blood."

Particularly in light of the reemergence of white supremacist
groups in recent years, not only nationally but locally, some
students have voiced discomfort with the claim that being a
Mountaineer is "in our blood." That kind of language seems too
close for comfort to turn-of-the-last century ideas about racial
hierarchies and eugenics.

Having worked first to disconnect Mountaineer identity from a human body, the campaign more recently has been making a concerted effort to attach Mountaineer identity to unexpected bodies. The June 2017 issue of the alumni magazine, for example, features profiles of international students and students who are naturalized US citizens. The article begins by noting that

> Our future alumni come from 107 countries. Some of them immigrated to the U.S. as children. Others are the children of immigrants. And some just arrived in the U.S. to attend college.
>
> The current freshman class is the most diverse in WVU's history. . . . But true diversity can't be expressed accurately in statistics. Our students live in stories, such as: Speaks Urdu at home. Visits Costa Rica every year. Grandmother emigrated from India.
>
> Here, we share with you some of their stories, tying them together with what they all have in common:
>
> They're Mountaineers.[62]

Notably, the article inverts the dynamic of the first wave of the Go First campaign; rather than disconnecting Mountaineer identity from a specific Mountaineer body, the article deliberately connects Mountaineer identity to these specific, non-traditional "bodies." Each student is photographed (including one woman wearing a hijab; fig. 5.5) and includes a profile describing the student's background and ending with the word *Mountaineer*.

The alumni magazine article seems to be part of the university's ongoing effort to move Mountaineer identity away from the exclusively white and almost exclusively male body. We might refer to this new iteration as the "inclusive Mountaineer." While the initial Go First campaign materials were determined to reconstruct Mountaineer identity completely through words and ideas, with no reference to the body or physical appearance at all, this newer phase links Mountaineer identity to a wide and perhaps unexpected range of bodies. This is undoubtedly one way the university is working to extend the label of *Mountaineer* to an increasingly diverse student body.

As the alumni magazine article notes, the Morgantown campus increased minority freshman enrollment by 27 percent in the fall of 2016.[63] In addition to more African American and Latinx students, WVU has attracted an increasing number of international students, particularly from Gulf countries such as Saudi Arabia, Kuwait, Bahrain, and Oman. Before and after the 2016 election, many of these students reported being verbally harassed or threatened. Sara Berzingi, the president of WVU's Muslim Students Association in 2016, wrote,

> In my two-term presidency of West Virginia University's Muslim Students Association, I've heard and documented close to 30 incidents of verbal harassment, many of which have gone unreported due to students' lack of faith in the system. Often, students are targeted by a passerby who runs or drives off shortly after committing these injustices, leaving victims with little to no substantive evidence for a report or claim. Muslim students at WVU describe instances where they've been called everything from towelheads to terrorists and a whole host of other colorful expletives while walking around campus.[64]

In an email, Berzingi also reported two incidents during the 2016–17 academic year when someone urinated on the group's prayer rugs.[65] And a climate survey of students released in early 2017 reported that "almost 29 percent of respondents perceived an atmosphere of 'unfriendliness' toward Muslims, 27 percent toward transgender students, 19 percent toward gay men/lesbians and 24 percent toward feminists. Thirty percent of respondents reported they had experienced a verbal hate- or bias-motivated assault." In response to the climate survey, the university reasserted its commitment to protecting marginalized students, with president Gordon Gee saying, "Inclusion and respect are core values that anchor all of us at West Virginia

Figure 5.5. Mays Ibraheem, Mountaineer, in an Instagram post, 2017.

University."[66] Clearly, the intended inclusivity of the Go First campaign has a long way to go to create real change in how marginalized individuals are treated on campus and whether they are perceived as "authentic" Mountaineers.

The university is not alone in its efforts to expand popular notions of who gets to call themselves a Mountaineer and what counts as West Virginian and Appalachian culture. Folklorist Emily Hilliard has been documenting folk traditions and cultural contributions throughout the state for the West Virginia Humanities Council, making a particular effort to record the traditions of underrepresented groups and recent immigrants. Queer Appalachia, an arts and culture collective based in Mercer

County, West Virginia, began as an Instagram account and has since emerged as a huge social media influencer and grant-making organization that publishes *Electric Dirt*, a journal that provides multilayered support to anyone in Appalachia and the South who is gender nonconforming. Chef Michael Costello, featured in the West Virginia episode of the late Anthony Bourdain's *Parts Unknown*, works to honor traditional Appalachian farming methods and foodways and to promote the locavore movement and sustainability. These and other efforts push back against the notion that West Virginia is a culturally and ethnically homogenous place and give marginalized people the ability to claim the moniker of Mountaineer or Appalachian as just one of many identities.

Exclusivity and Inclusivity: Dangers to the Mountaineer (Student) Body

As I was readying the final manuscript of this book during the spring semester of 2019, several events occurred that caused me to think anew about the Mountaineer: more evidence, as if I needed it, that this potent figure continues to be a vital and adaptable symbol of institutional and state identity. One was the snow day riot previously discussed; the other was the advancement in the West Virginia legislature of a bill that would allow individuals to carry concealed guns on campus, including in classrooms: House Bill 2519, the so-called Campus Self-Defense Act.

Similar legislation had been proposed in previous years, but those bills died quickly and quietly before reaching a floor vote. However, the 2019 bill seemed poised to pass, and the administration of West Virginia University—in particular the university's vice president for Strategic Initiatives, Rob Alsop—began a series of campus conversations to prepare faculty, staff, and students for the passage and implementation of the bill, which

Alsop implied was likely to pass.[67] The administration said that while it had fought the bill the previous two years, this year it had negotiated a group of exemptions that would allow guns in classrooms and common areas of dorms, but not in places like the university's daycare center, campus police headquarters, faculty offices, or "venues or arenas with a capacity of more than 1,000 spectators"—meaning the football stadium or the coliseum where basketball games are played.

As these campus conversations continued, members of the community—students, faculty, and staff—became increasingly bewildered by the administration's seemingly resigned approach to the bill. Why weren't they fighting it more strenuously? Why hadn't representatives of the groups that would be most directly affected by the bill been involved in discussions earlier? Why hadn't the university marshaled the forces of the larger community to fight it, instead of taking on the role of *in loco parentis* and making decisions that many in the community didn't agree with?

As the bill worked its way through the legislature, tensions between the administration and faculty increased significantly. A group of WVU faculty staged a walkout on February 21 and began working together to oppose the bill, making trips to Charleston to talk to legislators about the bill's shortsighted approach to campus safety; coordinating opposition efforts with faculty, students, and administrators at WVU and at other public colleges and universities across the state; and asking faculty and staff, including those at the Health Sciences Center, to prepare expert testimony to give to the senate judiciary committee.

The WVU Mountaineer's musket—one of the signature pieces of the figure's kit—suddenly took on new significance. The "frequently asked questions" sheet about HB 2519 on the university's website included a list of people currently allowed to carry firearms on campus. The list started, as one might expect, with law enforcement officers, military personnel, and Department of Corrections employees but ended with a surprising individual: the WVU Mountaineer.[68] Initially the Mountaineer's appearance on the list seemed a bit absurd; certainly the Mountaineer's reasons for being armed are very different from those of a law enforcement officer. And the firearm in question, a muzzle-loading musket, is in a completely different category from the handguns the bill proposed to allow on campus—not to mention that it would be difficult to carry a musket concealed. However, the fact that the WVU Mountaineer was on the list was a reminder of how atypical a mascot the Mountaineer is. Not only is the person a recognized individual rather than an anonymous student in a foam mask, but he or she is also currently the only student authorized to carry a firearm on campus. The campus carry bill would have allowed all students to be like the Mountaineer and carry a firearm.

To many in the legislature and the state at large, there was no irony in this proposed change at all; rather, allowing all WVU Mountaineers to be armed if they so chose was a way of enacting the motto *Montani semper liberi*: Mountaineers should be free to carry firearms wherever they like, especially since West Virginia is a permitless carry state. In its series of campus conversations, the university's administration seemed to suggest that it was lucky to have carved out any exemptions at all, since the exemptions were perceived by those favoring the bill—in particular the West Virginia Citizens Defense League (WVCDL)—as infringing on that freedom.

But for others, myself included, extending the WVU Mountaineer's right to bear arms to all Mountaineers was not merely ironic but a tragic indication of how fixating on one piece of the Mountaineer's kit, the rifle, as the most important symbol of the figure's freedom mutes the more important, if less visible, aspects of the Mountaineer's free-spiritedness. As the Go First campaign has been trying to emphasize, the WVU Mountaineer's freedom has never been explicitly or directly linked to his carrying a musket. Far from it: the backwoodsman, we might recall, put down the offending dandy with his fists, not with a firearm. And the WVU Mountaineer was, in fact, forbidden to carry a rifle for a long span from the late 1960s to the early 1980s. Suggesting that the rifle is the most significant symbol of the Mountaineer's freedom overshadows the far more important, if more abstract, qualities that empower the figure, including the Mountaineer's willingness to stand up to authority and to show hospitality to strangers.

That last quality seems to be one that is underappreciated these days, even though many WVU sports fans pride themselves on being courteous and gracious hosts to opposing teams' fans who have traveled to Morgantown for games. Hospitality, even when one has little to share, was a crucial aspect of the frontiersman Mountaineer's identity. One recent way the university has attempted to enact this part of Mountaineer identity is by extending the label *Mountaineer* to students who have generally been excluded from that identity, as in the examples from the Go First campaign mentioned above. Given these efforts to make Mountaineer identity more inclusive, it was painful to listen to campus conversations as international students, students of color, LGBTQ+ students, and Muslim students expressed their fears that the bill would make them feel less safe on campus. The kind of harassment that Muslim students experience, as described by Sara Berzingi, becomes even more menacing on a campus that allows concealed weapons. The freedom some Mountaineers associate with carrying a gun threatens other Mountaineers, whose status as Mountaineers is newer and less secure. While the Go First campaign worked hard to include marginalized students in the scope of Mountaineer identity, the university's apparent resignation to campus carry sent many of those same students the message that their university excluded them from its protection.

At the campus carry conversations and in other more informal settings, I listened as female students, students of color, LGBTQ+ students, international students, and others spoke about how they would feel less safe on campus knowing that other students might be carrying guns. I listened as they told stories about being harassed on campus and in the classroom, and I heard their fear that these verbal attacks could turn deadly. Then I listened as delegate Brandon Steele said that he "[didn't] care if we lose international students at our schools,"[69] and I was appalled a few days later by anti-Muslim propaganda that an extremist group openly displayed at the capitol on West Virginia GOP Day.[70]

In my young-adult literature class, I was teaching a novel about a transgender teenager who fears that she won't survive high school, much less make it to college, while delegate Eric Porterfield jokingly suggested in an interview that he would drown his own children if they came out to him as gay.[71] A few days later, I was in the gallery of the house of delegates when that body voted not to discharge from committee a bill that would have added "sexual orientation" and "gender identity" to the state's Human Rights Act. Back on campus, in the gun-free space of the coliseum, Brooke Ashby, the lone female finalist for the position of the 2019–20 Mountaineer, lost her bid for the position to a bearded male. Two days later, delegates on the floor of the house—in particular, Brandon Steele—claimed that campus carry was, at heart, a bill designed to help women: by carrying guns, college women would be safer on campus. Even as Steele and other state legislators railed against sending young women to campus unarmed, the one WVU student allowed to carry a firearm on campus remained a white male, as has been the case sixty-four of the sixty-six times the university has selected an official Mountaineer.[72] The idea of college women collectively carrying guns to protect themselves may be reassuring to some, but the idea of an individual woman and/or a person of color bearing the Mountaineer's rifle, and the title of the Mountaineer, is still controversial.

We live in a world where the Mountaineer's musket is both an anachronism—a throwback to that romanticized era of the frontiersman—and a potent symbol of the perceived link between freedom and firearms. Both the musket and the motto *Montani semper liberi* were marshaled into arguments on both sides of the campus carry controversy. The West Virginia Citizens Defense League's logo prominently features the motto beneath overlapping images of a hunting rifle and a military-style assault rifle. Taylor Giles, a WVU student and the WVU NRA campus coordinator, ended a *Daily Athenaeum* op-ed in support of campus carry by writing, "Our own mascot carries a gun. Why should that right be taken away from everyone else?"[73] And it should be noted that each newly selected WVU Mountaineer only becomes the official mascot after the Passing of the Rifle Ceremony in the spring. This tradition would seem to suggest that the musket is, in fact, the most crucial part of the WVU Mountaineer's kit.

However, opponents of campus carry used the same argument against the bill, saying that the *only* student they wanted carrying a gun on campus was the official Mountaineer—or WVU student Ginny Thrasher, a member of the varsity rifle team who won a gold medal in the women's ten-meter air rifle event at the 2016 Olympics in Rio.[74] Monongalia County delegate Danielle Walker, an opponent of campus carry, referenced the state motto when she noted that "Mountaineers are free, but you should be free to walk the campus and not be in fear of not knowing what the person walking on the side of you is holding."[75] It should come as no surprise that *Montani semper liberi* and the figure of the Mountaineer were woven through the fabric of the campus carry debate, since the issue touches on so many tangible and intangible aspects of Mountaineer identity. The concrete link between the WVU Mountaineer's rifle and students carrying guns is the obvious connection, but so are the abstract ideas about Mountaineer values, including freedom, dissent, and standing up to a perceived threat.

For faculty, staff, and students involved in the campus carry debate on both sides of the issue, it was those intangible characteristics that resonated in a new way, engendering stronger feelings of identification with the figure of the Mountaineer, and in particular with the Mountaineer's plainspoken and rebellious attitude toward authority. The university administration seemed surprised by the pushback from faculty, staff, and students opposed to HB 2519, despite years of promoting the idea that Mountaineers Go First and offering constant reminders that Mountaineers are individuals who speak out, act up, and follow their own path. One faculty member opposed to HB 2519 told me that she had never felt more proud to be a Mountaineer than while working against the bill. For some, what had seemed like empty public relations jargon suddenly came to life, as the Mountaineer transformed from a one-dimensional mascot into a blueprint on how to live. In short, they became Mountaineers in the process. Like the men of postwar Trinity Hall who seized the title of Mountaineers for themselves and others like them, the campus carry debate provided some faculty and students with a far more grounded and visceral sense of what it means to be a Mountaineer.

It makes sense to end here, with a very recent instance in this book's long list of similar moments when notions about the WVU Mountaineer, as defined and curated officially by the university have been challenged by folkloric, grassroots notions about Mountaineer identity. The term *Mountaineer* was born more than two hundred years ago, when John G. Jackson signed off as "A Mountaineer" in his letter to the editor of the *Richmond Examiner* decrying the lack of legislative representation for residents of western Virginia. Then, as now, claiming the Mountaineer title announces one's unwillingness to be silenced or marginalized, one's determination to act independently, and one's willingness to fight the legislature, whether it be in Richmond or Charleston.

Onward and Outward:
An (In)conclusion

———

In light of these recent events, what's next for the Mountaineer? How will the figure be constructed and embodied in the years to come? The acrimony of the 2019 legislative session suggests that West Virginia is at a crossroads, deciding between digging our heels in and continuing to promote the version of the Mountaineer that represents a romanticized, safe, and anachronistic past or embracing the version of the Mountaineer who thinks independently, resists oppression, and welcomes strangers. One indicator of which direction we are moving in will certainly be the physical embodiment of the WVU Mountaineer. As we have seen, the two women who have served as Mountaineer faced stiff opposition for not matching some students' and fans' expectations of what a Mountaineer should look like.

Other universities have contended with similar challenges, such as the University of Wyoming's controversy about its cowboy mascot, as discussed above, and also the University of Notre Dame, whose leprechaun mascot is one of the few college mascots whose identity isn't obscured by a foam head. On one hand, West Virginia University can feel good about the fact it chose its two female Mountaineers long before the University of Notre Dame chose the first woman to serve as its leprechaun. That just happened in April 2019, when Notre Dame selected Lynnette Wukie as its first female leprechaun mascot. However, Notre Dame is far ahead of the curve in terms of the ethnic diversity of its mascots. As a woman of color, Wukie is Notre Dame's second African American leprechaun, following the first, Michael Brown, who served from 1999–2000.[76] Because Notre Dame chooses three students to serve as the leprechaun in a single year, it also announced that one of the other individuals chosen to serve in 2019–20, Samuel Jackson, will be the university's third African American student to serve as the leprechaun. And an international student from Ireland, Conal Fagan, has also served in the role.[77]

A person of color has never served as Mountaineer. No international student has served as Mountaineer. Will the university's efforts to separate Mountaineer identity from a specific type of body make it easier or less controversial for a nonwhite or

Figure 5.6. Mural of the *Black Triangle* at Charleston's Grace Bible Church, created by children in the Hope Community Development project along with artists Calvin Jones and Crystal Good.

international student to serve as the Mountaineer? As Tennant's and Durst's experiences show us, whoever breaks those barriers will need to have a thick skin. It will be interesting to see whether the rhetorical strategies used to oppose or support the two female Mountaineers' service will get redeployed when a person of color or an international student becomes Mountaineer. The true test of the effectiveness of the Go First campaign will be when the first Mountaineer of color is selected. Then we can believe that the selection was truly based on the content of that individual's Mountaineer character, and not on his or her physical resemblance to a nonexistent bodily ideal. Children working on a project with the HOPE Community Development Corporation in Charleston have already imagined this in the mural they created with artists Calvin Jones and Crystal Good, depicting an African American Mountaineer standing behind the West Virginia capitol building (fig. 5.6).

I wish I could say I believed that the Go First campaign has this kind of revolutionary potential. But informal, grassroots ideas about who the Mountaineer is and what it represents have a far longer and deeper history in the state and at the university than the university's official, top-down version of the Mountaineer. And, as I have noted before, when folk and official versions of any tradition collide, the folk version almost always wins. That is not to say that the folk version doesn't change and adapt to new circumstances over time. In fact, what has been most remarkable to me about the long history of the Mountaineer is how flexible the term *Mountaineer* has proven to be. From its narrow origin as a term to describe residents of western Virginia, Mountaineer identity has grown to embrace an enormous variety of people, and all without losing its core characteristics: the Mountaineer was, and is, a freethinking (if sometimes rebellious), generous (if sometimes resentful), hardworking, and stalwart individual. The fact that such a particular set of traits should still be attached to the Mountaineer and still be relevant and desirable more than two hundred years after the term was first used is nothing short of astonishing.

Notes

INTRODUCTION

1. "Yosef," Appalachian State University Athletics, May 30, 2017, https://appstatesports.com/news/2017/5/30/athletics-yosef .aspx.
2. "Yosef."
3. Hyde, *Trickster*, 7.
4. Hyde, *Trickster*, 13, 9.
5. See the prefatory note to Paul Radin's seminal *The Trickster*.
6. For a good summary of this debate, see Babcock-Abrahams, "A Tolerated Margin of Mess," 161–64.
7. Babcock-Abrahams, "Tolerated Margin," 162.
8. Babcock-Abrahams, "Tolerated Margin," 161.
9. Hyde, *Trickster*, 13.
10. Ingrid Crepeau, interview by author, August 8, 2015.
11. *Cambridge Academic Content Dictionary*, s.v. "kit," accessed April 16, 2019, http://dictionary.cambridge.org/us/dictionary/english/kit.
12. "Mountaineer Mascot," West Virginia University, accessed April 16, 2019, https://birthday.wvu.edu/traditions/mountaineer -mascot.
13. Doddridge, *Dialogue*, 43.
14. Doddridge, *Dialogue*, 43.

CHAPTER I

1. "Senator Manchin's Newsletter: A West Virginia Day Message," email received by author, June 20, 2017.

2. "West Virginia Statehood," West Virginia Department of Arts, Culture and History, accessed July 11, 2017, http://www .wvculture.org/history/archives/statehoo.html.
3. "West Virginia Statehood."
4. "West Virginia Statehood."
5. Williams, *West Virginia*, 36.
6. Harkins, *Hillbilly*, 14.
7. Harkins, *Hillbilly*, 14.
8. Isenberg, *White Trash*, 53.
9. Isenberg, *White Trash*, 115.
10. Isenberg, *White Trash*, 107–8.
11. Isenberg, *White Trash*, 106.
12. Isenberg, *White Trash*, 106–7.
13. Isenberg, *White Trash*, 114.
14. Isenberg, *White Trash*, 149.
15. "Why Do So Many Americans Think They Have Cherokee Blood?" *Slate*, October 1, 2015, http://www.slate.com/articles/news_and _politics/history/2015/10/cherokee_blood_why_do_so_many _americans_believe_they_have_cherokee_ancestry.html.
16. Isenberg, *White Trash*, 114–15.
17. Isenberg, *White Trash*, 112.
18. Eby, "Dandy versus Squatter," 33–34.
19. Twain, "The Dandy Frightening the Squatter," 6.
20. Doddridge, *Dialogue*, 43.
21. Doddridge, *Dialogue*, 49.
22. Doddridge, *Dialogue*, 49.
23. Doddridge, *Dialogue*, 46.
24. Eby, "Dandy versus Squatter," 36.
25. Doddridge, *Dialogue*, 43–44.
26. Doddridge, *Dialogue*, 41–42.
27. Heale, "Role of the Frontier," 409, 411.
28. Heale, "Role of the Frontier," 407.
29. Botkin, A Treasury of American Folklore, 3.
30. Isenberg, *White Trash*, 105.
31. Eby, "Dandy versus Squatter," 34.
32. Isenberg, *White Trash*, 116.
33. Isenberg, *White Trash*, 113.
34. Heale, "Role of the Frontier," 423.
35. Isenberg, *White Trash*, 124.
36. Isenberg, *White Trash*, 119.
37. Isenberg, *White Trash*, 119.
38. Isenberg, *White Trash*, 117.
39. Isenberg, *White Trash*, 117.
40. Heale, "Role of the Frontier," 406.
41. Heale, "Role of the Frontier," 415, 417.

42. Isenberg, *White Trash*, 129.
43. Heale, "Role of the Frontier," 423.
44. Stoll, *Ramp Hollow*, 28.
45. Isenberg, *White Trash*, 135.
46. Isenberg, *White Trash*, 167.
47. Klotter, "Black South," 837.
48. Williams, *West Virginia*, 38.
49. Williams, *West Virginia*, 38.
50. Stoll, *Ramp Hollow*, 15.
51. Isenberg, *White Trash*, 118.
52. Harkins, *Hillbilly*, 15.
53. Isenberg, *White Trash*, 172.
54. Harkins, *Hillbilly*, 19.
55. Harkins, *Hillbilly*, 26–27.
56. Twain, *Huckleberry Finn*, 195.
57. Harkins, *Hillbilly*, 127.
58. Harkins, *Hillbilly*, 35–36.
59. Harkins, *Hillbilly*, 35–36.
60. Harkins, *Hillbilly*, 37–38.
61. Williams, *West Virginia*, 108, 126.
62. Williams, *West Virginia*, 127, 129.
63. Williams, *West Virginia*, 108.
64. Williams, *West Virginia*, 100–101.
65. Williams, *West Virginia*, 101.
66. Williams, *West Virginia*, 101.
67. Catte, *What You Are Getting Wrong*, 43.
68. Williams, *West Virginia*, 103, 115.
69. Williams, *West Virginia*, 104.
70. Williams, *West Virginia*, 105.
71. Williams, *West Virginia*, 106.
72. Batteau, *Invention of Appalachia*, 59–60.
73. Batteau, *Invention of Appalachia*, 61; Stoll, *Ramp Hollow*, 205.
74. Batteau, *Invention of Appalachia*, 63. There is more to say about the enormous influence of Fox's novels and stories on perceptions of Appalachia. See Batteau's thorough and insightful analysis of the themes of Fox's fictions in *Invention of Appalachia*, 64–74, and Stoll's interesting analysis of Fox's work in light of turn-of-the-century industrial and environmental change in Appalachia in *Ramp Hollow*, 202–7.
75. Stoll, *Ramp Hollow*, 205.
76. Batteau, *Invention of Appalachia*, 74.
77. Frost, "Contemporary Ancestors," 311.
78. Frost, "Contemporary Ancestors," 316.
79. Klotter, "Black South," 844.
80. Klotter, "Black South," 844.

81. Klotter, "Black South," 840.
82. Klotter, "Black South," 842.
83. Klotter, "Black South," 845.
84. Frost, "Contemporary Ancestors," 311.
85. Frost, "Contemporary Ancestors," 312, 313.
86. Frost, "Contemporary Ancestors," 316.
87. Frost, "Contemporary Ancestors," 313.
88. Frost bends the facts to suit his purposes with some regularity. In "Southern Mountaineer," he claims that in the Civil War, "the whole mountain region was loyal" to the Union (304). Nothing could be further from the truth, but given Frost's goal of prompting northern philanthropists to donate generously to Berea, it makes a good story. Loyal mountaineers are far more deserving of aid than their Confederacy-supporting, poor white trash brethren.
89. Frost, "Contemporary Ancestors," 319 (emphasis added).
90. Frost, "Contemporary Ancestors," 318.
91. Frost, "Contemporary Ancestors," 319.
92. Klotter, "Black South," 846.
93. Klotter, "Black South," 847.
94. Harkins, *Hillbilly*, 44.
95. Harkins, *Hillbilly*, 49.

CHAPTER 2

1. "WVU's Mountain Honorary to Celebrate Centennial," WVU Today Archive, West Virginia University, April 15, 2004, http://wvutoday-archive.wvu.edu/n/2004/04/15/3998.html.
2. Clay Crouse acted as the first unofficial Mountaineer in 1927, but Hill was the first officially selected WVU Mountaineer. See "History of the Mountaineer," West Virginia University, updated January 29, 2019, https://mountaineer.wvu.edu/history.
3. Sonja Wilson, WVU employee, in discussion with author, June 27, 2014; "150 Years of Mountaineers Going First," *Daily Athenaeum*, February 6, 2016; "Mountaineer Mascot," West Virginia University, accessed April 16, 2019, https://birthday.wvu.edu/traditions/mountaineer-mascot.
4. Doherty and Summers, *West Virginia University*, 104.
5. Doherty and Summers, *West Virginia University*, 57.
6. Bobcats versus Mountaineers, souvenir program, November 18, 1933, 14.
7. Harkins, *Hillbilly*, 49.
8. Abramson and Campbell, "Race, Ethnicity, and Identity," 239.
9. Doddridge, *Dialogue*, 46.
10. Williams, *West Virginia*, 97, 101.

11. Williams, *West Virginia*, 199–200.
12. Harkins, *Hillbilly*, 49.
13. Gainer, "Hillbilly."
14. Harkins, *Hillbilly*, 76.
15. Harkins, *Hillbilly*, 86.
16. Harkins, *Hillbilly*, 103.
17. Harkins, *Hillbilly*, 155.
18. Harkins, *Hillbilly*, 154–55.
19. Harmon, *Hillbilly Ballads*, n.p.
20. "Roy Lee Harmon," Hillbilly Music, accessed April 16, 2019, http://www.hillbilly-music.com/artists/story/index.php?id=16352.
21. *Li'l Abner*, Wikipedia, edited March 29, 2019, https://en.wikipedia.org/wiki/Li%27l_Abner#Setting_and_fictitious_locales.
22. Harkins, *Hillbilly*, 84–85.
23. "Mountaineer Mascot," West Virginia University, accessed April 16, 2019, https://birthday.wvu.edu/traditions/mountaineer-mascot.
24. "The Mountaineer," WVUSports, accessed April 16, 2019, https://web.archive.org/web/20140204025837/www.wvusports.com/page.cfm?section=9614.
25. Jerry Bruce Thomas, "The Great Depression," West Virginia Encyclopedia, revised August 9, 2012, https://www.wvencyclopedia.org/articles/2155.
26. Mangione, *The Dream and the Deal*, 45–46.
27. Thomas, "Nearly Perfect State," 105.
28. Thomas, "Nearly Perfect State," 100.
29. Thomas, "Nearly Perfect State," 99.
30. Thomas, "Perfect State," 102.
31. Thomas, "Perfect State," 99.
32. Armstrong, "Southern Mountaineers," 539.
33. Armstrong, "Southern Mountaineers," 540.
34. Armstrong, "Southern Mountaineers," 540.
35. Armstrong, "Southern Mountaineers," 541.
36. Hurston, *Mules and Men*, 2–3.
37. Harkins, *Hillbilly*, 141.
38. Harkins, *Hillbilly*, 136.
39. Howe, "History of WVU," West Virginia University, accessed July 27, 2018, http://www.as.wvu.edu/cwc/WVU-history-bhowe.html.
40. Howe, "History of WVU."
41. Doherty and Summers, *West Virginia University*, 193.
42. "Timeline," 12.
43. Howe, "History of WVU."
44. Upton, "Hillbilly," 23.
45. WVU *Monticola*, 1948, 97.
46. WVU *Monticola*, 1948, 97.

47. Shirley Doubleday Baker, letter to Trinity Hall reunion group via Tom Ferris, April 17, 2007.
48. WVU *Monticola*, 1947, 1 and 14–20. The 1947 yearbook apparently also served as a way to honor those students who were killed in the war. WVU president Irvin Stewart writes in a letter to the parents of a dead serviceman, "The students at West Virginia University, most of them veterans, dedicated their yearbook to the students and alumni of the university who had lost their lives in their country's service during the course of World War II. They are sending you a copy [of the 1947 yearbook] because your son was one of those to whom it is dedicated." Irvin Stewart to Mr. and Mrs. Samuel Urbanoff, January 16, 1948, Stewart Display, Correspondence, A&M 690, box 331.
49. WVU *Monticola*, 1947, 12–13, 272–73.
50. "Yosef."
51. Nello Anotonucci, William Howard Atkinson, Daniel J. Dowling, Tom Ferris, David B. Hathaway, Don Kersey, and George Lewis in discussion with the author, April 20, 2007.
52. Anotonucci et al. in discussion with the author.
53. WVU *Monticola*, 1948, 8.
54. David B. Hathaway, email message to author, October 29, 2007. The phrase *thin veneer of civilization* was not coined by Brawner. Google Ngram shows that it had been in use since the 1870s. And perhaps most notably, it is used in Appalachian writer John Fox Jr.'s novel *The Kentuckians*, when the character Reynolds tells a journalist that "Until a man has lived a year in the mountains he doesn't know what a thin veneer civilization is" (quoted in Stoll's *Ramp Hollow*, 205). Though I'm quite sure Brawner was not quoting Fox, it is interesting that both Brawner and Fox explain "hillbilly behavior" as the result of that veneer's erosion.
55. "Mountaineer Week," West Virginia University, last updated April 10, 2019, https://mountaineerweek.wvu.edu/about.
56. See Bakhtin's *Rabelais and His World* for more of Bakhtin's theories of the carnivalesque.
57. Doherty and Summers, *West Virginia University*, 189.
58. *West Virginia University Bulletin*, 36.
59. Barra, "Davy Crockett Returns (on DVD)," 31.
60. King, "The Recycled Hero," 138.
61. Griffin, "Kings of the Wild Backyard," 102.
62. Griffin, "Kings of the Wild Backyard," 102.
63. Griffin, "Kings of the Wild Backyard," 112–13.
64. The star of Disney's *Davy Crockett*, Fess Parker, would go on to play Daniel Boone in a later TV series that ran from 1964 to 1970 on NBC. This crossover underscores the way Crockett and Boone merged to become a single folk-hero type in the 1950s and 1960s.
65. King, "Recycled Hero," 151.

66. Nadel, "Johnny Yuma Was a Rebel," 57.
67. Blair, "Six Davy Crocketts," 449.
68. Blair, "Six Davy Crocketts," 455–59.
69. Roger Tompkins to Irvin Stewart, May 15, 1957. Stewart Display, Correspondence, A&M 690, box 331, WVRHC.
70. Irvin Stewart to Roger Tompkins, May 22, 1957. Stewart Display, Correspondence, A&M 690, box 331, WVRHC.
71. Irvin Stewart to Boris Belpuliti, May 22, 1957. Stewart Display, Correspondence.
72. Irvin Stewart to Ruth Robinson, May 22, 1957. Stewart Display, Correspondence.
73. Ruth Robinson to Irvin Stewart, May 28, 1957. Stewart Display, Correspondence.
74. Griffin, "Kings of the Wild Backyard," 110.
75. Smith-Rosenberg, "Davy Crockett as Trickster," 93–95.
76. In late 2012, a video titled "WVU Mountaineer Kills Bear with His Musket" appeared on YouTube. In it, the 2012–14 Mountaineer, Jonathan Kimble, is shown shooting and killing a young bear with his official Mountaineer rifle while the WVU fight song plays. Though the video was quickly removed and Kimble subsequently apologized, it nevertheless adds ongoing resonance to the Davy Crockett–Mountaineer connection, since a large part of Crockett's legend had to do with his killing a bear "when he was only three," as the TV theme song goes.
77. Nadel discusses the possible connections between the *Brown* case and the Crockett craze in his article. See note 66 above.

CHAPTER 3

1. "State Official Speaks to Fayette Association," *Beckley (West Virginia) Post-Herald*, July 11, 1967, 6.
2. Haines, *West Virginia*.
3. Thorn and Rubin, *Mountaineer Statue*, 7.
4. Thorn and Rubin, *Mountaineer Statue*, 9.
5. Thorn and Rubin, *Mountaineer Statue*, 11, 15.
6. Thorn and Rubin, *Mountaineer Statue*, 13–25.
7. "Vietnam War," History.com, updated February 22, 2019, http://www.history.com/topics/vietnam-war/vietnam-war-history.
8. Thorn and Rubin, *Mountaineer Statue*, 15.
9. "William Richar [sic] McPherson," Wall of Faces, Vietnam Veterans Memorial Fund, accessed June 20, 2019, https://www.vvmf.org/Wall-of-Faces/37237/WILLIAM-R-MCPHERSON/.
10. "William Richar [sic] McPherson," Wall of Faces.
11. Jeffrey M. Leatherwood, "Vietnam War," The West Virginia Encyclopedia, revised November 5, 2010, https://www

.wvencyclopedia.org/articles/869; Dennis Imbrogno, "Vietnam Seen through West Virginians' Eyes," *Charleston Gazette-Mail*, September 14, 2017, https://www.wvgazettemail.com/_arts __entertainment/vietnam-seen-through-west-virginians-eyes /article_8fdc333c-78e1-5e19-a74f-83d177e9a8d5.html.

12. For a brilliant account of this work, see Whisnant, *All That Is Native and Fine*.
13. Catte, *What You Are Getting Wrong*, 82.
14. Webb-Sunderhaus and Donehower, eds., *Rereading Appalachia*, 4.
15. Bingman, "Stopping the Bulldozers," 29.
16. Hennen, "Struggle for Recognition," 130–31.
17. FBI reports obtained by SDS member Scott Bills, Bills papers, A&M 2828, WVRHC.
18. "Dadministration," flier for the WVU chapter of SDS, WVU Student Anti-War Movement papers, A&M 2506, WVRHC.
19. "Dadministration," flier, WVRHC.
20. "Dadministration," flier, WVRHC.
21. Bills papers, A&M 2828, WVRHC.
22. Hennen, "Struggle for Recognition," 140.
23. Drobney, "A Generation in Revolt," 107. For additional information about coordinated antiwar activities at WVU and in the larger Morgantown community, see Sutton's excellent article "Have You Bought Enough Vietnam?"
24. "There Are 'Radicals' Here, but Confrontation Unlikely," *Morgantown Post*, October 1, 1969, 1B, 8B.
25. "Join MFP," brochure, WVU Student Anti-War Movement papers, A&M 2506, WVRHC.
26. "Join MFP," brochure, WVRHC.
27. "Join MFP," brochure, WVRHC.
28. Doddridge, *Dialogue*, 50.
29. Scott Bills MFP campaign posters, Bills papers, A&M 2828, WVRHC.
30. "Reagan Nominated for Governor of California," History.com, updated March 1, 2019, http://www.history.com/this-day-in -history/reagan-nominated-for-governor-of-california.
31. "Profile: James A. Rhodes," History Commons, accessed April 19, 2019, http://www.historycommons.org/entity.jsp?entity=james _a__rhodes_1.
32. "May 1970 Student Antiwar Strikes," Mapping American Social Movements, University of Washington, accessed June 20, 2019, http://depts.washington.edu/moves/antiwar_may1970.shtml.
33. Doug Townshend in discussion with the author, July 1, 2015.
34. Robert Lowe in discussion with the author, August 7, 2015.
35. Lynne D. Boomer, "'We've Got to Go beyond Surface' of Frustrations," letter to the editor, Morgantown *Dominion News*, May 9, 1970, 6A.

36. Boomer, "Go beyond Surface," 6A.
37. Lowe, discussion.
38. Doug Townshend, voice mail message to author, June 7, 2016.
39. Lowe, discussion.
40. Oldstone-Moore, *Of Beards and Men*," 235.
41. Oldstone-Moore, *Of Beards and Men*, 239.
42. Oldstone-Moore, *Of Beards and Men*, 243.
43. Oldstone-Moore, *Of Beards and Men*, 242.
44. Oldstone-Moore, *Of Beards and Men*, 244.
45. "Mountaineer Photos," West Virginia University, updated February 3, 2017, https://birthday.wvu.edu/traditions/mountaineer-mascot /list-of-mountaineers/mountaineer-photos.
46. "Accused Win Continuance," *Daily Athenaeum*, June 25, 1970, 1.
47. "Accused Win Continuance," 1.
48. "Morgantown Six Petition; No University Reply Yet," *Daily Athenaeum*, July 2, 970, 1A.
49. "Solidarity," flier 1, n.d., Bills papers, A&M 2828, WVRHC.
50. "Information," flier, n.d., Bills papers, A&M 2828, WVRHC.
51. "Solidarity," flier 2, n.d., Bills papers, A&M 2828, WVRHC.
52. "Rappers Reap Harvest of Reaction," *Daily Athenaeum*, June 25, 1970, n.p.
53. "Haymond Plans No Appeal on His Demotion," *Daily Athenaeum*, June 25, 1970, 1A.
54. "Rappers Reap Harvest," n.p.
55. "Three Bomb Threats Slow Lair, Towers Activities," *Daily Athenaeum*, July 23, 1970, 1.
56. "'Security Measures' Close 'Lair; Students Angered by Mass Eviction," *Daily Athenaeum*, July 23, 1970, 1.
57. "'Security Measures' Close 'Lair," 1.
58. "'Security Measures' Close 'Lair," 1.
59. "Sunrise at WVU: To the People, By the People," booklet, Bills papers, A&M 2828, WVRHC.
60. "Sunrise at WVU," booklet, Bills papers.
61. "Brothers—Sisters!" flier, Scott Bills papers, A&M 2828, WVRHC.
62. "Brothers—Sisters!," flier, Bills papers.
63. "Sunrise at WVU," booklet, Bills papers.
64. "Sunrise at WVU," booklet, Bills papers.
65. "State Joins Move to Curb Campus Disorders," *Daily Athenaeum*, July 23, 1970, 8.
66. "State Joins Move," 8.
67. "Students Attack Code," *Daily Athenaeum*, September 19, 1968, 1.
68. "Students attack code," 1.
69. "North Bend Statement," Bills papers, A&M 2828, WVRHC.
70. "North Bend Statement," Bills papers.
71. "Citizens Circulate Petition to Fight WVU 'Radicalism," *Daily Athenaeum*, July 9, 1970, 1.

72. "VFW Leader, Citizens Hit at Radicalism," Morgantown *Dominion News*, June 24, 1970.
73. "VFW Leader."
74. "VFW Leader."
75. "VFW Leader."
76. "VFW Leader."
77. "Hite Selected Sub Mountie for Tomorrow," *Daily Athenaeum*, November 1, 1968, 1.
78. Steven Hite in discussion with the author, July 18, 2018.
79. Hite, discussion.
80. Hite, discussion.
81. Townshend, discussion; Lou Garvin in discussion with the author, August 2, 2015.
82. Townshend, discussion; Garvin, discussion.
83. "West Virginia University Mountaineer Mascot Application 2018–19," West Virginia University, accessed August 1, 2018, https://students.wvu.edu/files/d/6c6bc93d-acc4-488d-a934 -af384b0f9bc6/mountianeer-mascot-application-18-19.pdf.
84. "'Buckskin Babes' New Coliseum Attraction," *Dominion Post* (evening edition), December 3, 1973, 2B.

CHAPTER 4

1. Christine M. Kreiser, "Mad Anne Bailey," West Virginia Encyclopedia, revised September 25, 2012, https://www .wvencyclopedia.org/articles/327.
2. McNeill, *Gauley Mountain*, 15.
3. Lofstead, "Trailblazers at the College of Law," 18.
4. Doherty and Summers, *West Virginia University*, 43–44.
5. Doherty and Summers, *West Virginia University*, 36.
6. Doherty and Summers, *West Virginia University*, 45.
7. Doherty and Summers, *West Virginia University*, 64.
8. "New Look for W. Virginia Mascot," *USA Today*, March 26, 1990, 2C.
9. "Eye Openers," *St. Louis Post Dispatch*, August 31, 1990, 2D.
10. Rebecca Durst in discussion with the author, July 7, 2015.
11. "Female Mascot Applicant Just Enthusiastic," *Daily Athenaeum*, February 27, 1990, 3.
12. "First Woman Performs as Mountaineer Mascot," *Daily Athenaeum*, February 28, 1990.
13. "First Woman Vying for Mountaineer," *Daily Athenaeum*, February 23, 1990, 1, 12.
14. "First Woman Vying for Mountaineer."
15. "First Woman Vying for Mountaineer."
16. "Tennant U's First Female Mascot," *Daily Athenaeum*, March 2, 1990, 1.

17. Kirk Bridges, "The Best Man Should Have Won," editorial, *Daily Athenaeum*, March 21, 1990, 4.
18. Letter to the editor, *Daily Athenaeum*, April 16, 1990, 4.
19. Bridges, "The Best Man Should Have Won."
20. Letter to the editor, *Daily Athenaeum*, April 4, 1990, 4.
21. Bridges, "The Best Man Should Have Won."
22. Letter to the editor, *Daily Athenaeum*, April 10, 1990, 4.
23. Letter to the editor, *Daily Athenaeum*, April 18, 1990, 4.
24. Letter to the editor, *Daily Athenaeum*, April 18, 1990, 4.
25. Letter to the editor, *Daily Athenaeum*, April 23, 1990, 4.
26. "Pathetic: Fan Conduct Shocking," *Daily Athenaeum*, March 1, 1990, 4.
27. "U Men Should Grow Up, Save Hostility for Terps," *Daily Athenaeum*, September 7, 1990, 4.
28. "Pathetic: Fan Conduct Shocking," 4.
29. "Can a Female Incite the Crowd?" *Daily Athenaeum*, March 1, 1990, 4.
30. "Female Mascot Applicant Just Enthusiastic," *Daily Athenaeum*, February 27, 1990, 3.
31. Letter to the editor, *Wall Street Journal*, November 1, 1990, A23.
32. "Eye Openers," *St. Louis Post Dispatch*, August 31, 1990, 2D.
33. Natalie Tennant in discussion with the author, July 7, 2014.
34. Tennant, discussion.
35. "Mountaineer Mascot Set to Face Challenges of Job," *Daily Athenaeum*, August 30, 1990.
36. "In West Virginia, a Mascot's Gender Is No Trivial Thing," *Wall Street Journal* (eastern edition), September 26, 1990, A1.
37. "University Should Have Mr. and Ms. Mountaineer," *Daily Athenaeum*, September 14, 1990, 4.
38. Tennant was not the only target of these "cup fights," which appear to have been a widespread practice in the student section at the time, since a number of *Daily Athenaeum* articles and editorials discuss it.
39. "Tennant: Doing Her Job with Class," *Daily Athenaeum*, September 4, 1990, 4.
40. "Tennant Booed because She Doesn't Raise Morale," *Daily Athenaeum*, September 26, 1990, 4.
41. "Mascot: Sexist Attitudes Making State and U Look Bad," *Daily Athenaeum*, September 28, 1990, 4.
42. "Thanks, Saps, for Making State Look Bad," *Daily Athenaeum*, October 4, 1990, 4.
43. "Mascot Controversy Makes U Look Bad," *Daily Athenaeum*, October 4, 1990, 4.
44. "University Haven for Stereotyped Jerks," *Daily Athenaeum*, October 3, 1990, 4.
45. "Mascot Controversy," *Daily Athenaeum*, 4.
46. "These Days, the Joke's on Us," *Daily Athenaeum*, October 3, 1990, 4.
47. "True Mountaineer Character: People That Harass Natalie Tennant Just Don't Have It," *Daily Athenaeum*, October 8, 1990, 5.

48. "Natalie Tennant Didn't Deserve Parade Abuse," *Daily Athenaeum*, October 16, 1990, 4.
49. "Mountaineer Showed No Spirit at Season Finale," *Daily Athenaeum*, December 6, 1990.
50. "Mascot Controversy Result of Biased Selection Process," *Daily Athenaeum*, October 16, 1990, 4.
51. "New Selection Process Needed for U Mascot," *Daily Athenaeum*, October 17, 1990, 4.
52. "Interviews Upcoming for New Mountaineer," *Daily Athenaeum*, January 24, 1991, 3.
53. "Women, Minorities Should Try to Become Next Mascot," *Daily Athenaeum*, January 30, 1991, 4.
54. "Four Candidates Try for Mascot," *Daily Athenaeum*, February 18, 1991, 2.
55. "Mountaineers Shear Rams, 94–61," *Daily Athenaeum*, February 15, 1991.
56. "Tennant Toon Was a Piece of Needless Nonsense," *Daily Athenaeum*, February 26, 1991, 4.
57. "New Mountaineer Finds Tennant Treatment Unfair," *Daily Athenaeum*, April 29, 1991.
58. "Tennant Treatment Unfair," *Daily Athenaeum*, 1.
59. Tennant, discussion.
60. Durst, discussion.
61. Tennant, discussion; Durst, discussion.
62. Tennant, discussion.
63. Durst, discussion.
64. Tennant, discussion.
65. "The Year of the Woman, 1992," US House of Representatives, accessed April 19, 2019, https://history.house.gov/Exhibitions-and-Publications/WIC/Historical-Essays/Assembling-Amplifying-Ascending/Women-Decade/; Alix Strauss, "Key Moments Since 1992, 'The Year of the Woman,'" *New York Times*, April 2, 2017, https://www.nytimes.com/interactive/2017/04/02/us/02timeline-listy.html.
66. Tennant, discussion.
67. For an excellent discussion of the prevalence, variety, and significance of these jokes, see Pershing, "His Wife Seized His Prize and Cut It to Size," 1–35.
68. "Committee Selects Second Female Mountaineer in University History," *Daily Athenaeum*, March 9, 2009, https://www.thedaonline.com/committee-selects-second-female-mountaineer-in-university-history/article_36ed52a5-bf07-5a56-b23e-8d7e8a9614d4.html.
69. "The Tale of No Beard," *Daily Athenaeum*, April 21, 2009, https://www.thedaonline.com/the-tale-of-no-beard/article_5fc6442c-bcbe-5ec1-9ffe-005384f37c4b.html.

70. "Tale of No Beard," *Daily Athenaeum*.
71. "Selection of New Mountaineer Mascot Raises Eyebrows," *Daily Athenaeum*, August 8, 2013, https://www.thedaonline.com /selection-of-new-mountaineer-mascot-raises-eyebrows/article _de3ef4a4-0676-5376-b5f6-47fd6369245e.html.
72. "Mascot Raises Eyebrows," *Daily Athenaeum*.
73. "Mascot Finalists to Compete in Cheer-off Tonight," *Daily Athenaeum*, March 4, 2009, https://www.thedaonline.com /mascot-finalists-to-compete-in-cheer-off-tonight/article _d7d1f970-152b-5940-ab4b-f1fb3fe7b7de.html.
74. "Embrace Our New Mountaineer Mascot," *Daily Athenaeum*, March 9, 2009, https://www.thedaonline.com/embrace-our -new-mountaineer-mascot/article_cd4b8c3e-3b98-5f0f-8390 -8c6b77ad256e.html.
75. Will Turner, Jason Zucarri, Whitney Rae Peters, Cassie Werner, Jason Parsons, and Tommy Napier, letter to the editor, *Daily Athenaeum*, April 23, 2009, https://www.thedaonline.com/letters-to-the-editor /article_8984bdf7-9c79-5b25-a7b4-8584e0e41d61.html.
76. Turner et al., letter to the editor.
77. "Buckskins and Rifles and Cheers—Oh My," *Daily Athenaeum*, March 5, 2009, https://www.thedaonline.com/buckskins-and -rifles-and-cheers—oh-my/article_6c84cc9e-0dbd-5ead-a5ad -ccadd1849460.html.
78. "WVU Students Weigh-in on Rebecca Durst's Performance," *Daily Athenaeum*, September 8, 2009, http://www.thedaonline.com /news/wvu-students-weigh-in-on-rebecca-durst-s-performance /article_fdcb49e1-b672-5688-adb5-98bc276855f6.html.
79. Durst, discussion.
80. Durst, discussion.
81. Durst, discussion.
82. Durst, discussion.
83. "Tale of No Beard," *Daily Athenaeum*.
84. "On Football Gamedays, the Life of a Mascot Is Never Boring," *Daily Athenaeum*, December 1, 2009, https://www.thedaonline .com/on-football-gamedays-the-life-of-a-mascot-is-never /article_7965522f-2d77-5f6c-9bba-d094111ddc48.html.
85. "Life of a Mascot Is Never Boring," *Daily Athenaeum*.
86. Durst, discussion.

CHAPTER 5

1. Ed O'Keefe, "Joe Manchin Objects to MTV's 'Buckwild' Reality Show," *Washington Post*, December 7, 2012, https://www.washing tonpost.com/blogs/2chambers/wp/2012/12/07/joe-manchin -objects-to-mtvs-buckwild-reality-show/?utm_term=.762095046c4.

2. Philiana Ng, "MTV Renews 'Buckwild,'" *Hollywood Reporter*, accessed August 1, 2017, http://www.hollywoodreporter.com /live-feed/mtv-renews-buckwild-418757.
3. Krishnadev Calamur, "MTV Cancels 'Buckwild' after Star's Death," National Public Radio, April 10, 2013, http://www.npr.org /sections/thetwo-way/2013/04/10/176851845/mtv-cancels -buckwild-after-star-s-death.
4. Hollie McKay, "Should MTV Cancel 'Buckwild' Following Star Shain Gandee's Death?," Fox News, http://www.foxnews.com /entertainment/2013/04/02/should-mtv-cancel-buckwild -following-star-shain-gandees-death.html.
5. Tony Rutherford, "Buckwilders Would Have Hollered in Huntington during Second Season," HuntingtonNews.net, accessed July 31, 2013, http://www.huntingtonnews.net/68125.
6. Rutherford, "Buckwilders."
7. Rutherford, "Buckwilders."
8. Rutherford, "Buckwilders."
9. Elizabeth Catte characterizes such stories as belonging to the "Trump Country genre" and notes that they "shore up narratives of an 'extreme America' that can be condemned or redeemed to suit one's purpose" (*What You Are Getting Wrong*, 35).
10. Rod Dreher, "J. D. Vance's Straight Talk about Poverty," *American Conservative*, July 25, 2016, http://www.theamericanconservative .com/dreher/jd-vance-straight-talk-about-poverty/.
11. Rod Dreher, "Trump: Tribune of Poor White People," *American Conservative*, July 22, 2016, http://www.theamericanconservative .com/dreher/trump-us-politics-poor-whites/.
12. StefanieRose Miles, "Author J. D. Vance Does Have Hillbilly Cred—Like It or Not," *Lexington Herald Leader*, September 9, 2016, https://www.kentucky.com/opinion/op-ed /article100925787.html.
13. Vance, *Hillbilly Elegy*, 41.
14. Vance, *Hillbilly Elegy*, 24.
15. Vance, *Hillbilly Elegy*, 126.
16. Vance, *Hillbilly Elegy*, 40.
17. Vance, *Hillbilly Elegy*, 43.
18. Vance, *Hillbilly Elegy*, 230.
19. Vance, *Hillbilly Elegy*, 230.
20. Vance, *Hillbilly Elegy*, 8.
21. Catte, *What You Are Getting Wrong*, 89–90.
22. John Thomason, "Hillbilly Ethnography," *New Inquiry*, November 29, 2016, https://thenewinquiry.com/hillbilly-ethnography/.
23. Thomason, "Hillbilly Ethnography."
24. Thomason, "Hillbilly Ethnography."
25. "W. Va. Governor Talks Work Stoppage in Wheeling Town Hall," WTRF.com, February 26, 2018, https://www.wtrf.com/news

/education/w-va-governor-talks-work-stoppage-in-wheeling-town
-hall/992616486.

26. "Sharing Our Story: Mountaineers Go First," West Virginia
   University, February 2, 2015, https://presidentgee.wvu.edu
   /messages/mountaineers-go-first.
27. Vicki Smith, "W.Va. University Tops Party School List,"
   Washington Post, August 21, 2007, http://www.washingtonpost
   .com/wp-dyn/content/article/2007/08/20/AR2007082001242
   _pf.html.
28. Peter Jacobs, "The Top 10 Party Schools in America According to
   Playboy," *Business Insider*, September 26, 2013, http://www
   .businessinsider.com/playboy-west-virginia-university-top-party
   -school-2013-9.
29. "22 fires Set Following Bin Laden's Death in Morgantown," *Daily
   Athenaeum*, May 2, 2011, http://www.thedaonline.com
   /article_72ca393e-a39b-5050-b757-e71342148fa3.html.
30. "St. Patrick's Day Sends WVU through Culture Changes," *Daily
   Athenaeum*, March 17, 2017, http://www.thedaonline.com/news
   /article_32ceb3f0-0acb-11e7-996c-2f0a9232c9dd.html.
31. "WVU, City Officials Discuss Fire Plans," *Daily Athenaeum*,
   October 12, 2012, http://www.thedaonline.com/article
   _f38a74b0-79f4-5b90-903d-2bd0c38d7d7e.html.
32. "Victory Spawns Riot, Destruction," *Daily Athenaeum*, October 20,
   2014, http://www.thedaonline.com/news/article_63625906
   -5824-11e4-abd0-001a4bcf6878.html.
33. "Roughly $45k Worth of Damage from Riots," *Daily Athenaeum*,
   October 28, 2014, http://www.thedaonline.com/news/article
   _f8122d32-5e5b-11e4-86b8-0017a43b2370.html.
34. Marcus Constantino, "3 WVU Students Expelled over Postgame
   Riots," *Charleston Gazette-Mail*, October 23, 2014, http://www
   .wvgazettemail.com/article/20141023/DM01/141029588.
35. "President Gee to WVU Community: 'Time to Take Our University
   Back,'" West Virginia University, October 20, 2014, http://
   wvutoday-archive.wvu.edu/n/2014/10/20/president-gee-to-wvu
   -community-time-to-take-our-university-back.html.
36. "Time to Take Our University Back."
37. Constantino, "3 WVU Students Expelled."
38. Doherty and Summers, *West Virginia University*, 111.
39. Doherty and Summers, *West Virginia University*, 211.
40. Nick Madigan, "Peace Plan in Boulder Bans Sofas on Porches,"
   New York Times, May 30, 2002, http://www.nytimes.com/2002
   /05/30/us/peace-plan-in-boulder-bans-sofas-on-porches.html.
41. Madigan, "Peace Plan in Boulder."
42. Tomas Engle, "University Should Sanction Official Couch
   Burning Event," *Daily Athenaeum*, November 16, 2011, https://
   www.thedaonline.com/column---university-should-sanction

-official-couch burning-event/article_84bd2dca-a49e-577e-9d1f -1fe828c8db41.html.

43. Football Jesus (@westva75), "#kroger wouldn't sell us a burning couch cake bc apparently it 'promotes bad behavior.' Settled for football Jesus," Twitter, November 18, 2017, https://twitter.com /westva75/status/931931375107805184.

44. Bryan Bumgardner, "Couch Fires Really a True WVU Tradition," *Daily Athenaeum*, December 5, 2012, http://www.thedaonline .com/article_5ec897ac-0002-52ca-846f-cc008f4a428b.html.

45. Taylor Jobin, "For Better or for Worse, Mountaineers Go Hard," *Daily Athenaeum* (graduation edition), May 2015, 20–21.

46. "The Battle of Spruce Street," *Daily Athenaeum*, February 4, 2019, 1.

47. William Dean, "Police Disperse Spruce Street Block Party after Crowd Hurls Bottles," *Dominion Post*, February 1, 2019, https:// www.dominionpost.com/2019/02/01/spruce-street-party-turns -to-riot/.

48. Bronner, *Campus Traditions*, 202.

49. Mazzella, "Where Do We Go from Here?," 20.

50. Evelyn Merithew, "Recuperating from News of Riot," *Daily Athenaeum*, October 21, 2014, http://www.thedaonline.com /news/article_5c320dc8-58da-11e4-abe6-001a4bcf6878.html.

51. Alexis Randolph, "SGA Discusses Aquatic, Community Center, Club Hockey Team," *Daily Athenaeum*, October 23, 2014, http:// www.thedaonline.com/news/article_8e296544-5a7c-11e4-9582 -0017a43b2370.html.

52. Constantino, "3 WVU Students Expelled."

53. William Dean, "Eleven Facing Charges for February Snow Day Riot," *Dominion Post*, March 6, 2019, https://www.dominionpost .com/2019/03/06/eleven-facing-charges-for-february-snow-day -riot/.

54. "WVU Student Population: Who Goes Here?" Collegefactual.com, accessed April 19, 2019, https://www.collegefactual.com/colleges /west-virginia-university/student-life/diversity/.

55. It has been a constant wonder to me that the conflicts between these two vastly different groups of students don't flare up more often in the classroom. To be sure, I've seen some eye-rolling from native West Virginians when an out-of-state student boasts about some exceptional aspect of their home state. But in general, the two groups coexist peacefully, at least in the classroom.

56. "Personality," West Virginia University Brand Center, accessed April 21, 2019, https://brand.wvu.edu/brand-guide/voice /personality.

57. "Identity," West Virginia University Brand Center, accessed April 21, 2019, https://brand.wvu.edu/brand-guide/identity.

58. "Queer Nation NY: Our History," Queer Nation NY, updated August 25, 2016, https://queernationny.org/history.
59. Anecdotally, I heard that surveys about the university's branding revealed that people recognized the Flying WV logo and found it appealing, but they were neutral about the logo of the Mountaineer, based on the statue in front of the Lair. Some respondents apparently claimed that the Mountaineer logo suggested that only white men could be Mountaineers, potentially excluding some students from identifying with the university's brand.
60. "Our Audiences," West Virginia University Brand Center, accessed April 21, 2019, https://brand.wvu.edu/brand-positioning/our-audiences.
61. Claire Hansen, "A Flagship's Proposed Slogan—'The World Needs More Cowboys'—Draws Fire Out West," *Chronicle of Higher Education*, July 10, 2018, https://www.chronicle.com/article/A-Flagship-s-Proposed-Slogan/243883.
62. Diana Mazzella, "Home among the Hills," *WVU Magazine*, March 29, 2017, https://magazine.wvu.edu/stories/2017/03/29/home-among-the-hills.
63. Mazzella, "Home among the Hills."
64. Sara Berzingi, "A Letter from the WVU Muslim Student Association President," *Daily Athenaeum*, November 3, 2016, http://www.thedaonline.com/opinion/a-letter-from-the-wvu-muslim-student-association-president/article_b1df514a-a239-11e6-a459-0392c88a817a.html.
65. Sara Berzingi, email message to author, July 2, 2018.
66. "'Climate Survey' Shows General Feeling of Safety, but Acknowledges Issues," WVU Today, West Virginia University, February 17, 2017, https://wvutoday.wvu.edu/stories/2017/02/17/-climate-survey-shows-general-feeling-of-safety-but-acknowledges-issues.
67. "What Campus Carry Could Look Like on WVU's Campus," *Daily Athenaeum*, February 17, 2019, http://www.thedaonline.com/news/what-campus-carry-could-look-like-on-wvu-s-campus/article_f363e9ea-331a-11e9-a48a-43fffd74bd71.html.
68. Although the university has taken down the original FAQ sheet about HB 2519, a cached html version is available at https://governmentrelations.wvu.edu/files/d/ce5599a3-5511-4a7a-9b2e-f1925d828198/campuscarry.pdf.
69. WV House Bill 2519, Campus Carry, 3rd reading, YouTube, https://youtu.be/YulkQBlZ5VQ?t=7234.
70. Jake Zuckerman, "Anti-Muslim Display Sparks Conflict at WV Capitol," *Charleston Gazette-Mail*, March 1, 2019, https://www.wvgazettemail.com/news/legislative_session/anti-muslim-display-sparks-con;ict-at-wv-capitol/article_728c7654-9b4c-5b32-b45f-5b224ce866bb.html.

71. "Porterfield Stands by Statements on LGBTQ Community," WVVA.com, February 10, 2019, https://wvva.com/news/top-stories/2019/02/10/delegate-porterfield-stands-by-his-statements-regarding-the-lgbtq-community/.
72. Bill Schackner, "At WVU, 'Passing the Rifle' Christens New Mountaineer, Ends 'The Greatest Experience' for Another," *Pittsburgh Post-Gazette*, March 11, 2019, https://www.post-gazette.com/news/education/2019/03/11/West-Virginia-University-WVU-Mountaineer-mascot-Eads-Kiess-colllege-football-higher-education/stories/201903080084.
73. Taylor Giles, "The Truth about Campus Carry," *Daily Athenaeum*, February 24, 2019, http://www.thedaonline.com/opinion/the-truth-about-campus-carry/article_f732ac42-38a5-11e9-9ecb-3f11d3235ef6.html.
74. "All-time WVU Olympians (by Olympiad)," WVU Sports, accessed April 28, 2019, https://wvusports.com/sports/2018/1/31/all-time-wvu-olympians-by-olympiad.aspx.
75. "Update: Bill to Allow Concealed Carry on W.Va. Campuses Fails," WTAP.com, March 5, 2019, https://www.wtap.com/content/news/WVa-lawmakers-listen-to-comments-on-campus-carry-bill-505686431.html.
76. "Michael Brown: My Years as the Notre Dame Leprechaun," WBUR, October 17, 2015, https://www.wbur.org/onlyagame/2015/10/17/notre-dame-leprechaun-mascot.
77. "University of Notre Dame to Have First Woman Serve as Leprechaun Mascot," *The Hill*, April 18, 2019, https://thehill.com/blogs/blog-briefing-room/news/439614-university-of-notre-dame-to-have-first-female-leprechaun-mascot.

Bibliography

Abramson, Rudy, and Roberta M. Campbell. "Race, Ethnicity, and Identity." In *Encyclopedia of Appalachia*, edited by Rudy Abramson and Jean Haskell, 239–45. Knoxville: University of Tennessee Press, 2006.

Armstrong, Anne. "The Southern Mountaineers." *Yale Review* 24 (March 1935): 539–43.

Babcock-Abrahams, Barbara. "'A Tolerated Margin of Mess': The Trickster and His Tales Reconsidered." *Journal of the Folklore Institute* 11, no. 3 (1975): 147–86.

Bakhtin, Mikhail. *Rabelais and His World*. Bloomington: Indiana University Press, 2009.

Barra, Allen. "Davy Crockett Returns (on DVD)." *American Heritage* 53, no. 2 (May 2002): 31.

Batteau, Allen W. *The Invention of Appalachia*. Tucson: University of Arizona Press, 1990.

Bills, Scott. Papers. A&M 2828. West Virginia and Regional History Center, West Virginia University Libraries, Morgantown.

Bingman, Mary Beth. "Stopping the Bulldozers: What Difference Did It Make?" In *Fighting Back in Appalachia: Traditions of Resistance and Change*, edited by Stephen L. Fisher, 17–30. Philadelphia: Temple University Press, 1993.

Blair, Walter. "Six Davy Crocketts." *Southwest Review* 25 (1940): 443–62.

"Bobcats versus Mountaineers." Souvenir program, November 18, 1933.

Botkin, B. A., ed. *A Treasury of American Folklore: Stories, Ballads, and Traditions of the People*. New York: Crown Publishers, 1944.

Bronner, Simon. *Campus Traditions: Folklore from the Old-Time College to the Modern Mega-University*. Jackson: University Press of Mississippi, 2012.

Catte, Elizabeth. *What You Are Getting Wrong about Appalachia*. Cleveland: Belt Publishing, 2018.

Doddridge, Joseph. *The Dialogue of the Backwoodsman and the Dandy, in Logan: The Last Race of Shikellemus, Chief of the Cayuga Nation. A Dramatic Piece to which Is Added the Dialogue of the Backwoodsman and the Dandy, First Recited at the Buffaloe Seminary, July the 1st, 1821*. Cincinnati: Robert Clarke & Co., 1868.

Doherty, William T., Jr., and Festus P. Summers. *West Virginia University: Symbol of Unity in a Sectionalized State*. Morgantown: West Virginia University Press, 2013.

Drobney, Jeffrey. "A Generation in Revolt: Student Dissent and Political Repression at West Virginia University." *West Virginia History* 54 (1995): 105–22.

Eby, Cecil D. "Dandy versus Squatter: An Earlier Round." *Southern Literary Journal* 20, no. 1 (1987): 33–36.

Frost, William G. "Our Contemporary Ancestors in the Southern Mountains." *Atlantic Monthly*, March 1899, 311–19.

————. "The Southern Mountaineer: Our Kindred of the Boone and Lincoln Type." *American Review of Reviews* 21 (1900): 304–5.

Gainer, Patrick Ward. "Hillbilly." Unpublished, undated manuscript. Ward Papers. A&M 3003. West Virginia and Regional History Center, West Virginia University Libraries, Morgantown.

Griffin, Sean. "Kings of the Wild Backyard: Davy Crockett and Children's Space." In *Kids' Media Culture*, edited by Marsha Kinder, 102–19. Durham: Duke University Press, 1999.

Haines, Thomas. *West Virginia as Seen by Man Child-Tom*. Charleston, WV: Faith Workshop, n.d.

Harkins, Anthony. *Hillbilly: A Cultural History of an American Icon*. Oxford: Oxford University Press, 2004.

Harmon, Roy Lee. *Hillbilly Ballads*. Beckley, WV: Beckley Newspapers Corporation, 1938.

Heale, M. J. "The Role of the Frontier in Jacksonian Politics: David Crockett and the Myth of the Self-Made Man." *Western Historical Quarterly* 4, no. 4 (1973): 405–23.

Hennen, John. "Struggle for Recognition: The Marshall University Students for a Democratic Society and the Red Scare in Huntington, 1965–1969," *West Virginia History* 52 (1993): 127–47.

Hurston, Zora Neale. *Mules and Men*. Philadelphia: J. B. Lippincott & Co., 1935. Reprinted with a foreword by Arnold Rampersad and an afterword by Henry Louis Gates Jr. New York: HarperCollins, 1990.

Hyde, Lewis. *Trickster Makes This World: Mischief, Myth, and Art*. New York: Farrar, Straus and Giroux, 1998.

Isenberg, Nancy. *White Trash: The 400-Year Untold History of Class in America*. New York: Penguin, 2016.

King, Margaret J. "The Recycled Hero: Walt Disney's Davy Crockett." In *Davy Crockett: The Man, the Legend, the Legacy, 1786–1986*, edited by Michael A. Lofaro, 137–58. Knoxville: University of Tennessee Press, 1985.

Klotter, James C. "The Black South and White Appalachia." *Journal of American History* 66, no. 4 (March 1980): 832–49.

Lofstead, Becky. "Trailblazers at the College of Law." *West Virginia University Alumni Magazine* 23, no. 1 (Winter 2000): 18.

Mangione, Jerre. *The Dream and the Deal: The Federal Writers' Project, 1935–1943*. New York: Avon Books, 1972.

Mazzella, Diana. "Where Do We Go from Here?," *WVU Magazine*, Fall 2014, 20.

McNeill, Louise. "Ballad of Mad Ann Bailey." *Gauley Mountain*. New York: Harcourt, Brace and Company, 1939.

Nadel, Alan. "'Johnny Yuma Was a Rebel; He Roamed through the West': Television, Race, and the Real West." In *Reality Squared: Televisual Discourse on the Real*, edited by James Friedman, 50–74. New Brunswick: Rutgers University Press, 2002.

Oldstone-Moore, Christopher. *Of Beards and Men: The Revealing History of Facial Hair*. Chicago: University of Chicago Press, 2016.

Pershing, Linda. "'His Wife Seized His Prize and Cut It to Size': Folk and Popular Commentary on Lorena Bobbitt." *NWSA Journal* 8, no. 3 (1996): 1–35.

Radin, Paul. *The Trickster: A Study in American Indian Mythology*. London: Routledge and Paul, 1956.

Smith-Rosenberg, Carroll. "Davy Crockett as Trickster: Pornography, Liminality, and Sexuality." In *Disorderly Conduct: Visions of Gender in Victorian America*, 90–108. New York: Knopf, 1985.

Stewart Display, Correspondence. West Virginia and Regional History Center, West Virginia University Libraries, Morgantown, West Virginia.

Stoll, Steven. *Ramp Hollow: The Ordeal of Appalachia*. New York: Hill and Wang, 2017.

Sutton, Nora. "'Have You Bought Enough Vietnam?': The Vietnam Antiwar Movement at West Virginia University, 1967–1970." *West Virginia History* 13, no. 1 (Spring 2019): 27–55.

Thomas, Jerry B. "'The Nearly Perfect State': Governor Homer Adams Holt, the WPA Writers' Project and the Making of West Virginia: A Guide to the Mountain State." *West Virginia History* 52 (1993): 91–109.

Thorn, Gordon R., and Scott B. Rubin. *The Mountaineer Statue*. Morgantown: West Virginia University, 2006.

"Timeline." *West Virginia University Alumni Magazine* 34, no. 1 (2011): 4–18.

Twain, Mark. *The Adventures of Huckleberry Finn*. New York: Charles L. Webster and Company, 1885. Reprinted with a foreword by Victor Fischer and Lin Salamo. Berkeley and Los Angeles: University of California Press, 2001.

———. "The Dandy Frightening the Squatter." *Carpet-Bag* 2, no. 5 (1852): 6.

Upton, Elsie. "Hillbilly." *Rayburn's Ozark Guide* 19 (1948): 22–23.

Vance, J. D. *Hillbilly Elegy: A Memoir of a Family and Culture in Crisis.* New York: HarperCollins, 2016.

Webb-Sunderhaus, Sara, and Kim Donehower, eds. *Rereading Appalachia: Literacy, Place, and Cultural Resistance.* Lexington: University Press of Kentucky, 2015.

West Virginia University Bulletin 51, nos. 12–22 (June 1951), 36.

West Virginia University Student Anti-War Movement papers. A&M 2506. West Virginia and Regional History Center, West Virginia University Libraries, Morgantown, West Virginia.

West Virginia University. *Monticola* yearbook. Morgantown, West Virginia: 1947. Accessed June 20, 2019. https://archive.org/details /monticola1947west.

———. *Monticola* yearbook. Morgantown, West Virginia: 1948. Accessed June 20, 2019. https://archive.org/details/monticola 1948west.

Whisnant, David E. *All That Is Native and Fine: The Politics of Culture in an American Region.* Chapel Hill: University of North Carolina Press, 1983.

Williams, John Alexander. *West Virginia: A History.* New York: W. W. Norton, 1984.

Illustration Credits

Fig. 1.1. West Virginia Secretary of State website.
Fig. 1.2. Wikimedia Commons.
Fig. 1.3. Library of Congress, Prints & Photographs Division, LC-DIG-pga-04179, https://www.loc.gov/item/93511184/.
Fig. 1.4. Justin Howard, illustrator. "Sut Lovingood's Daddy-Acting Horse," from *Sut Lovingood Yarns* by George Washington Harris. New York: Dick & Fitzgerald, 1867.
Fig. 1.5. A&M 2537, Ballard Collection, West Virginia and Regional History Center, West Virginia University Libraries.
Fig. 2.1. West Virginia and Regional History Center, West Virginia University Libraries.
Fig. 2.2. West Virginia and Regional History Center, West Virginia University Libraries.
Fig. 2.3. Image courtesy of Randy McNutt, author of *King Records of Cincinnati* (Mount Pleasant, SC: Arcadia Publishing, 2009).
Fig. 2.4. Paul Webb, "The Mountain Boys," promotional booklet distributed by the Electric Auto-Lite Company, Toledo, Ohio, n.d. This artwork is copyright of its owner(s) (if applicable) and is used solely for historical and scholarly purposes.
Fig. 2.5. Author's collection.
Fig. 2.6. Author's collection.
Fig. 2.7. *Monticola*, West Virginia University yearbook, 1948.
Fig. 2.8. *Monticola*, West Virginia University yearbook, 1947.
Fig. 2.9. *Monticola*, West Virginia University yearbook, 1947.
Fig. 2.10. *Monticola*, West Virginia University yearbook, 1947.
Fig. 2.11. *Moonshine* 3, no. 5, 1949, 1.
Fig. 2.12. Author's collection.
Fig. 2.13. Author's collection.

Fig. 2.14. *Monticola*, West Virginia University yearbook, 1948.
Fig. 2.15. *West Virginia University Bulletin* 51, nos. 12–22 (1951): 36.
Fig. 2.16. Publicity photograph.
Fig. 3.1. Haines, Thomas. *West Virginia as Seen by Man Child-Tom.* Charleston, WV: Faith Workshop, n.d. This artwork is copyright of its owner(s) (if applicable) and is used solely for historical and scholarly purposes.
Fig. 3.2. Haines, Thomas. *West Virginia as Seen by Man Child-Tom.* Charleston, WV: Faith Workshop, n.d. This artwork is copyright of its owner(s) (if applicable) and is used solely for historical and scholarly purposes.
Fig. 3.3. West Virginia and Regional History Center, West Virginia University Libraries.
Fig. 3.4. West Virginia and Regional History Center, West Virginia University Libraries.
Fig. 3.5. Scott Bills papers, A&M 2828, West Virginia and Regional History Center, West Virginia University Libraries.
Fig. 3.6. WVU Student Anti-War Movement papers, A&M 2506, West Virginia and Regional History Center, West Virginia University Libraries.
Fig. 3.7. Scott Bills papers, A&M 2828, West Virginia and Regional History Center, West Virginia University Libraries.
Fig. 3.8. Scott Bills papers, A&M 2828, West Virginia and Regional History Center, West Virginia University Libraries.
Fig. 3.9. Courtesy of Doug Townshend.
Fig. 3.10. WVU University Relations Photography.
Fig. 3.11. West Virginia and Regional History Center, West Virginia University Libraries.
Fig. 3.12. Photo by Richard P. Rogers, West Virginia and Regional History Center, West Virginia University Libraries.
Fig. 4.1. West Virginia and Regional History Center, West Virginia University Libraries.
Fig. 4.2. West Virginia and Regional History Center, West Virginia University Libraries.
Fig. 4.3. Illustration from the *American Magazine* 12 (1881): 605. Science History Images / Alamy Stock Photo.
Fig. 4.4. WVU University Relations Photography.
Fig. 5.1. Publicity photograph.
Fig. 5.2. Author's photograph.
Fig. 5.3. Author's photograph.
Fig. 5.4. Author's photograph.
Fig. 5.5. WVU University Relations Instagram post; photo by Raymond Thompson Jr.
Fig. 5.6. Courtesy of Pastor Matthew J. Watts and the artists.

Index

backwoodsman (*continued*)
149, 220; versus the dandy in
contemporary culture, 192–93,
196–99; early conceptions of,
25–28, 33–34; garb of, 16, 76;
and influence on Mountaineer,
22, 24, 34, 103, 106, 149; as
noble/role model, 70, 103, 106,
112; parallels of, with hillbillies,
74
Bailey, "Mad" Anne, 153, 157
Bailey, Tim, 170
Bakhtin, Mikhail, 101, 234n56
"Ballad of Davy Crockett, The"
(song), 105
Barra, Allen, 104, 105
Batteau, Allen, 51, 231n74
Battle of Point Pleasant (1774), 153
beards: changing social norms and,
138–41, 150; hillbilly appearance
and, 48, *93*, 110–11, *112*; as part
of Mountaineer kit, 16, 111, 121;
and sexism against female Moun-
taineers, 156, 159, 177–78, 182,
186, 222; and Yosef (mascot), 3,
93. *See also* Mountaineer kit
Belpuliti, Boris, 108
Berea College, 3, 51–55, 57, 64
Berzingi, Sara, 216, 221
Betz, Frank, 162
Beverly Hillbillies, The (television
series), 119
Black Triangle, 226
Blair, Walter, 106
Bills, Scott, xi, 122–24, 127, *128*,
141–44
Bingman, Mary Beth, 120
Boas, Franz, 7
Bobbitt, Lorena, 176
Boggs, Mark, x
Boomer, Lynne D., 135–36
Boone, Daniel, 105, 157, 162,
234n64
Botkin, Benjamin, 33–34, 36
Boulder, CO, 202
Bourdain, Anthony, 218

Boyd, Belle, 162
Brawner, James Paul, 100–101, 148,
204, 234n54
Bridges, Kirk, 159, 161
Brown, Michael (University of Notre
Dame mascot), 225
Brown, Michael (of Ferguson, MO),
199, 201
Brown v. Board of Education (US
Supreme Court case), 84, 109
Brutus Buckeye (Ohio State
University mascot), 2
Bucca, Daniel, 147–48
Bucca, Frank, 147–48
Buckskin Babes, 152
buckskins, 16, 25, 75, 82, 90, 94,
102, 105–6, 183–85, 188. *See also*
Mountaineer kit
Buckwild (television series), 11,
189–92
Burwell, Brock, x, 180
Bush, George H. W. (US president),
170
Byrd, Robert (US senator), 124
Byrd, William, 23–24

Cambodia, US invasion of. *See under*
Vietnam War
Campbell, Brady, x, 173
Campbell, Roberta, 65
Campus Self-Defense Act (HB
2519), 218–19, 224, 245n68
Capp, Al, and *L'il Abner* comics, 46,
70, 74–75, 166
Caravasos, Mark, 200
Carlow University, 130
Carnegie Mellon University, 130
carnivalesque, 101, 234n56
Cassell, Bob, 120
Catte, Elizabeth, 49, 195, 242n9
Cerulli, Diane, 182
Charleston, WV, 110, 190, 219, 224,
226
Chatham University, 130
cheer-off, 159, 162, 170–71, 178,

Metropolitan Theater, Morgantown, 2

Meyer, Billy, 62

Middletown, OH, 194

Milan Puskar Stadium (at WVU), 151

Miller, Al, 123

Miller, Dawn, 162

Miller, Mitch, 105

Mississippi, 192

moccasins, 16, 25, 29, 105, 212. *See also* Mountaineer kit

montani semper liberi (WV state motto), 4, 19–20, 127, 220, 222–23

Monticola (WVU yearbook), 87–92, 94, 99, 234n48

Moonshine (campus humor magazine), 91–92, *93*

Moore, Arch (WV governor), 114

Morgan, John, 167

Morgantown, WV, 2, 4, 84, 120, 134–35, 147, 153, 155, 190, 198–99, 207, 221

Morgantown Female Seminary, 154

Morgantown Post, 124

Morgantown Six, 141–44, 146–47, 149

Morrison, Agnes J., 155

Moses, Herman, 172

Mountain Boys at WVU, 99–100. *See also* Webb, Paul, and *Mountain Boys* comics

Mountain Honorary (WVU student group), 60, 75, 115, 151, 157–60, 162, 169–72, 178

Mountaineer Advisory Board, 183, 185

Mountaineer Day, 11, 99–102, 148, 204, 206

Mountaineer Freedom Party (MFP), 123–29

Mountaineers Go First (WVU publicity campaign), 12, 188, 198, 206–11, 213–15, 217, 220–21, 224, 226

Mountaineer kit, 16, 17, 75–76, 105, 110, 140, 219. *See also* beard; buckskins; coonskin cap; moccasins; musket; rifle

Mountaineer statue, 111–12, 114–15, 118, 129, 140, 150, 152, 156, 187, 211, 245n59

Mountaineer Week, 11, 101. *See also* Mountaineer Day; Mountaineer Weekend

Mountaineer Weekend, 102–3, 150

Mountainlair (WVU student center), 108, 111, 114, 122, 131, 135, 143–45, 149–50, 211, 213–14

mountain whites, 52–58, 62–63, 68, 70

Mount St. Mary's University (Maryland), 3

Murphy, Joe, 192

Murray, Charles, 195

music. *See* "Ballad of Davy Crockett"; country music; hillbilly: hillbilly music; race: "race music"

musket, 3, 16, 151, 172, 178, 184, 219–20, 222. *See also* Mountaineer kit; rifle

Nadel, Alan, 105–6, 235n77

National Hillbilly News, 73–74

Native Americans, 25–26, 37–38, 43, 48, 64, 212; dress, 25–26. *See also* buckskins; moccasins

Natural Bridge, VA, 27, 34, 64

Neff, Charles (WVU vice president), 201

Nelson, Roland (Marshall University president), 123–24

Newsweek, 139

New York Journal, 58, 68

New York Times, 193, 196, 202

Nixon, Richard (US president), 129–30

North Bend Statement, 144, 146–47

ROTC, 116, 122, 130. *See also* West
Virginia University: Cadet Corps
Rubin, Jerry, 139

Sacajawea, 162
Schreiner University (Texas), 3
Schroeder, Fred, 62
Schwartz, Louis D., 171
Scott, Nathan B. (WV state senator),
154
Scott, Sir Walter, 33
Scottish (or "Scots-Irish") heritage,
46–47, 56, 66, 194–96
Scribner, Charles, 52
segregation, racial, 53. *See also*
"separate but equal"; *Plessy v.
Ferguson*
Semple, Ellen Churchill, 58, 64
"separate but equal," 57
sexism, 11, 159–63, 165–69, 171,
174–78, 180–86, 194, 201
Silard, Kevin, 168
Sissonville, WV, 190
slavery, 7, 19, 20, 22, 26, 38, 52–53,
56, 64
Snakers, 62
Snuffy Smith, 23, 70, 75
social media, 177, 185, 207–8, 217.
See also Facebook, Twitter
sorority, 156, 163
South Carolina University, 96, 169
Southern Vermont College, 3
southern whites, 22, 43, 45
squatters, 22, 24–29, 31, 34–39,
41–43, 48, 66, 103, 197, 209
Squires, Michael, x, 178
Stansbury Hall (WVU building), 2
Steele, Brandon (WV legislative
delegate), 222
Stewart, Irvin (WVU president), 84,
106, 108, 111, 211, 234n48
Stoll, Steven, 14, 41, 52, 231n74
Student Government Association
(SGA), 207

Students for a Democratic Society
(SDS), 120, 123–24; Marshall
University chapter, 123–24; WVU
chapter, 121–25
Swart, James A., 166

teachers. *See* West Virginia
teachers' strike
tear gas, 136, 137, 200, 201, 203
Tennant, Ken, 203
Tennant, Natalie, x, 4, 11, 140, 152,
156–78, 180–85, 226, 239n38
Tennessee, 34, 36, 74, 192
Tennessee Valley Project, 78
Thomas, Clarence, 174–75
Thomason, John, 195, 196
Thorn, Gordon, 111, 114, 162, 172
Thrasher, Ginny, 223
Tompkins, Roger, 106–8
Townshend, Doug, 129, 131–32,
135–38, 141, 148, 150–52
transgender identity and students,
216, 222
Treaty of Greenville (1795), 153
trickster, 5–8, 24, 74, 81–82, 88,
97, 116
Trinity Episcopal Church, Morgan-
town, WV, 2, 84
Trinity Hall (residence hall
associated with WVU), 84, 85,
87–89, 94–99, 102, 200, 204,
210, 224
Trump, Donald (US President),
149, 192–94
Twain, Mark (Samuel L. Clemens),
28–29, 45–46, 149
Twitter, 185

United Mine Workers, 125
University of Kentucky, 130
University of Notre Dame, 168, 225.
See also leprechaun (University of
Notre Dame mascot)

CPSIA information can be obtained
at www.ICGtesting.com
Printed in the USA
JSHW010059180120
3654JS00005B/6